# MEMORY : SELF

T.Collins Logan

**First Edition, August 2010**
**ISBN 0-9770336-4-3**


*Published by the Integral Lifework Center*
*PO Box 221082*
*San Diego, CA 92192*
*www.integrallifework.com*

*Everything is Memory*

## SPECIAL THANKS

This book would not have been possible without my biological parents, who brought me into this world and provided me with many rich experiences from which to build a complex and thriving sense of self. Thanks dad for being such a great sounding board, skeptic and advocate for all those compelling ideas over the years – and especially for our lively discussions about memory. Thanks mom for letting me use your poems in this book, for sharing the many letters you wrote years ago along with some wonderful photographs from our past, and for inspiring me to view the world through my own muse. I am also indebted to the many quirky and wonderful people throughout my childhood and early adolescence who took it upon themselves to help parent me with kindness, humor, timely encouragement and invaluable insight. In particular I owe a debt of gratitude to Ann, Rick, Margie and Jerry for their steadfast interest, support and exhortations. Thanks also to my uncle Dale and aunt Wendy for being so patient with me, for their willingness to share their thoughts and listen to my own, and for their enduring enthusiasm about our shared passions.

# TABLE OF CONTENTS

## INTRODUCTION

My father doesn't believe in memory, or at least he doesn't trust it. Especially the recollection of long past events from childhood. We remember what we believe is true, he will say, we assemble things – images, feelings, thoughts, associations – but how we put them together is entirely an exercise of our imagination. There is no such thing as a "real" memory, because most people's brains don't store information in an infallible way. Basically, we're just making it all up as we go along. I've challenged him on this many times over the years, trying to poke holes in his assertions and affirm the objective veracity of my own recall, but he has remained steadfast. Memories are like dreams – manufactured things, a fabrication from incomplete perceptions, illusory impressions of the past filtered through an evolving understanding in the present. At least I think that is how my father understands the workings of the human psyche…but I may be remembering it wrong.

Ultimately, after railing against the impermanence and malleability of my own thoughts, I now tend to concede that the structure of every memory is assembled on-demand. Like dehydrated meals, each memory requires reconstitution within the fluidity of immediate experience. I must heat the water of my introspection, mix in the spices of my emotional state, and pour all of this into the bowl of my life's context in the present moment. Then I stir this messy concoction with the power of my will and whatever appetites and qualities of intention I have carried into the kitchen. Then, like magic, the dry flakes of stored data begin to fill out, swelling into three-dimensional shapes that look, smell and taste like real experiences. When the food is ready, I take a bite, savoring the flavor, and swallow it down as a new experience – that is, a new experience of remembering an old experience. Eventually, my meal will be absorbed into the background noise of my life once again. A dry, flaky assemblage of potential meaning, adding to strata of existing data that reinforce my beliefs about myself and the world.

As we grow older, these patterns of recollection begin to solidify. They become a complex, interconnected web of associations that shape our self-concept and self-worth. Over time, our patterns of memory begin to equate the pattern of our identity. We can no longer differentiate between what we remember about our past and who we are. Understandably, any memory we summon will be reshaped into the image we have made of ourselves. If I feel I am a victim, I will remember all those instances that readily conform to this self-concept – or that can be manipulated in my imagination to support this belief. If I feel empowered and successful, I will recall those moments from my past where I felt most powerful, rearranging memories to comply with this idea of who I am. And the more invested I become in any one view of myself and the world, the more likely I will unconsciously reshape past experiences to agree with that view. And so the daily emotional cycles of my being will come to depend on the patterns of memory I continually disgorge – both consciously and involuntarily. My emotional choices in the present will of necessity mimic and amplify the chain of past emotional experiences, kept alive by my current sense of self and resulting orientation to others.

In this way identity, emotions and memory are inseparably linked. They reinforce and support each other with or without our conscious participation. So if we want to shift our emotional cycles or revise our identity in positive ways, how we interact with our memories becomes the centerpiece of that transformation. How can we change the nature of this interaction? If we continue deferring to the habits of interior processing and exterior relating that led to our current understanding of who we are, we will only amplify the construct that we are trying to change. If we forcibly rebel against our own inner rigidity and the established patterns that inform our sense of self, we will tend create stress, strife and crisis for ourselves and those we love. In fact it can seem as if there is no way out of this fixed dynamic, that we will forever be enslaved to the emotional cycles, memories and identity that constantly instigate and shore each other up.

For those who are happy with who they are and how they react, who have no compelling need to question the status quo, this self-reinforcement may be entirely acceptable. For others, exploring such questions may be too painful even to contemplate, because it threatens to undermine their ideas about reality or a barely maintained sense of well-being. As Marcel Proust wrote regarding sleep in *Cities of the Plain*, "What hammer-blow has the person or thing that is lying there received to make it unconscious of everything, stupefied until the moment when memory, flooding back, restores to it consciousness or personality?" It is indeed a frightening thought to acknowledge our sense of self could be so tenuous. But for those who are ready to embrace a little self-doubt and explore the unknown, for those who have heard a call from the center of Self to awaken, heal, grow and perhaps even evolve, the prospect of reinventing these interior relationships is an exciting and compelling opportunity.

So what inspires a person to explore new ways of being and becoming? I think it is our inherent desire for freedom. Freedom from emotional hurt and psychological suffering, freedom from physical illness, freedom to be ourselves without hesitancy or protectiveness, freedom to become something amazing, something we as yet only vaguely intuit or imagine – all of these things. And whenever we choose freedom, we must let go of our former selves. What we believe about ourselves, what we've been told, what we suspect, what we fear, what we hope, and each and every emotion and memory that supports those suppositions. No matter how attached we seem to be to that long, heavy chain of associations that links the present with the past, we must raise our anchor. We must set ourselves adrift on an adventurous sea, relying on the beacons of insight, understanding and discernment to chart our course. To hoist sail and move forward, we loosen our grasp on the familiar and let the wind of chance surge forth. It's a risk, to be sure, but as we learn to trust our instincts in this new journey, both our confidence and our navigational competency become easier and easier.

What is really happening here? We are rewriting our personal history. We're not necessarily changing the facts – although we should be open to the possibility that those facts are different than what we remember or assume – but we are revising the tone and characterization of our core material. With a stroke of conscious effort, we turn drama into comedy, tragedy into parable, embarrassing farce into action-adventure. Each memory and its emotional content become points of departure for transformation, an exercise in creative invention. We are, after all, making it all up as we go along anyway, so why not make up a story that we enjoy for ourselves and relish sharing with our loved ones?

There is no better way of demonstrating the processes being suggested here than by sharing my own life story with you. Not as a conventional memoir, but as a series of semantic themes and the most distinct and formative episodic memories that have supported those themes over time. I have tried to be as transparent and grounded as possible in my recollections, avoiding the use of entertaining embellishments or overemphasis of sensational elements. These are truthful memories inasmuch as my imperfect, impermanent and malleable mind permits them to be. More importantly, they are the result of how I see myself, and how that self has evolved into its current state.

Unlike much of my previous writing, I will not attempt to entirely conceal the identities of the people involved in the stories from my past, though I have excluded surnames to provide a modicum of privacy. During the course of writing this book, I have in fact sought to verify the names of people and places – with mixed success – by discussing these memories with some of the folks involved. I am grateful that those frank, open discussions have become a substantial part of my own ongoing healing process. I certainly don't want to injure anyone through my disclosures (which is why I have hesitated to use real names before now), but naming everything as accurately as possible has become an important component of my inner truth-telling, and underlines for me the role integrity has in my self-concept.

In the same spirit of honesty, these stories are as much a cathartic release as an instructive example, and I hope they will entertain even as they inspire. Life is mysterious, motivations are complex, and all creative effort is an unfolding of unexpected twists and turns. I encountered many surprises as I whittled back into the past, while at the same time those with whom I shared these stories found strong resonances with their own personal experiences. We are all so much more alike than different, and no matter how strange or uncomfortable some memories may be for us, there will always be someone in the world who knows exactly how we feel. At the same time, there are particular events that still do not make sense to me. That is, I do not yet understand their nature, what lessons I might glean from them, or what mark they have left on my soul. I think that's a good thing, a reminder that my pilgrimage into a more complete understanding is still underway.

So now we begin our journey together. I hope you enjoy the ride.

## OVERVIEW: METASTRUCTURES OF BEING

In order to understand the relationship between our memory and our identity, we need to adopt a working model for how memory and identity operate in our consciousness and being. As yet, there is still an unresolved and lively debate within and between cognitive psychology, neurophysiology, philosophy and various spiritual traditions regarding this issue, so our working model will include insights and language from all of these disciplines, while at the same time departing from the theories of memory, identity and consciousness we might find among them. For now, let's divide the crucial components of this interaction into two broad categories: metastructures of being and supportive structures of being. Metastructures contain top-level organizing principles for all supporting structures, and the supporting structures in turn organize various types of experiential input and cognitive information critical to establishing, expanding, enriching and reinforcing the more abstract, higher-level metastructures.

First, we require a metastructure that defines the totality of memory inclusive of everything that contributes to our general sense of self. I like to use the terms *mnemosphere* and *memory field* interchangeably to represent this metastructure. The mnemosphere is our broadest metastructure and contains all others. It is a fluid, dynamic, self-creating field of information and processes that is constantly evolving. It involves mental activity, of course, but it also involves many other components not always associated with cognition. To define the composition of a greater mnemosphere, I'll offer seven contributing metastructures and begin to describe their relationships to each other. We'll call these *regions* of the memory field. These metastructures include our *integrative buffer*, our *narrative self*, our *governing beliefs*, our *unconscious substrata*, our *somatic memory,* our *spiritual ground* and our *emotional disposition.* Each of these regions has a powerful influence on the formation and maintenance of our memory field, and interacts with every other in some way. They are also not completely self-contained, but overlap each other. That is, each region is a building block in every other, organizing themselves dynamically according to current conscious and unconscious energy allocation. But before we define each of these, we should touch on some important distinctions in this conception of the mnemosphere that differ from previous memory models.

Memory theories often distinguished between *short-term* ("primary" or "active" memory), and *long-term* memory ("secondary" memory). Short-term memory has been ascribed a very short duration – mere seconds – with very limited information capacity, whereas long-term could apparently increase its store continually, to be retained indefinitely. Today the concept of *working* memory has overlaid these distinctions, in some cases bridging the two. Working memory is often defined in terms of focus of attention, conceptual capacity, rehearsal patterns and frequency, perceptual components and a host of other qualitative descriptors that hint at both short and long-term memory's interactions with volition, perception, consciousness and learning.

Another modern characterization is to separate *explicit* memory from *implicit* memory, where explicit represents any material that is intentionally introduced into memory and is readily accessible; and implicit memory is that which is less readily available and involuntarily or incidentally becomes part of our memory. Substitute concepts are frequently encountered – such as "declarative," "optional," "procedural," or "obligatory" – alternately clarifying or muddying the discourse. This multiplicity of terms seems to occur a great deal across different specializations of memory study, and even within the same research communities. However, despite the many different theories of memory and the role of each component, there is broad agreement about the conceptual placeholders for explicit and implicit functions.

While agreeing with many of these functional conceptions, the memory field metastructure discussed here does not entirely embrace such components or definitions. Instead, the mnemosphere is comprised of an interrelated continuum of memory processes, where each system and subsystem is a fractal representation of the whole and remains entirely fluid in its organization and exchanges. Explicit and implicit are described in terms of four energy levels of increasing memory activation. Short-term, long-term and working memory are approached via independent agents and passive components that aggregate to facilitate these and other, higher-level functions. In a further digression from contemporary theory, we will also explore how different systems and subsystems of being that have traditionally been excluded from memory theory also contribute to the mnemosphere.

The classic conceptions of preconscious and unconscious (Freud) as well as the further refinements of personal unconscious and collective unconscious (Jung) have influenced this proposed framework. As have Pierre Janet's ideas about the relationship between dissociated memories and automatic thoughts and behavior. The seminal work of Endel Turving on semantic memory and episodic memory also makes a critical contribution. And of course Erik Erikson and James Marcia's explorations of identity formation have influenced my thinking as well. So short-term, working, long-term, explicit and implicit memory functions – in concert with the unconscious, dissociation, automatism and identity formation – are all represented here in some way, we'll just arrive at them via a different set of assumptions. All of this is covered with more detail in the chapters ahead, but for now it is enough to say that every region of the memory field is part of every other, and the level of activity of any region of memory within our consciousness is dependent on dynamic relationships of agents and energy levels within and between them at any given moment.

The mnemosphere has a profound influence on all mental processes, especially regarding the content of those processes. As we absorb more information into our memory field, that information becomes ever more pertinent to our perception-cognition. How we react, interact, conceptualize, interpret, decide, learn, confirm, anticipate and a host of other cognitive phenomena relies on the organization and stored material of our memory field. We could even say that "consciousness" is as much an act of remembering as it is a transitive awareness of internal and external experiential conditions. Yes, we can possess a sort of raw, unmitigated attention to all such phenomena in the present moment – and this is in fact a desirable condition in many mystical spiritual disciplines. But without the intrusions of memory, the differential qualities of those phenomena would be indecipherable. The mnemosphere as we will define it contextualizes all experience, providing a backdrop of relations and valuations that facilitate everything we could conceive as consciousness: the executive functions of the mind, a continuous sense of self, the tacit interpretation that occurs during perception-cognition, the boundaries of our interiority and its relation to the world around us, the formation of ideas and so on.

Our ultimate goal here is to create a viable therapeutic model that explores the relationship between memory and self, and facilitates modification of that relationship when required. So let's begin with a brief overview of the leading edge of the mnemosphere, its first point of contact with all other components of our being, followed by a sketch of each successive metastructural region. After that, we'll take a look at the internal supportive structures of the mnemosphere, and then the shared components and characteristics of every region and structure. Lastly, we'll examine how the memory field relates to self-nourishment. By the end of this chapter, it will become clear how all of these concepts integrate into a single theory of memory; and by the end of this book, it will be clear how that theory can be practically applied to successfully reinvent self-concept.

### Regions of the Memory Field

**Integrative Buffer.** Whenever we are exposed to new information, the raw data requires evaluation and organization before it can be fully incorporated into our memory field, and the *integrative buffer* provides a neutral space to hold information so that this can occur. Such information might include sensations, thoughts, perceptions, reactions, tentative connections or associations, or any other tidbits of data that might potentially become useful or meaningful to us in some way. A contributing function of every other region of the memory field is to provide contexts for data to be defined, prioritized and integrated, so there is a high intensity of exchange between the integrative buffer and all other metastructures.

Another function of the integrative buffer is to act as a safe zone where preexisting memories freed from past associations can be revisited and re-integrated into our memory with revised valuations. That is, a neutral place to reintroduce data that has already been integrated into other regions. As such, this region is pivotal in any memory reorganizing efforts. The integrative buffer is also the region through which dissociated material – experiences or information that is challenging or perhaps even threatening in some way – must be reintroduced in order to be successfully integrated into other regions.

**Governing Beliefs.** Our *governing beliefs* are just that: the primary values and conclusions we have accepted as valid and integrated into our routine reasoning. They influence many of our other mental operations. They inform our conscience, energize our evaluation and planning, and help guide our efforts in-the-moment. Governing beliefs attempt to answer the *whys* of our intentions and actions. They also influence how we process all new information. Interestingly, we may not always be aware of what all of these beliefs are, how we learned them, or whether we would even completely agree with all of them if we consciously considered them.

**Narrative Self.** Our *narrative self* is the story we continually construct for ourselves about who we are in relationship to everyone and everything around us. More specifically, it represents an ongoing effort to connect our experiences together in a certain way so that they make sense to us and support our sense of self. Our narrative self not only influences what we choose to remember, but also how new experiences are evaluated in every area of our lives. Who are we spiritually? Emotionally? Intellectually? Socially? What is our individual purpose? What are our personal strengths and weaknesses? And so on. Our narrative self is also the story of how the rest of the world interacts with us. As with governing beliefs, we may not always have a clear, conscious picture of our narrative self, but we nevertheless depend on it to navigate our environment and weigh our decisions. Also, our narrative self isn't strictly oriented to the past – it is also a projection of our personal story into a desired or presumed future.

**Emotional Disposition.** Our *emotional disposition* is our state of readiness to experience a particular emotion or category of emotion. Am I on the verge of sadness, or on the verge of joy? Am I quick to become angry, or quick to laugh? Much of the time, emotions can be an almost reflexive reaction to our experiences, rooted in basic social instincts or the unconscious conditioning of previous experiences and exposure to strong feelings. Our emotional disposition determines the emotional vocabulary most readily available to us; in a sense, it represents the predominant content of our most accessible emotional memories – or at least the energy level of selective, reinforcing content. At other times, we may choose to moderate or transform our emotional state based on what we believe has helped us in similar situations, or what we have been taught is the most appropriate response, and this can of course modify our disposition. However, whatever the emotional state at which we eventually arrive, it will have a tremendous influence on what events we remember in other regions, how we contextualize our memories, and how we interpret and respond to new situations.

At one level, our emotional disposition is encoded in the neural pathways of our brain. At another level, it is encoded in our endocrine system throughout the body, as well as muscles, fascia and tendons. It patterns itself right down to the cellular level in our physiology. And it is encoded in both the energy pathways that course through us and the fields and frequencies that emanate from us. Even at a quantum level, I would offer that our emotional disposition is also part of an ongoing record of the events associated with our being. All of this occurs as the result of our genetic propensities, exposure to the emotional modeling of others, other environmental influences ranging from nutrition to toxic pollution, and our own classical conditioning. Although every region of the mnemosphere engages an equivalent breadth of encoding across all systems, our emotional disposition is a particular potent organizing force for material stored in all other regions, and is particularly susceptible to external influences.

**Somatic Memory.** Our *somatic memory* consists of several threads. Many of our instinctual or reflexive responses can be defined as body memories carried forward by our genes – for example our ability to heal, or digest food, or become sexually aroused. Then there is the memory of life events that have been embedded in our physical being in some way, which modify, enhance or even negate our instinctual responses. Our tissue may be scarred by an injury, or there may be changes in cell function resulting from exposure to certain energies, chemicals, strong emotions or even powerful ideas. As with our emotional disposition, somatic memory is stored across all systems of being and percolates into all other regions of the memory field.

The concept of somatic memory combines several ideas about what is stored in our bodily tissues and energies. There is the intelligence, language, wisdom and physiological memory as conceived of in therapeutic practices like Hakomi, Somatic Experiencing, Jin Shin Do and other body-centered techniques. There are genetically programmed autonomic systems, reflexes and functions. There is the possibility of a biological mind, a cellular intelligence that includes and transcends instinct, such as Rolando Toro's "vital unconscious." There is collective biological memory, perhaps a product of what Rupert Sheldrake describes as morphic fields and morphic resonance. There are the vital energy centers of the body as conceived of in various Yoga, Chinese Medicine and Taoist practices. And there is the concept of a type of procedural memory for learned tasks that at least in part resides in muscle tissues. There is all of this and more.

Thus somatic memory is a sun tan, a muscle made stronger through exercise, chronic illness in tissues we associate with some traumatic experience, a chakra that is out-of-balance, an involuntary rush of pleasure when we see someone we love, a meridian that is blocked, a reflexive motor pattern we have learned through training, an iris contracting in bright light or some other biological reflex or impulse inherent to our species. All of these physiological patterns fall into this region of the mnemosphere. Somatic memory can be just as complex and multifaceted as the information stored in any other region, but it is stored mainly in the cells, tissues and energies of the body rather than the neurons of the brain.

**Spiritual Ground.** Our *spiritual ground* is the memory conveyed by our spiritual being. In previous writings I have referred to this region as "shared understanding," the instinct of the spirit, that gift of universal wisdom that our soul knows but our mind sometimes has to consciously relearn. This aspect of spiritual ground is similar to Jung's idea of a collective unconscious, but with less emphasis on mythic representations. There are aspects of Yogacara Buddhism's *ālaya-vijñāna* or "storehouse consciousness" as well.   It also borrows from Sri Aurobindo's concept of the evolving soul or "pscychic being," a transpersonal and transcendent spiritual nature.  Spiritual ground would also include a karmic record of our actions, an endless chain of cause-and-effect that bears on current conditions in all other regions.

Most  importantly, this metastructure also tracks our interactions and relationship with the ground of being; that is, it characterizes our orientation to and connection with the Divine, the source of Light and Life, the Absolute, the Universe or however else we might want to describe the foundation and essence of spiritual causality.  Along with all of these characteristics, this region's essential role is remembering a felt connection with our own soul and conveying our soul's insights and urgings to our conscious mind.  Of course, such language presumes an acceptance of spiritual concepts, so another non-spiritual way to approach this region might be to describe it as quantum knowledge or information and associations stored in a quantum field.  Ervin Laszlo's proposal that scientifically observable nonlocal coherence correlates to the Hindu concept of Akasha is one example of this alternative approach.

**Unconscious Substrata.**  This region includes information from every other region – and is in fact integral to every one of them – while at the same time combining all of them into a unified processing space in the mnemosphere.  For most of us, this is the large but invisible portion of an iceberg that actually makes up a majority of our memory field.  What are the substrata of this region?  These are several loosely associated, non-hierarchical memory processes, but it is important that this region as a whole be viewed much like the mnemosphere itself: as a fluid, organic field in which data and energy flow relatively freely between various components.  That said, here are some proposed unconscious substrata:

> **Adjacent** – Any material lying just below the surface of our conscious thoughts, often readily accessible but requiring directed effort to restore into active memory – active memory being the short-term aspect of working memory that excites our conscious attention.  This is similar to Sigmund Freud's idea of the preconscious.  Sometimes the adjacent unconscious resists active recollection, however, so it also includes the idea of tacit

knowledge that we "know" quite well, but don't consciously realize that we know, can't articulate or aren't able to restore to active memory. The key concept here is that, either way, adjacent material is highly energized and influential, but just outside of our conscious attention. Thus the adjacent unconscious contributes to our most routine automatic thoughts, emotional responses and behaviors.

**Dissociated & Repressed** – Material that has been isolated or compartmentalized within unconscious memory, and made inaccessible to voluntary recall either temporarily or permanently. *Repressed* material can include individual emotions, sensations, ideations or any other perception-cognition that has strongly negative, antagonistic associations. Also included are entire traumatic episodic memories made inaccessible to active memory as a coping mechanism. However, *dissociated* material is not always antagonistic – it may only be information that doesn't readily conform to our existing metathemes or regional organization, or is otherwise difficult to integrate. So there are varying degrees of dissociation. Still, if we consider this material challenging enough – for example, if it produces an unmanageable level of cognitive dissonance – we may reflexively repress it. Dissociated and repressed material is often responsible for self-limiting, nourishment-obstructive or even pathological automatic thoughts, emotions and behaviors.

**Decayed** – Material where associations have atrophied to the point where only fragments without clear context or meaning can be recalled. Unlike dissociation or repression, where material represents a challenge or threat that must be managed, decay is an inevitable process of memory loss over time due to inattention to the material – usually a result of its perceived lack of relevance to our daily lives – and its consequent de-energizing. Adjacent, dissociated and repressed material can drift into decayed substrata, but only if it loses its importance in how we construct and maintain other metastructures and our overall self-concept. With effort, decayed memories can be reconstituted, but great care must be taken to correlate and re-energize such fragments, as these are most likely to lend themselves to creative fabrication.

**Deep Unconscious** – Material that by design is not available without special conditions of consciousness. Examples would be somatic memory accessed through therapeutic bodywork, or shared spiritual understanding made available through mystic activation, or the emotional and somatic intelligence that surfaces through invited intuition. We might consider this material dormant but fully available for integration under special effort or conditions. Our deep unconscious has only indirect influence over our conscious or automatic thoughts and responses, bypassing both adjacent and dissociated substrata, while at the same time resisting decay. It can, however, facilitate access to all other substrata, helping create alternate pathways to repressed or adjacent material we would otherwise be unable to assemble in active memory.

The key to understanding the unconscious substrata region is its inclusion of material stored in different systems of memory. Neural patterns residing in the brain are of course represented here, but also other patterns stored in other tissues and in other energy matrixes of our being. Somatic memory encodes experiences and information differently than governing beliefs or narrative self. Emotional disposition likewise encodes differently than either the latter two or somatic memory. And spiritual ground encodes in yet another, entirely different way than these others. And yet all of these regions congregate in our unconscious in a perpetual dance of exchanges and revisions, modifying the energy and priority of all memory. Information from all unconscious substrata regularly contributes to processes in each region without our awareness, often with a surprising amount of force. And together they create a magnificent continuum for our unconscious sense of self.

Beyond and inclusive of our unconscious substrata, the constant, active interplay of all metastructural regions generates all sorts of unique conditions of being, but most importantly that interplay defines a totality that is greater than the sum of its parts. Our memory field encompasses all that we empirically are and have been, all that we observe or theorize to be beyond ourselves, all that we might intuit via contact with our spiritual and emotional self, everything that our experiences and genes have shaped in our body, all that we conceive ourselves to become in our imagination, and all the unconscious information that simmers below the surface of what we routinely recall. Thus our mnemosphere supports our greater Self – inclusive of egoic, unconscious, and transpersonal aspects – as well as an ever-expanding understanding of the reality around us. The interdependence of all memory regions creates an additive synergy.

It is important to describe this as a perpetual, regenerative process that occurs in the moment. There are static components to memory – bits and bundles of information that are called upon when needed to support this dynamic system – but the mnemosphere itself is a continually revised landscape that offers constantly updated representations of ourselves and All That Is. Self, other, the Universe, all knowledge, all creative imagination, the Divine, all emotion, all intention, all sensation, all interdependent being…everything in varying degrees of complexity and abstraction in the current moment. This ongoing synthesis, this creation and re-creation, generates our fluid sense of identity, place, context and meaning in the Universe.

Of course, all of these seemingly different conceptual representations are really part of a unified interior progression. Although my memory field encompasses objects I perceive outside of myself, those objects exist for me as part of my interior operations. I may subjectively differentiate between self and other, but everything I perceive as *other* is referenced through my own perception and conception. Even the most abstract theory about the furthest reaches of space-time is a product of my cognitive and sensory processes, and is ultimately bound to my own experience of being and becoming. As far as the mnemosphere is concerned, everything organized as outside of my *narrative self* is merely an aspect of my *governing beliefs*, an artifact of my *unconscious substrata*, an upwelling of my *spiritual ground*, a reflection of my current *emotional disposition* or an expression of *somatic memory*, or it is awaiting further processing in the *integrative buffer*. Ergo: external objects persist as part of my interiority regardless; my mnemosphere is a virtual reconstruction of all exterior realities within my interior landscape.

We should also briefly touch upon what the memory field is not. As mentioned earlier, it is not consciousness, but rather the backdrop against which consciousness can develop and interact with itself. The mnemosphere is not where conscious executive functions such as evaluation or decision-making take place, though it does act as a resource for such functions and participates in unconscious valuation and prioritization. It is not the unitary awareness we might associate with our general sense of self at any given moment, but rather the fertile soil in which that unitary awareness can take root, grow and be instantaneously reassembled. And although everything we learn and experience is stored in our memory field in some way, and that field has tremendous influence on how we learn new things, the self-aware learning process itself is not a function of the mnemosphere. So although we are describing something that is both active and perpetually regenerative, it is not metacognitive; that is, the memory structures and metastructures being described do not require our consciously thinking about them to function. That said, we will nevertheless explore how self-directed thought processes have remarkable influence over the organization and ongoing impact of our memory field.

This top-level cluster of seven metastructures depends on an array of supporting structures, with each successive component interacting with and relying upon every other. In fact, we could say that all supportive structures and metastructures are fundamentally equal and interdependent. Even though terms like "greater," "top-level" or "subordinate" will be used to isolate the scope and role of each, these descriptions have less to do with hierarchy and more to do with temporary relationships that facilitate collaborative synergy. Each metastructure draws upon several dynamically interconnected supportive structures, and those structures contribute equally to all metastructures. A brief description of these subordinate structures follows, as defined by the primary functions or characteristics of each.

### *Semantic Objects, Types, Themes, Metathemes & Containers*

Those familiar with cognitive memory theory will recognize the term "semantic" as recalling Endel Turving's differentiation of generalized knowledge memory (semantic memory) from memories of autobiographical events (episodic memory), and the subsequent development of this idea in cognitive psychology over several decades. Although Turving's conception has been widely adopted and expanded upon in intervening years, there remain countless competing theories of how semantic memory is organized, and equally plentiful research supporting one view over another using all manner of scientific data-gathering techniques. After reviewing a broad sampling of this research and theory, I was not able to embrace any one model as the most appropriate for an integral approach. So I am proposing a simplified model in order to inform a practical and effective therapeutic method for active memory reorganization. In this approach, semantic memory is divided into the progressively abstract descriptors of *objects, types, themes, metathemes* and *containers*. All of these then constitute supportive structures for the higher level metastructures.

*Semantic objects* are the identifications and differentiations of the least abstract items in our vocabulary of thought. These are concepts that are easy to observe directly and concretely. For instance, physical items like a ball, a leaf, a hand, a dog; or the ideas of easily reproducible actions like grabbing, running, giving, taking, jumping; or readily observable traits like big, small, heavy, loud, rough, stinky. These are the basic building blocks of semantic memory because they are the basic building blocks of understanding our observed environment. As individual semantic objects, however, they do not yet describe sophisticated or nuanced relationships with other objects. In fact, until associations are established between them, semantic objects are in essence just gobs of extraneous data floating around inside our heads. However, this accumulation creates a necessary and useful reserve, which in turn allows us to create or enhance all future associations. This accumulation of a semantic object data store seems to be a reflexive habit for the human mind.

*Semantic types* are simple groupings of semantic objects according to a few of their basic properties or traits, and begins to address how these observable concepts interact and relate to each other. For example: balls that are different sizes and textures, balls that bounce, balls that can be thrown; or nice dogs, mean dogs, fast dogs, stinky dogs; or loud actions, quiet actions, actions that hurt, and so on. Notice that many different *objects* can be associated with many different *types*, and any temporary hierarchy or organization can easily and fluidly change. Initially, when our exposure to certain objects is limited, we may generalize from one or two interactions that "all dogs bite, but don't bounce" and that "all balls bounce, but don't hurt." As we gain more exposure to larger and larger groups of similar objects, we can then recognize that "things that bounce" or "things that hurt" could include both particular dogs and particular balls – that is, particular objects associated with different types. You can see how precarious any rigid relationships in memory become, especially as we gain more and more experience and information that modifies our interpretations. This is why, understandably, our comprehension of simple objects precedes any organization of objects into types, and must of necessity be followed by more abstract evaluations.

*Semantic themes* are the next level of abstraction, allowing us to identify causal patterns for different objects and types, then organize and prioritize those patterns for our own understanding and the successful navigation of our environment. Again, this requires more experience with types and objects relating to each other and to us. As an example, over time I may learn a certain way of interacting with dogs that generates positive outcomes: I can instigate a playful demeanor with them and they will become playful, I can throw a ball for them and they will retrieve it, I can speak to them in a certain way and they will bark back, and so on. Over the course of experimentation and reinforcement, a repeating pattern of cause and effect generates the semantic theme of "how to have positive interactions with dogs." It describes specific causal relationships that combine into desired outcomes. Such themes facilitate our basic survival and successful interaction with others, and of necessity are developed after we have integrated a broad vocabulary of basic semantic objects and simple semantic types. Another way to conceptualize semantic themes is to describe them as the causal operating assumptions upon which we base many of our beliefs about the world, and which we rely upon to make decisions about our course of action.

The next level of abstraction is the *semantic metatheme*. Metathemes organize our semantic themes into yet another layer of cohesive association, one that is most readily identifiable as beliefs and conclusions about more complex causal relationships. For example, we might observe that the amount of assertive force required to manage positive interactions with dogs is roughly mid-way between complete passivity and maximum assertiveness; we don't want to injure the dog or make the dog feel chastised or punished, but at the same time the dog won't respond to us at all if we don't speak in a certain volume or tone, act with a certain level of confidence or enthusiasm, or assert a modicum of authority in certain situations.

We might then observe that a similar principle holds true regarding asking for help from other people when we are in need; if we aren't assertive enough or don't make our needs clear, we might not receive sufficient help, but if we are overly forceful, demanding or aggressive we might alienate potential resources who would otherwise come to our aid. Once we begin to observe this higher level association in multiple contexts, we can move away from situational operating assumptions into more generalized principles. In this case, to a belief that there is an appropriate middle ground for assertiveness or forcefulness in many if not most situations. And the more new contexts and variables we can include in our evaluation, the more generalized an concretized our *metathematic* conclusions can become.

These do not always result in consciously held beliefs, of course – we may accumulate thousands of semantic metathemes without realizing they have become part of our worldview or "belief tree." What makes this semantic evolution unique for each person is how we chain certain associations together to maintain our beliefs, whether we are conscious of them or not. And once we are particularly impressed with a set of cooperative conclusions about ourselves and the world around us, we will tend to align all subsequent evaluations with previously chained associations, thus lengthening and strengthening the chain. In fact, in order to ensure that our conclusions are valid – and therefore useful for our survival – we will tend to conform all of our decisions and behavior to previously established associations, and carefully insulate our beliefs from any dissonant material. Why? Because whenever we encounter something that does not integrate with guiding conclusions in some arena of thought or action – that is, within an established theme or metatheme – it creates cognitive dissonance, confusion, stress and, in extreme cases, existential crisis. It undermines our confidence in what has been a successful way of processing reality and thriving in our environment. This is one reason we require the next level of semantic abstraction, the *semantic container*, as we are exposed to more and more situations that modify and expand our understanding.

*Semantic containers* segregate semantic themes and metathemes into cooperative groups that are relevant only in certain contexts. What makes these groups "contained" is that they each maintain a psychic boundary around themselves whenever they are invoked in consciousness – a boundary that disallows interaction with the contradictory or disruptive themes and metathemes present in other containers. These boundaries allow seemingly incompatible or antagonistic principles to coexist in our mnemosphere without completely debilitating all conscious processes. Containers allow us to operate from one set of interdependent principles or beliefs while navigating workplace politics, another set when playing team sports, another set when engaging in high risk behaviors, another set when interacting with family members at dinnertime, another set when celebrating a special occasion with friends, and yet another set when immersed in period of spiritual renewal. In each divergent situation or environment, we abandon the semantic metathemes that functioned well for us elsewhere, and reflexively encourage a new container of metathemes to kick in.

Perhaps the most striking example of how semantic containers are formed is when a person is abruptly transported from an environment of familiar and acceptable rules and relationships to one they have never encountered before, where acceptable rules and relationships are completely different. A young soldier from a peaceful community who goes off to war. Someone who grew up in a rural town moving to a big city. The first year of schooling for a young child. A new romantic relationship or the loss of an established one. In each situation, a new container must quickly be formed to accommodate a new combination of cooperative metathemes and the addition of new metathemes.

The same themes and metathemes may also belong to multiple containers, and one or more whole containers may be present in many other containers. Often, even though we may believe we are fairly rigid in our beliefs and organization of information, there is an underlying fluidity of exchange between different containers, and many may be formed ad hoc when new situations demand them. However, the more practiced we become in utilizing one or more containers to successfully navigate our world, the more rigidified and resilient those containers subjectively become. Especially if we are in constant crises, our dominant containers will present themselves as islands and fortresses to preserve our well-being, dominating all our insights and interactions; we will cling to them because they feel like safe, high ground to us.

How rigid the boundaries become around each of these containers is an important area of examination, as is the question of whether semantic containers are always a psychologically healthy means of self-organization. They seem to have variable permeability, depending on our innate or learned tolerances for cognitive dissonance – that is, the less tolerant we are, the more impermeable our containers. Containers are an understandable necessity to survive in a seemingly chaotic, rapidly changing world with many conflicting demands. But the unconscious record keeper within our memory field – that most wise and insightful observer of all our conscious processes – recognizes and tracks the conflicts between different containers. As we increase our level of self-awareness – that is, the integration of our unconscious observations with our conscious thoughts – those conflicts will become more and more evident and potentially disruptive to our well-being. At the opposite end of the spectrum, a deficit in self-awareness might help explain a ready capacity for multiple contradictory containers.

Of course we all have different capacities for all of our supportive structures as well, and this also influences our ability to be flexible and fluid. One person with highly developed semantic object capacity can store and recall oodles of as-yet-unassociated knowledge – individual facts that don't seem to relate to anything else but nevertheless persist in the mnemosphere. Another person is able to congregate an exceptionally high number of semantic types and themes in working memory, and thus create much more complex, conditional or nuanced associations and metathemes on-the-fly. Someone else may have an intrinsic ability to create strong, rigid barriers between countless numbers of containers, where others find creating or maintaining separate containers nigh unto impossible.

In fact, I think exploring the characteristics of these supportive structures and the interactions between them in more detail would explain much of the natural variation in human reasoning ability, differences in personality and even natural propensities toward certain belief systems. For instance, if I find it challenging to manage a lot of contradictory metathemes, I may gravitate towards inflexible, black-and-white belief systems where both ambiguity and opposing viewpoints are less tolerated. If, on the other hand, I have a natural facility for integrating diverse metathemes more easily, perhaps I will be more flexible and tolerant in my acceptance of ambiguity and opposing viewpoints. We could even say that various survival personas we adopt over the course of our development to cope with new life challenges are themselves highly refined semantic containers; they are not our true identity, but they may be the part of ourselves that we show the world in different situations because they offer the most appropriate or effective groupings of metathemes.

In one way, each of these successive semantic abstractions is a means of navigating and managing everything subordinate to it. In another, these are all part of the same endless arc of continuous, dynamic organization. There is both a dependent structure and an amorphous continuum – a definable set of hierarchical functions and a chaos of information that spontaneously forms meaningful organization. Certainly a miracle of mind. Once again, above all of these semantic structures are the metastructures *integrative buffer, governing beliefs, narrative self, emotional disposition, spiritual ground, somatic memory* and *unconscious substrata.* Although these expansive metastructures contain semantic elements and could in part be defined in terms of semantic memory, they are also synthesized from many additional input streams and a larger set of processes and structures. So now we'll explore some of those.

## Other Supportive Structures & Processes

What else contributes to the formation of our chief metastructures of being? I think we are only beginning to understand how deep the river of our being actually flows, and how diverse the influences upon the course of that river may be. Not only are the sources of information our mnemosphere calls upon to assemble itself varied, but their prioritization and emphasis is also constantly changing.    Of prime importance is that many are cognitive in nature, but many are not – or that they combine cognitive elements with other dimensions of being not traditionally associated with cognitive processes.

**Episodic Patterns**.    Episodic memory is mainly autobiographical – it contains events we have experienced that relate specifically to us. *Episodic patterns* are the way we organize these events into similar categories.    These categories may be semantic in nature, progressing in complexity and abstraction – first as *objects, types,* then as *themes* and *metathemes,* and finally as *containers* – or they may rely on other, non-semantic mechanisms of organization.    For example, in somatic memory, information may be organized according the type of physical energy or process it facilitates; in spiritual ground, information may be organized by its spiritual resonance or frequency; in emotional disposition, information may be organized by the emotion it evokes.    These categories are not static, and the same episodes may appear as part of different patterns, but the autobiographical events of our past naturally gravitate into some level of organization within the mnemosphere.    We can hypothesize that this is mainly due to the inherent importance of experiential knowledge in our learning and development.

Of necessity, our being quickly introduces ways to prioritize these episodic recollections, determining what is more important to remember than something else.    Much of this prioritization is governed by our existing metastructures – that is, by what perpetuates our current narrative self, what supports our existing governing beliefs, what reinforces or facilitates our dominant emotional disposition, what readily aligns with a preponderance of data in our unconscious substrata, what sympathizes with our somatic memory or harmonizes with our spiritual ground.    So this is one way autobiographical data migrates from our integrative buffer into other metastructures.    However, early on in our lives specific episodes may have a more formative effect, creating categories of meaning and priority that hadn't previously existed. Perhaps an experience was particularly unusual, or evoked strong emotions, or had a dramatic impact on our environment, or was traumatic in some way.    Perhaps it strongly agreed with what is already present in our memory field, or strongly contradicted it.

These are the sorts of flags that signal our being to prioritize certain experiences over others. It is important to reference "being" rather than "mind" because such episodic impressions may be stored anywhere in our mnemosphere – in the tissues of our body, in our karmic record, as components of our semantic themes and metathemes, and so on. In turn, these circumstantially amplified memories actually contribute to the formation of our higher metastructural regions, and will subsequently be called upon to reinforce them. Thus episodic patterns are critical in exploring ways to evaluate and reorganize memory.

**Influential Memes and Memeplexes**. Think of memes as cultural concept-viruses that we have either consciously integrated or that influence us without our being aware of them. They are, in effect, *semantic themes* and *metathemes* that have been projected into the world around us, acquiring a life of their own and the capability of reproducing independently, spreading from one person to the next. They aren't actually viruses, of course, but like computer viruses or prions, they exist outside our normal biological definitions of self-replicating organisms. I like to think of them as energy matrices we simply haven't yet found a way to scientifically isolate or measure.

As examples, a meme can be as seemingly simple as an advertising jingle that persuades us of the value of some product or service, or a story or joke that influences our judgments about a person, place or thing. This would be roughly equivalent to an externally projected semantic theme. Or a meme can be as complex as abstract religious doctrines, far-fetched conspiracy theories, or convoluted dieting regimens that influence our judgments about larger groups of concepts. This would be a memeplex, which is more like an externally projected semantic metatheme.

Influential memes and memeplexes are usually introduced to us through our family of origin and our surrounding culture. The methods of meme propagation and delivery vary widely. They include things we would readily recognize as influential, such as mass media and the arts, or educational institutions, or the tribal groupthink of family and peers. But influential memes may also be introduced through other means. For instance, our interactions in the realm of spirit or via unidentified quantum mechanisms. Physiological means such as psychotropic drugs or physically induced mental states may transmit memes. Major life events can introduce radical new perspectives that imprint as memes. And memes or even whole memeplexes can be transmitted by physical objects or places that have somehow maintained the residual energies of memetic events – that is, events that powerfully express certain memes.

So although the traditional idea of memes usually places them in the semantic structures of the mind – affecting our knowledge, attitudes, assumptions and beliefs – I would not restrict them to this realm. Even though they often originate as semantic themes and metathemes, and most closely identify with these memory structures, they can in fact support any region of the mnemosphere. Why? Because they have been projected outside of the mind. If my violent thought becomes a violent action, I leave evidence of that thought in physical form. The same is true of loving thoughts, thoughts that stem from a particular prejudice or belief, and so on. All of these can be transmitted through action. If I do this often enough, with consistent enough set of intentions, memes and whole memeplexes begin to take shape in other realms of existence – the physical realm, the spiritual realm, the emotional realm and so on. So my expressive actions generate and reinforce unconscious memes, emotional memes, spiritual memes, somatic memes and narrative memes until those memes take on a life of their own.

To illustrate this point, think of a cathedral or a symphony. What do these represent? A memeplex transmitted across time and culture in elaborate creative form, received by our aesthetic senses and influencing our being without our necessarily being aware of the intentions that inspired them. What about a pattern of tissue scarring resulting from repeated childhood abuse? This becomes a somatic meme embedded in our body. And a helpful way to describe karma is a persistent memeplex that penetrates and encompasses spiritual aspects of self. Thus memes can influence every dimension of self and every region of our memory field.

What makes a meme or memeplex more potent or influential than another depends on many things. The receptivity of each metastructure of being, for example, or the vulnerability of our semantic containers to external influences, or the strength of our intentions and will, or the presence of other memeplexes that are more cohesive, harmonizing and unifying within our being. If we already have a strong sense of purpose, well-defined boundaries of self, and a powerfully harmonious system of governing beliefs that tends to incorporate or subjugate all other memes, we will naturally resist or subordinate any new meme. Otherwise, we can be carried along by the momentum of each new memeplex and inadvertently sacrifice our interior and exterior continuity of self.

**Primary Drives & Fulfillment Impulses.**  Here we are addressing the issue of volition by borrowing some terms from *Integral Lifework*, the umbrella philosophy and system of self-care for which the process of active memory reorganization was developed.  How does volition interact with memory?  Of central interest is its influence on memory encoding and retrieval through prioritizing the input and output for our mnemosphere.  In this case that prioritization is generated through whatever facilitates our fundamental motivations.  Whatever information is flagged as enabling our will – as satisfying our primary drives and fulfillment impulses – is allocated space, energy and interactive priority within our memory field.  There are other systems that assist in this prioritization, but our will is a central guiding force.

*Integral Lifework* defines four primary drives and sixteen fulfillment impulses that govern motivations, mainly by determining what nourishment looks like in each dimension of self.  Primary drives are the fundamental motivators for everything we do, and include the imperatives to *exist, experience, adapt* and *affect*.  These drives in turn create higher level fulfillment impulses; that is, more sophisticated ways of satisfying our primary drives in various environments and through different dimensions of being.  For instance, a fulfillment impulse of *belonging* might allow me to exist, experience, adapt or affect in a tightly knit social group.  A fulfillment impulse of *imagination* might permit me to exist, experience, adapt or affect in a realm of ideas and creative or intellectual exchanges.  A fulfillment impulse of *avoidance* might protect me from harm when I am confronted with a risky or threatening situation, thus allowing me to exist, experience, adapt or affect for a little bit longer.  A fulfillment impulse of *mastery* allows me to become better and better at existing, experiencing, adapting or affecting.  And so on. Understanding the full array of impulses isn't critical in appreciating how these structures support other metastructures, but a chart is included here to help describe the full array of these motivational influences.

| FULFILLMENT IMPULSE | ACTIVE EXPRESSION | FELT SENSE |
|---|---|---|
| Discovery | Observe/Explore/Expand/Experiment | Sense of adventure, risk, opportunity |
| Understanding | Contextualize/Evaluate/Identify/Interpret | Sense of purpose, meaning, context, structure |
| Effectiveness | Impact/Shape/Actuate/Realize | Sense of activity, success, achievement, accomplishment |
| Perpetuation | Stabilize/Maintain/Secure/Contain | Sense of safety, family, security, "home" |
| Reproduction | Sexualize/Gratify/Stimulate/Attract | Sense of attraction, arousal, satisfaction, release, pleasure |
| Maturation | Nurture/Support/Grow/Thrive | Sense of caring, supporting, growing, maturing |
| Fulfillment | Complete/Transform/Transcend/Become | Sense of wonder, awe, fulfillment, transcendence, self-transformation |
| Sustenance | Taste/Consume/Quench/Savor | Sense of fullness, enjoyment, contentment, satiation |
| Avoidance | Escape/Evade/Deny/Reject | Sense of fearfulness, self-protectiveness, wariness, stubbornness |
| Union | Accept/Embrace/Incorporate/Combine | Sense of "being," union, interdependence, continuity |
| Autonomy | Differentiate/Individuate/Rebel/Isolate | Sense of distinct self, uniqueness, freedom, personal potential |
| Belonging | Cooperate/Conform/Commit/Submit | Sense of belonging, trust, community, acceptance |
| Affirmation | Appreciate/Enjoy/Celebrate/Create | Sense of "I am," play, gratitude, aesthetics, inspiration |
| Mastery | Empower/Compete/Dominate/Destroy | Sense of strength, power, control, skill, competence |
| Imagination | Hypothesize/Consider/Extrapolate/Project | Sense of limitlessness, possibility, inventiveness, "aha" |
| Exchange | Communicate/Engage/Share/Interact | Sense of connection, intimacy, sharing, expression |

As with all other supportive structures, our primary drives and fulfillment impulses are directly involved in the creation and maintenance of all metastructures. They define the nature and efficacy of nourishment in every dimension of self, and thereby determine the prioritization of our experiences in the mnemosphere. Did I learn something in this situation that helps me exist, experience, adapt or be effective in some area? Then I'd better offer it a prominent place in my memory field. Note also that each fulfillment impulse also has a specific quality of *felt sense* associated with it. This demonstrates how our emotional disposition relates to our fundamental drives, and how emotional arousal contributes to memory formation and prioritization. For example, if a certain activity evokes a sense of "uniqueness, freedom and personal potential," then we will associate that activity not only with those emotions, but also with the underlying *autonomy* fulfillment those emotions evidence.

**Moral Development.** The strata of moral valuation in the following chart are a proposed natural progression and maturation through moral orientations over time. These strata describe the evolutionary consequence of exposing every aspect of our being to diverse life experiences, and processing those experiences through empathy and compassion. Within the *Integral Lifework* worldview, this progression is available to everyone, and indeed inevitable – provided we have sufficient opportunity to explore every facet of love and integrate those facets into routine consciousness. My ideas in this area have been influenced by my own mystical practice, the poetry and musings of mystics of all faiths, the theories of several developmental psychologists, the many voices of the human potential movement, and other integral thinkers like Ken Wilber. These strata reflect a distinct hierarchy of values that I believe to be universal.

How do these strata manifest in our mnemosphere? Among other things, they encourage an increasingly positive emotional disposition. They continually expand the scope, function and relatedness of our narrative self. They mold the shape of our integrative buffer, so that our most cherished governing beliefs are continually reinforced. They encourage communion with our spiritual ground. They also govern how we respond to other supportive structures and processes – that is, which fulfillment impulses we amplify, the memes we embrace, and the prioritization of episodic memory. In concert with these other components, moral valuation strata sculpt our memory field and maintain its depth and breadth according to an evolving moral compass.

Our moral development has a distinct impact on the evolution of our self-concept, and the "self-identification" column in the following chart illustrates that relationship. What begins as an unformed identity progresses along with ever-widening conceptions of self until that self is inclusive of everything, even the formless infinite that precedes existence. Along the way, our concept of what effective compassion looks and feels like expands to include larger and larger arenas of affection and action – an idea explored more fully in my book *True Love*. In many ways, this progression represents the increasing permeability, cross-pollination and integration of all regions of the mnemosphere. Thus each stratum of moral valuation becomes a supportive structure for all other metastructures, and our moral evolution becomes a supportive, integrative process for the entirety of our memory field.

| SELF-IDENTIFICATION | STRATA OF MORAL VALUATION |
|---|---|
| **Formless Infinite**<br>Self Equates both Being and Non-Being (or Non-Identification) and Compassionate Integration of All Other Self-Identifications | **Applied Nonduality**<br>Translation of mystical, nondual consciousness into unfettered being where loving kindness harmonizes with spiritual understanding; a persistent, all-inclusive love-consciousness that integrates previous value orientations and current intentions into a balanced, purposeful flow |
| **All-Being**<br>Identification with Progressively Broader Inclusion of Consciousness & Being Together with All Supportive Systems | **Spiritual Universality**<br>Through intimate connection with an absolute, universal inclusiveness of being, moral function is defined by a guiding intentionality of "the good of All" as revealed by a successive unfolding of spiritual awareness, intuition and dialectic processing |
| **Shared Spirit**<br>Identification with All Beings as Defined by Shared Spiritual Understanding | **Transpersonal Holism**<br>Appreciation and acceptance of pluralistic value systems and the necessity of moral ambiguity – as guided by discernment of intentional, strategic outcomes that benefit the largest majority possible |
| **Earth Life**<br>Identification with Every Living System on Earth – All Its Individual Components & Supportive Environments | **World-Centric**<br>Appreciation and acceptance of interdependent, globally inclusive systems and the need for individual and communal responsibility with compassionate effort in support of those systems |

| **Human Society**<br>Identification with All People Everywhere | **Principled Rationalism**<br>Commitment to a clearly defined set of reasoned moral principles that intend to benefit all of humanity, with a corresponding individuation of identity from affinitive and beneficial communities |
|---|---|
| **Affinitive Community**<br>Identification with All People Who Share the Same Values or Experience | **Cooperative Communalism**<br>Acceptance of communal role and necessity of collaborative contribution to human welfare without a need for competition or positional authority, with facilitative conformance to a community's shared values |
| **Beneficial Community**<br>Identification with All People Who Benefit Each Other in Some Way | **Competitive Communalism**<br>Acceptance of communal role to participate in mutually beneficial community, usually in competition with others for personal positional power and influence, and without necessarily conforming to that community's shared values |
| **Committed Greater Self**<br>Acceptance of the Identify of "Self" as Larger Than Associations with Group(s) or Ideas | **Contributive Individualism**<br>Fully individuated from tribe and committed to own well-being and wholeness, and interested in efforts that appear "good" or helpful to others as framed by (morally relativistic) individual experience and interaction |
| **Tentative Greater Self**<br>Identification with a Possible "Self" Larger Than Associations with Group(s) or Ideas | **Opportunistic Individualism**<br>In the process of individuating from tribe, morally adrift except for a sense of obligation to own well-being and wholeness, with minimal concern for the impact of that process on others |
| **Secure Tribal Position**<br>Identification with "My People" | **Defensive Tribalism**<br>Championing correctness of primary social group(s) and propagating the distinct definitions of rigid rules (law & order, right & wrong, black & white) of the group(s) defines most moral function |
| **Insecure Tribal Position**<br>Identification with "The People I Want to be My People" | **Tribal Acceptance**<br>Conformance with and approval or acceptance from primary social group(s) governs moral function; what is "right" or "wrong" is defined by what gains or loses social standing within the group(s) |
| **Ego Identity**<br>Identification with Ego | **Self-Protective Egoism**<br>Acquisitive, consumptive, hedonistic patterns to protect and sustain ego in a self-absorbed and self-centered moral orientation with indifference to the needs of others, as moderated by fear of personal gains being lost |
| **Formative Identity**<br>Developing Ego and Ego-Identity | **Self-Assertive Egoism**<br>Aggressive promotion of own wants and whims above those of others as a moral imperative in most situations, as moderated by fear of personal pain or punishment |
| **Unformed Identity** | **Egoless "Raw Need"**<br>Naïve state: volition is centered around unrestrained basic needs fulfillment in every moment |

In conclusion, all of our supportive structures and processes continually interact with all other components, changing the substance and texture of our memory field. Each one influences our integrative buffer, governing beliefs, narrative self, unconscious substrata, somatic memory, spiritual ground and emotional disposition differently. In a way, we could say that what we experience as memory is really the unique synergy of these components and other information in the current moment, with the current moment itself constantly being re-remembered. That is not to say that our mind does not contain static, permanently stored information – it is just that such information is contextualized in an interdependent, continually evolving way, mainly as influenced by these structures and the regions they support. In all but a few exceptional circumstances, the subjective experience of being right here, right now is really the perception-cognition of how and where we were a few hundred milliseconds ago, subtly combined with every thought and experience we have ever had. Thus…*everything is memory.*

## Shared Components & Characteristics

Even though these structures and metastructures of being each have unique roles and contributions regarding our development and maintenance of self-concept, they share the same internal composition; that is, they are made up of the same functional components. We'll touch on that composition briefly, but the important point is to think of all structures and metastructures as running in parallel with each other within the same set of rules. Even with respect to subordinate, supporting structures in one direction, and the overarching mnemosphere and all-inclusive sense of self in the other, these are all mirror images of each other, like fractals containing the same characteristics expressed on different scales.

**Shared Components: Agents & Passive Repositories.** Every structure and metastructure has components that carry out its basic functions. On the active side of the equation are agents with various roles. There is the *observer* who tracks what occurs there. The *arbitrator* who decides what is to be stored, recalled or integrated, the pathways and endpoints the data will travel, and how all of that encoding and recall is to be associated. The *recorder* who encodes memories relating to a specific structure or region. The *retriever* who activates (excites, energizes) relevant material whenever it is needed. The *gopher* who transports incoming and outgoing information between each metastructure and our perception-cognition. And the *coordinator* who interfaces and coordinates agent functions within a structure or metastructure, and mediates between agents of different regions. Again, all of these agents exist independently within every supportive structure and metastructure.

On the more passive side of the equation are *repositories* where static information is stored. A repository can be a simple dataset without contextual relationships, or complex and multidimensional matrix of valuations and prioritizations. However, without active agents to interact with that data, the matrix would be forever inaccessible to working memory, or would slowly decay into obscurity. Even repressed unconscious memories have active agents to manage their repression.

Following the fractal representation of these components to its conclusion means that each region has its own independently operating version of "self," mirroring each progressively enlarged nexus of structures and metastructures. For example, each regional observer agent is in fact a facet of an amalgam Observer for our entire consciousness. The regional retrievers likewise work in concert to recall multiple perspectives of the same event to generate unified conscious recall. The arbitrators, recorders and retrievers combine to manage the integrative buffer, create and maintain chained associations among data, and perhaps contribute to other global functions such as integration, intentionality, conscience and integrity. The gophers conspire to create an amalgam of working memory in the conventional sense, though what these agents transport is not always available to our conscious attention. The coordinators combine into a sort of glue for our unitary awareness, and so on.

If this model is accurate, then any complete picture of both memory and our overall consciousness would be expanded to include a broad array of contributions – from our somatic intelligence, our spiritual centers of being, our acquired memeplexes, our episodic patterns, our emotional state and from every other region and supportive structure of the memory field. Agents acting independently within each structure or metastructure to efficiently handle tasks with constrained scope, and then in concert to address more complex and even global functions, maximizes limited resources to support demanding and sophisticated processes. In other words, our being can do more with less. Perhaps at some point it will be possible to scientifically validate this model, either through cognitive research or neurophysiology; for now, it is just a working hypothesis.

**Shared Characteristics: Attention Priority & Energy Levels.** As all of us have experienced, each input stream into our mnemosphere has a different priority in our consciousness at different times. Sometimes our awareness is fixated on an episode in our autobiographical memory. Sometimes we are preoccupied with shape and texture of a particular personal belief – a particular semantic metatheme – and its relevance in our current situation. Sometimes we are tuned into our unconscious substrata via meditation, catharsis, epiphany or therapeutic technique. Sometimes our consciousness is filled with the felt contact of our spiritual ground. And sometimes we are completely overwhelmed by our emotional state. At any given moment, even though all metastructures of being are concurrently active in our memory field, just one or two of them are amplified by our focus, filling our consciousness to the brim. This describes the characteristic of *attention priority* within the mnemosphere. For example, throughout the autobiographical chapters to follow, the centerpiece of each chapter will be a semantic container that has a high attention priority for me – through both default and conscious self-organization.

In *Integral Lifework* the intersection of a metastructural region and our conscious awareness is called *processing space*. Sometimes the processing space we rely upon most reflects a natural propensity, and sometimes it represents how we were influenced or trained to interact with certain types of new data over the course of our development. For example, I might approach articles in a science magazine very intellectually, while I respond to a child's cries for help on a purely emotional level. In each instance, I draw upon comparative information offered through different regions of being; not exclusively, of course, because my memory field is always roiling with some kind of interaction between structures and metastructures, but at any given moment I am shifting my emphasis from one source of comparative information to another, and thus either consciously or reflexively shifting my preferred processing space. This in turn creates shifting attention priorities for the material stored in each region of the mnemosphere.

Although each processing space is an intersection between conscious attention and our memory field, and often involves unconscious processes within all regions, I think of them as part of the foundation of consciousness itself. In previous writing, I have described some of these as mental spacetime, emotional spacetime, somatic spacetime, spiritual spacetime and soul spacetime; and as a combined nexus they represent one of the twelve essential dimensions of nourishment: Flexible Processing Space. Really they are the crucible within which our understanding of self and our relationship to everything and everyone around us is germinated. They are the cauldron where the fires of our attention heat the magical stew of both memory and transitive experience. So to exercise, integrate and expand this dimension is to strengthen these conceptions and the muscles of consciousness itself, as well as balance and equalize the attention priorities allocated to all of our formative material.

What is particularly interesting is that we require input from each processing space to make what could be generally categorized as wise and discerning decisions. Relying solely upon intellect, emotion, physical responses or spiritual insights to guide us in any situation can confuse, paralyze or misinform us. For example, if I rely only on my appreciation of an automobile's aesthetics or handling characteristics to purchase it, I may end up with an unsafe or unreliable vehicle. If I rely only on technical data sheets and consumer statistics, I may end up with a safe and reliable vehicle that I nevertheless abhor driving. If I depend solely on the emotional approval and advice of my family and friends, I may end up with a car that is unsafe and unreliable, and which I also hate to drive despite its social acceptance. And so on. The more I can combine the input streams of all metastructures and supportive structures with my conscious intentions, in relatively neutral and evenly weighted way, the more balanced, insightful and discerning my decisions will be. This applies to nearly every evaluation process in any situation.

This becomes especially relevant in the relationship between our memory field, our processing spaces and our sense of self, because the same process is occurring there. If we restrict ourselves to just one or two metastructural regions or spacetimes in constructing or maintaining our self-concept, it will result in an incomplete, imbalanced, self-limiting and perhaps even injurious way of being. How can I perceive myself as whole if I ignore some major contributing factor to my own existence? I am intellectual, I am emotional, I am physical, I am spiritual, I am social, and so on. So to be effective, any memory reorganization technique will require that I learn how to both honor and balance all these disparate input streams, addressing all of them within increasingly integrated processing spaces. Of course, the reality of our moment-to-moment existence is also that our focus is constantly shifting, so we will have to take this into consideration as well.

Attention priority not only focuses conscious processing on specific material, it also elevates the energy of that material. The more I concentrate on a concept, or an autobiographical memory, or a remembered sensation, or the ineffable qualities of a spiritual interaction, the more I excite that information into higher and higher levels of energy. From one perspective this could be described an neuronic excitation; from another the amplification of vital energies in particular agents and repositories; from another the gating of primary drives and fulfillment impulses into mental activities according to instructions from memory. However we decide to describe it, the net effect is a reinforcement of established patterns in the mnemosphere and the establishing of new patterns. By composing and projecting these over and over again through each processing space, we create enduring matrixes that guide all subsequent energies.

To get an initial handle on this dynamic, we can identify the relative prioritization and energy level offered by our supportive structures and metastructures at any given moment. These could be divided into the following progressive conditions: *disconnected, inactive, standby* and *active*. These represent increasingly energized states of the content of our structures and metastructures, and also the increasing relevance of that content to any interior processes. Disconnected information has the lowest level of energy, it's just floating around without a ever having a coherent anchor or reference, destined to fade away into nothing unless it finds meaningful utilization; for example, we'll often encounter disconnected information in our decayed unconscious substratum. Inactive information has more energy, but it has been put on hold; it may have been active and useful at one time, but it is now no longer part of our current matrix of valued data. Perhaps it has been contradicted in some way, or has lost its regular day-to-day importance, or has been dissociated due to some interior conflict. Standby is just what it sounds like: readily accessible, energized, meaningful information that is waiting to be called upon by current contexts; one potent example of this is anything hovering in our adjacent unconscious. And of course active information is whatever receives the highest energy levels at any given time. As an example, we could say that working memory involves active material highly energized by our conscious processes.

All of these energy levels can exist within all of our metastructures. From our discussion of attention priority, we might assume that the level of energy directly corresponds to our level of conscious attention, but this is not always the case. For instance, some highly active material in our unconscious substrata – such as dissociated material in our unconscious, or somatic and spiritual information in our deep unconscious – may not even be available to conscious recollection, and yet still be extremely influential in the function of other metastructures. This is because mnemonic material can become energized through different mechanisms. There might be strong emotional associations, or a preponderance of episodic correlations, or a constant drumbeat of repetition, or a triggering of related spiritual instinct in our deep unconscious, or a spontaneous somatic release, or some arbitrary event or association that excites our neurons into action. Each of these then links with conclusions and valuations about what satisfies our primary drives and fulfillment impulses, and this will determine what receives the most energy in much the same way it would influence what demands our conscious attention.

In addition, the most energized elements of every other region become candidates for introduction into the integrative buffer, what is elevated to conscious attention there, and what is ultimately integrated into other regions. Because the agents in each region of being are microcosms of our global consciousness, their automatic attention to any information energizes that information just as our conscious attention does, even if the totality of our awareness does not engage or recognize that automatic attention. So, for example, this means the effort exerted to repress something into unconscious substrata – and keep it repressed there – actually elevates that information's energy. To reiterate, even in our unconscious substrata and integrative buffer, the same gradations of energy level occur.

To clarify all of this, consider the relative importance of some episode in autobiographical memory. I was hit by a car while riding a bicycle when I was ten. When I am riding a bike along a busy street in the present, this episodic memory may be allocated additional energy because of the increased relevancy of association with current activities or environments, facilitation of my primary drive to exist, and the amplification of past successes (or errors) in my ability to predict outcomes. I may not be immediately conscious of the memory – it may not have a high attention priority – but it is there in my unconscious, waiting to inform any evaluations or decisions I might make. In fact, there is a chained association of cause-and-effect stored there, and as I commit to making a turn across oncoming traffic, my unconscious memory asserts itself: "Look out! Look out!" It warns. If I want to continue existing and avoid past mistakes, my unconscious substrata will inform my conscious choices.

Without immediately knowing why, I become more alert, my heart rate increases, and I may experienced heightened fear or stress. Even if I have repressed the traumatic material of being hit by a car, the weight and pressure, the highly energized cognitive force of that unconscious information is generating increased vigilance, or anxiety, or some other direct influence on my conscious decisions. And should that unconscious, highly active material percolate up into conscious recollection, it will then add supportive rationale for my reaction: "Remember what happened when you did this before?" At this point, it has gained attention priority, perhaps even in multiple processing spaces, and I can then consciously include it in my decision-making.

### Other Identity and Personality Development Schemas

There have been many different approaches to the development and composition of personal identity and its ultimate expression in our personality. However, not all of these approaches address memory directly; often it is a presumed critical function, a lumbering but invisible elephant in the room. The metastructures and supportive structures of being introduced here are therefore intended to compliment such theories, inviting cooperation and even integration. What I am most interested in is an open framework within which many different models peacefully coexist, and which can rapidly be employed to support ongoing self-care and therapeutic regimens.

For example, we can integrate many developmental theories in the same way that *Integral Lifework's* moral valuation strata have been incorporated. Whether Jane Loevinger's ego stages, Erik Erikson's psychosocial stages, neo-Piagetian theories of development, James Fowler's stages of faith, Lawrence Kohlberg's moral stages, Robert Siegler's overlapping waves, the spiral dynamics of Don Beck and Chris Cowan, the developmental lines or streams of Ken Wilber's AQAL theory – all of these could be described in terms of their relationship to the different components of memory we've defined, as well as the energizing and prioritizing of those components over time. Whatever developmental philosophy we embrace, any progression will correlate to an evolving organization of memory that, of necessity, accommodates our revised values and identity.

Various personality trait or type theories – from Carl Jung, Gordon Allport, Raymond Cattell, C. Robert Cloninger, or Hans Eysenk – could be navigated in terms of the semantic containers those traits or types represent. More specifically, they could indicate the innate or default containers we have strengthened over time, and the current shape and condition of our self-concept. The question then becomes whether those containers should – or even can – be modified. One traditional view – echoed by some contemporary approaches such as Gallup's strengths-based development – is that we do best to embrace these traits and build upon them, rather than attempt to transform them. This is perhaps a useful approach for, as one example, quickly aligning a person's work performance with their natural propensities, but it does little to augment

healing or transformative practices.    How we resolve this issue
determines how trait or type theories might dovetail with metastructures
of being – and with the method of active memory reorganization
proposed in the next chapter.

To address this question, the concepts of the *real self* and the *ideal self* may
be helpful.   The real self is the idea of who we actually are – our current
state, traits and strengths – including our potential to self-actualize.  Our
ideal self is the conglomeration of societal expectations we accept or
project onto ourselves, an adopted simulacrum of who we *should be*.  The
difference between these two conceptions and experiences, between who
we are and who we think we should be, creates dissonance in our self-
concept.   Carl Rogers related to that dissonance as "incongruity," and
Karen Horney defined it as "neurosis,"  but the outcome is essentially
the same:   anyone steeped in this tension becomes stressed and
unhappy…potentially pathologically so.  So our goal here would not be
to create unrealistic ideals that contradict who we are.   On the other
hand, we also don't want to deny or restrict our own self-actualizing
potential.  The organic, experiential reality is that who we actually are
does change over time, and that with disciplined effort we can guide,
enhance and expand that evolution.   Otherwise we would never heal,
never strengthen, never grow, never learn, never become whole.  So trait
or type theories can help us explore and define our current state of being
at any given time – and specifically our current organization and
prioritization of the mnemosphere.  But they should not be relied upon
to rigidify who we are, or restrict who we can become.

Additional approaches, such as social learning theories from Julian
Rotter or Albert Bandura, could also be interfaced with relative ease.  For
instance, Bandura's four sources of self-efficacy – our experiences of
mastery, the social modeling we observe, the social persuasion we are
subject to, and our own psychological responses – can fairly easily be
mapped into the proposed mnemonic landscape.  These sources could be
viewed as additional ways of prioritizing and organizing supportive
structures and processes into semantic themes, metathemes and
containers for each region.   In the same way, motivational theories –
Abraham Maslow's hierarchy, Frederick Herzberg's dual factors, Steven
Reiss's basic desires, Edward Deci and Richard Ryan's self-
determination theory, etc. – offer us different hierarchical cross-sections

of mnemosphere and different prioritizations of exchanges, with the intended result that we become more effective in fulfilling our own needs. All of these concepts fit within the memory field framework, and indeed add value to it.

We could of course explore many more comparative ideas, but the point here is that the relationship between memory and identity can integrate with various schemas to create new synergies, rather than excluding any particular approach. Different approaches can, in fact, offer additional tools to enhance self-awareness, supplant or combine with the core AMR practices we'll cover in the next chapter, and generate a more comprehensive theory of the mnemosphere. Even B.F. Skinner's radical behaviorism – as set in stark contrast to cognitive approaches – offers us an understanding of reinforcement and conditioning that is indispensible in helping evaluate how our mnemosphere took shape, and how we can transform it.

Regardless, however, we want to allow enough room for different evolutions as new data is uncovered and new avenues of exploration are unveiled. In my view, one of the greatest pitfalls of the modern era is its insistence on competition between ideas – and the often deliberate subjugation of one meme by another – rather than holding as many concepts as possible in a gently synthesizing embrace. There is of course always the challenge of specialized vocabularies, incompatible methods, blinding philosophical biases, the unnecessary rivalries provoked by commercialism and so forth, but when we peek below the surface of different conceptual frameworks, we may find enough common threads to weave a stunning new tapestry that is much stronger and more vibrant than what has come before. In my view, continual openness, inclusiveness, dialogue and synergy are the chief characteristics of any integral system, and well worth striving for.

## THE METHOD: ACTIVE MEMORY REORGANIZATION (AMR)

There are many extant techniques that attempt to explore, expand or modify individual components of the mnemosphere. Usually, each approach targets one type of memory and relies upon a particular philosophical orientation regarding the most effective mechanisms for doing so. At one end of the spectrum are body-centered techniques that utilize structural manipulation to access and change memory patterns stored in our physiology. At the other end of the spectrum are cognitive approaches that rely on talk therapy, guided imagery or introspection to explore formative events from our past. And of course there are countless other approaches as well, including techniques designed to access the experiences of previous lifetimes, rectify karma in some way, or heal injuries to the soul. But a common theme among all of these approaches is that our past determines our present; that we cannot escape the influences of our mnemosphere on every aspect of our being in navigating each new situation and environment.

Our goal here is therefore to create a method of active memory reorganization that involves all metastructures and supportive structures of the mnemosphere. Why? Because each memory or memory pattern does not exist in isolation. They are interconnected with every other component of the memory field, drawing on aspects of each to generate a whole. If we neglect any particular region or supportive structure, the rearrangement will be incomplete and likely to revert back to previous conclusions about our identity through the energetic force, weight and momentum of other unaddressed patterns or unaltered associations. And yet, in order to contextualize and learn from each event in our lives, we tend to first isolate them from each other, then group them into families of similar experiences that reinforce familiar themes and support our generalized conclusions about self, others and the world at large. We are constantly shifting from specific to general and back to specific again to navigate our perceptions and understanding, and the semantic containers that group our memories govern that process. This seems to be a permanent fixture of human consciousness.

At the heart of an integral method of memory reorganization is the recognition that the more material we accumulate under one heading, the more powerful that group of memories becomes in fixing our conclusions, establishing our most enduring beliefs and filtering our perceptions. And because these containers can be somewhat arbitrary – in both their creation and in how we distribute memory patterns among them – our entire worldview and method of navigating reality can become equally arbitrary. So rather than relying on this capriciousness, we can begin to group our memories more actively – that is, in a consciously directed and structured way that is beneficial to our wholeness and well-being.

The challenge is engineering a method that not only accesses all of the mnemosphere, but also appeals to as broad an audience as possible; an integral method that is integrally accessible. To attempt this, we will explore how my own memories shaped me over the course of my life and the ways I have reorganized my own episodic material. Our focus will remain primarily on episodic patterns, because among all of the supportive structures in our mnemosphere, this is one of the most accessible and the most powerful in creating positive, cascading changes in all other areas. The method proposed here also includes many additional components, but understanding, evaluating and rearranging episodic patterns will be our primary means of mnemonic leverage throughout.

What are we really trying to accomplish here? We want to identify what semantic themes, metathemes and containers dominate our experience. We want to appreciate how these elements are ordered and energized in our consciousness. And we want to enable both flexibility and malleability in how our mnemosphere is structured, while at the same time generating thoughtful priorities for that reorganization. That is, out of our own values, drives and specific needs for nourishment in each dimension, we want to formulate the most supportive and sustainable landscape of self. We want to consciously create who we are and where we are going from a cooperative nexus of thoughts, feelings, spirit, and physical awareness – from our past as well as our present. For however we choose to evaluate and re-integrate our past will determine how we interpret the present, and what vision we project onto our future.

With all of this in mind, the integral approach to active memory reorganization has five core practices applied in conjunction with a five-step process, successively evaluating and instigating changes in one or more regions of the mnemosphere – and in combination addressing all regions. First, let's summarize the core practices, the essential widgets in our toolbox of self-transformation. These include engaging in *neutral awareness*; invoking *gratitude and compassionate affection*; utilizing *therapeutic breathing* techniques; initiating *cognitive restructuring*, and ensuring *reinforcement and accountability*. Each is applied to the structures and metastructures of memory, resulting in a permanent transition from self-limiting or injurious patterns of self-concept to a healing, flourishing and empowered identity. Later we will explore some resources for routine application of these practices, but for now we will paint each with a broad brush.

## Five Core AMR Practices

**Neutral Awareness.** Consider the possibility of a near-perfect stillness of mind, body, heart and spirit. A receptive and observant state of introspection that witnesses what is occurring within every region of the mnemosphere without reacting to it in any way…other than to notice what arises and then, in turn, letting each observation go. Here we are detached but attentive, interested but calm, engaged but relaxed. This is in fact a state encouraged by different spiritual traditions as the deliberate result of meditative practice, or we could characterize it as a sort of non-meditation. After all, we are just remaining still, being watchful, noticing and releasing, recognizing and letting go, again and again until the neutral observer of our non-reactive consciousness becomes a primary reflex, quieting all other responses.

What is happening here? We are allowing the energy of our perceptions, experiences and judgments in the moment to dissipate on their own. We are, in effect, encouraging those phenomena to congregate in the neutral field of our integrative buffer rather than any other region. As long as we do not amplify that energy with our reactions, this is what will happen. In contrast, if we were to forcefully deny ourselves of any reaction, this would increase the energy of whatever was occurring – so this is not a process of suppressing our responses. Think of a pack of dogs reacting to a passing siren. One begins to howl, the rest join in, and the howling, whining, barking and general excited carrying on continues after the initial siren has attenuated. Achieving neutral awareness is essentially allowing ourselves to recognize that yes, there is a siren, but then relaxing our desire to howl in response. If we are more used to howling, of course, that may still be our first reflex, and so our neutral attention shifts to our own howling, observing it from a distance. "Oh look, I'm howling. Huh. Isn't that interesting."

At first this skill may feel like indifference, but it is anything but that. Instead, we are paying a very special type of attention to our inner life. We are noticing and honoring our physical sensations, our emotions, our thoughts, our thoughts about our thoughts, our intuitions and spiritual insights, material bubbling up from our unconscious and so on. We are just relinquishing our need for control over these things, along with our necessity to draw conclusions from them, or their drawing us into their orbit in some way. We are relaxing into neutrality because from within that space – the space of our integrative buffer region – all these phenomena have equal priority. And when everything has equal priority, we can consciously decide what we would like to do with each of the phenomena that arise. Eventually, neutral awareness will allow us to more carefully and consciously process and distribute information within our mnemosphere.

For that is the endgame in this particular exercise: providing a bit more freedom in how we organize the regions of our memory field. This tool allows us to shift from the reflexive, arbitrary and chaotic organization of past habits into a new world of conscious order. Once we induce neutral awareness, shifting episodic memories from one semantic container to another, and even associating different emotions with them, becomes much easier. But is learning to inhabit this stillness easy? It is difficult for some, and surprisingly easy for others, but once we experience the depths of a truly neutral awareness, subsequent efforts become ever more effortless. In truth, this is about mastering effortlessness, but if we are used to expending effort to achieve balance – or to feel calmer, or gain perspective – then this exercise may feel awkward and foreign at first. Once we get the hang of it, though, it's really as easy as breathing.

**Gratitude and Compassionate Affection.** Here again we aim to depart from previous patterns of emotional response to what arises within and without. But this time our goal is to generate a distinctly non-neutral emotional disposition. By practicing gratitude and compassionate affection on a daily basis, we condition ourselves to filter both what emanates from our mnemosphere and what is absorbed into it through these positive emotions. We prepare ourselves to respond with gratitude and affection as our first reflex, rather than with more antagonistic emotions such as anxiety, anger, sadness or disappointment. The more consistently we can condition our emotional disposition, the more likely we are to process all information in our memory field in its most positive light.

Remember that emotional disposition is a region of our mnemosphere precisely because it helps us contextualize memory. If my emotional disposition leans in the direction of joyful contentment, then not only will every episode in my autobiographical memory be colored with that positive emotion, but I will tend to prioritize and recall memories that support this condition. As we practice gratitude and affectionate compassion, we will call upon recent and long past episodic material to evoke and reinforce these emotions. In effect, we will energize positive supportive material with the combination of our mental focus and felt emotional state. And once this process has begun, it too will become a natural rhythm in our daily life, informing not only the quality of our thoughts and insights, but also our very identity. We become what we feel.

To differentiate, this is not a "positive thinking" practice, nor is it a Pollyannish approach to our memories or experiences. It is instead the training of our emotional heart muscles toward the most uplifting and constructive reflexes in the human emotive repertoire. We begin with gratitude and affection exercises relating to things that easily and naturally evoke those responses in us, then gradually move toward more challenging material. Like any practice, our effectiveness will grow with time. This becomes one more tool in mastering the reorganization of episodic patterns and disposing ourselves toward the most constructive responses during each new encounter within and without; one more way to be free of unhealthy reflexes that limit us, and create a brighter path for our minds and hearts.

**Therapeutic Breathing.**   Moderating our breathing patterns is an excellent physiological tool. There are many variations in technique, but we will rely mainly on just one type to augment our active memory reorganization. Not only can this technique calm turbulent emotions and jumbled thoughts, but it can also help us access our unconscious substrata by encouraging unconscious material to percolate up into our integrative buffer. In addition, when used in combination with any of the other techniques discussed here, therapeutic breathing tends to greatly amplify their effectiveness. Also, as a means of evoking and interacting with somatic memory, it is indispensible. As with any of the other methods we'll be exploring, experiencing is believing; however, therapeutic breathing has been used in spiritual traditions for centuries and more recently has been adopted by mainstream medicine for managing everything from emotional stress to high blood pressure.

Another important byproduct of this tool is the potential to encourage spiritual (or quantum?) perception-cognition. In this context therapeutic breathing becomes an aid to mystic activation and subsequent connection with the ground of being. Remember that we are trying to address all regions of our mnemosphere, so structuring an approach to spiritual information is a necessary process. It is of course possible – and even likely – that other methods will assist our exploration of spiritual ground. Gratitude and affectionate compassion could, after all, be directed toward the Divine, and neutral awareness can also open doors into the Absolute, so we shouldn't exclude those possibilities. However, therapeutic breathing has proven to be extremely effective in assisting exploration of this particular region of the memory field.

**Cognitive Restructuring.**   As the fourth item in our toolbox, cognitive restructuring draws upon the well-established principles of several cognitive techniques, including cognitive behavioral therapy (CBT) and motivational interviewing (MI), with additional tools defined by *Integral Lifework*. These methods most readily involve our narrative self and governing beliefs, but can easily be applied to all other regions as well the supportive structures of our memory field. Cognitive restructuring asks us to recognize our reflexive patterns of thought, emotion and behavior as experienced in our episodic memory and expressed in the present. We then evaluate the conclusions we have drawn from those patterns – that is, the semantic containers we have created to make sense of them. Are those conclusions valid? Do they align with our core values? Are they effective in supporting our fulfillment impulses and satisfying our twelve dimensions of nourishment? Do they conform to the evidence we observe around us in the present, or are they rooted in assumptions that aren't necessarily rational or founded on fact? Do we wish to change how our memory is organized to support a more constructive, harmonious and reasonable set of conclusions? From this point, we can experiment with new, alternative sets of assumptions and behaviors, and see how those align with our reality, until we settle on a semantic organization that work better for us in measurable ways.

As with each of the other tools, cognitive restructuring is about strengthening conscious choices. Do we wish to operate on an arbitrarily determined autopilot that disrupts healthy or sustainable results in certain areas, or do we wish to exercise a more thoughtful influence, enlivening positive outcomes that help us thrive? Our memory creates a backdrop for all our thought processes and a trajectory for our self-concept. Using cognitive tools to delink autobiographical material from unhelpful or destructive associations allows us to reshape both that backdrop and that trajectory.

**Reinforcement & Accountability.** If we think of the first four core practices as forces that shape the clay of our mnemosphere, this final practice is like a kiln that fires that shape into relative permanence. Without reinforcement and accountability, our narrative self, governing beliefs, emotional disposition and other metastructures will tend to revert back to their previous iterations. There are four helpers in this area of practice: the *goals* that we routinely set for ourselves; the *activities* we engage in each day; the *environments* in which we spend most of our time; and the *language* we use in our routine interactions. G-A-E-L. If you're a fan of Gaelic history, culture and language as I am, this might be a useful mnemonic.

The common thread among these four helpers is of course that our relationships with other people have tremendous influence on each one. In fact you could say that the quality of our relationships as defined by these four areas is a major determining factor in the success of AMR. If our relationships continually support goals, activities, environments and language that in turn support the deliberate revisioning of our self-concept, then our most positive efforts will constantly be energized. If our relationships and community undermine or contradict those efforts, we are likely engaging in a Sisyphean exercise. The goal here is to generate a sense of confidence and competence around our newly formed trajectory of self, and although we shouldn't become dependent on our relationships to maintain this sense, the reality of human social needs is that the relationships we choose will have a lasting impact on our ongoing development.

### The Five-Step AMR Process

At first we learn to use each of these five tools independently, in concentrated, focused exercises, until we become comfortable with all of them. The ultimate objective, however, is to apply all five tools simultaneously and continuously in deep integration with our unconscious processes. Through repetition and committed intention, we invigorate healing and constructive patterns in all regions of our mnemosphere, including our unconscious substrata. In one way we are setting ourselves free from one interpretation of our past, while in another we are training ourselves to adhere to a new vision of what that past means. By choosing to evaluate and change the patterns in each region of our memory field with the five tools outlined so far, we take the first steps toward a less automatic and more creative existence. Rather than acting or reacting out of imprinted cycles of being we learned when we were young, we initiate new patterns that conform to the values and ideals we choose to cherish. In concept, this approach is immediately recognizable; in practice, it requires a stubborn commitment to well-being and growth.

AMR offers a straightforward, five-step process:

**Step One:** Understand and initiate the five core practices independent of their application to memory reorganization. In other words, strengthen our interior muscles with each widget in preparation for ongoing AMR.

**Step Two:** Inventory the semantic themes, metathemes and containers we rely on most from day-to-day, and how these containers may be tied into our most formative autobiographical memory. How have certain episodic patterns organically organized and reinforced themselves?

**Step Three:** Evaluate the effectiveness and accuracy of our current memory organization and its expression in our identity. Does the current state of our mnemosphere facilitate outcomes that align with a realistic and positive self-concept? Does it reflect our most deeply held values? Is it creating barrier to nourishment, or facilitating self-nurturing? All of this is intended to occur without self-reproach or guilt, but rather in a crucible of neutral awareness that is warmed by gratitude and compassionate affection.

**Step Four:** Develop alternative arrangements of episodic memory – or alternative emphasis and conclusions for existing associations – that more effectively support our values, priorities and preferred self-concept. That is, envision a reorganization that creates and sustains healing, healthy and even transformational metastructures of being. Then we compare and contrast that vision to where we are. Here we are encouraging a freefall in our identity and memory organization, a mild but potent crisis that must be resolved.

**Step Five:** Condition our memory field to strengthen and integrate this new, regenerative memory organization. This is achieved through the continued utilization of the five core practices, with particular emphasis on creating goals, activities, environments and language that reinforce our consciously chosen patterns and the most positive facets of our ever-evolving self-concept. Inherent to this reinforcement is the balanced nourishment of the twelve essential dimensions of being, as well as a sincere commitment to our renewed identity. In this final step, it is critical that our intention, attention and follow-through support our chosen direction for all of this internal reorganization. While accepting wherever we are, we are at the same time drawn forward into the light of our own rejuvenating being.

Toward the end of each chapter, we'll touch on how some or all of these steps were involved in reorganization of the episodic material described in that chapter. However, it is important to acknowledge that no two people will have the same experience of AMR. It is a loose framework of practices and guiding principles, within which autobiographical material can be evaluated and rearranged, but the specific arrangement occurs differently for everyone depending on their proclivities, life experiences and context of the moment. In my own case, revisiting certain families of experience in my mnemosphere has encouraged continuous reorganization and subtle shifts in identity. The objective is therefore not to create a new fixed pattern of associations, but an organic way of managing our mnemosphere so that we can rediscover and re-create who we are throughout every step of our journey.

So now we have some of the concepts and vocabulary needed to navigate through the farthest reaches of memory. When we combine the five core practices in the five steps of AMR, barriers to compassionate and transformative self-care begin to evaporate. No well-rutted series of chained associations, no unassailable fortitude of antagonistic belief, and no intensity of trauma can stand for long before our efforts to mitigate them in this way. Any and all impedances to a constructive and vibrant sense of self and a flourishing capacity to nurture every dimension of being eventually crumble before this synthesis. If memory is everything, then empowering ourselves with a fluid ability to reorganize memory changes everything. We are not layering superficial adjustments on top of unaltered core material, but reshaping the core material itself, thereby becoming sculptors of our own lives.

A proposed primary motivation throughout all of these efforts – and in fact the very thing that motivated me to write this book – is an overwhelming desire for the good of All. We become whatever we consume, and whatever we become individually contributes to the evolution of the whole. Therefore, whatever drives what we consume individually is eventually expressed in the dominant memes of our surrounding culture. Although our motivations will always be multifaceted and complex, we can still aspire to place the greater good above both our own willful self-gratification and any codependent reflexes that might sabotage us. When we engage in any major adjustments to our interior processes, we can be guided by a sincerely compassionate impulse – compassion for our own well-being and for the constructive impact of our efforts on everyone around us. As within, so without.

## How Memory Reorganization Relates to Self-Nourishment

Within the context of holistic self-care, active memory restructuring is intended to remove barriers to essential nourishment. Since our memory-identity is the primary filter through which we view the world around us, it alternately allows or disallows various exchanges, trusting or mistrusting each interaction, evaluating and prioritizing each self-care dimension and self-nurturing practice. For example, if my self-concept does not include a spiritual dimension, I will tend to devalue spiritual nourishment as a necessary avenue of self-care. If I have struggled with traditional avenues to intellectual learning my entire life, I may minimize the importance of certain forms of mental stimulation. If my memories are brimming with failures whenever I have initiated physical intimacy, I will tend to deemphasize or even reject the role of such intimacy in my interactions. If my recollections are replete with themes of betrayal and mistrust, then I will struggle with vulnerability and reliance in my present relationships. Our current habits of self-nurturing are inseparable from how past nourishment experiences have shaped our mnemosphere.

*Integral Lifework* defines twelve dimensions of essential nourishment that support, sustain and transform us as individuals and as a society. As a natural outgrowth of our fulfillment impulses, all of these nourishment centers can both influence and be influenced by active memory reorganization. Here is a brief summary of those dimensions:

- **Healthy Body.** Sustaining and strengthening our physical being through conscious patterns of diet, exercise, sleep and other key factors uniquely suited to who we are.

- **Playful Heart.** Maintaining healthy emotional expression and connection with our inner life, and engaging in regular playfulness and creative self-expression from day to day.

- **Supportive Community.** Inviting love and acceptance into our lives, both in what we receive from others, how loving and accepting we are of others, and how actively we participate in our community.

- **Expanding Mind.** Building, broadening and routinely stimulating our knowledge, understanding and mental capacities and abilities.

- **Fulfilling Purpose.** Discovering and actuating a satisfying life-purpose that is perfectly matched to our authentic self, and which supports the focus, strength and healthy expression of our personal will.

- **Authentic Spirit.** Establishing and increasing our connection and interaction with the ground of being – described in different traditions as the fundamental essence, spiritual energy, universal soul or divine nature of reality – and translating that deepening connection into a spiritually authentic life.

- **Restorative History.** Acknowledging, honoring and, when necessary, reprocessing all the experiences of our lives – whether remembered or forgotten, integrated or rejected – that have contributed to our current state of being; every significant relationship, trauma, milestone, accomplishment, perception or influence that has led us to the present moment.

- **Pleasurable Legacy.** Creating and sustaining new life, pleasurable experiences that are shared, and an enduring and positive impression on our world, while at the same time maintaining a sense of safety and stability for ourselves and those we love.

- **Flexible Processing Space.** Being able to regularly and effortlessly transition through different modes of processing, with each centered in different facets of our being – the heart, mind, body, spirit and soul – so that we fully nourish those facets and create transparent access to the insights, wisdom and discernment each has to offer.

- **Empowered Self-Concept.** Tuning our self-awareness, self-worth and self-efficacy toward the most realistic, compassionate and supportive range of function, so that we both strengthen our nurturing capacity in all other nourishment centers, and continually address any barriers that arise.

- **Satisfying Sexuality.** Exploring the nature of our own sexuality – through the dynamics of our sexual relationships and our expectations of intimacy – in order to clarify and communicate our needs and desires and arrive at fulfilling nourishment for ourselves and those with whom we sexually engage.

- **Affirming Integrity.** Consciously aligning the unfolding essence of our being with our thoughts, feelings, words and actions, so that *how* we are from moment to moment authentically reflects *who* we are in our innermost depths.

One of these dimensions, Restorative History is the obvious placeholder for most of the concepts and practices of active memory reorganization. There is also a direct linkage between Empowered Self-Concept and the mnemosphere. The dimensions of Flexible Processing Space and Affirming Integrity have a prominent role as well. But really, all dimensions of nourishment are interdependent, and although it may appear we are restricting our focus to just a few at a time, the usefulness of adjusting our mnemosphere actually relies on holistic nurturing in all dimensions at once, even as memory reorganization likewise contributes to the nourishment of all twelve.

For example, I might become more physically healthy as I reorganize self-limiting memories into empowering ones – I might even become a more effective athlete – but I must concurrently address my physical well-being even as I engage memory's mainly interior dimension. I may be expanding my mind, or enhancing the relationships of my supportive community, or encouraging the playfulness of my heart, or even define a more fulfilling purpose. Once again, everything is memory. In terms of our individual and collective well-being, perhaps the greatest error of the modern era is the belief that different components of any living organism operate independently of each other, or can be addressed separately from their integral whole. As all dimensions work in concert to satisfy our primary drives and fulfillment impulses, every region of our mnemosphere works in concert to facilitate nourishment for all dimensions.

## How The Rest of This Book is Organized

In each of the following chapters, you will encounter the current organization of my own episodic memory into semantic themes, metathemes and containers. Each chapter roughly equates to a dominant family of experiences, with chapter sections summarizing recurring metathemes I have grouped within in that container. Some of these choices are the deliberate consequence of years of interior work. Others reflect my default evolution without much conscious evaluation. In the very process of recalling these events and writing about them, I have of necessity revisited many of the tools and steps required by active memory reorganization. Sometimes I was surprised at how easily and calmly I could re-experience both traumatic and inspirational moments from my past. Sometimes I was equally surprised at how powerful the emotions and reactions to some memories can still be. Sometimes I was appalled at how poorly I have tended my inner gardens of self. Sometimes I was delighted at the progress I have made.

And this is really how the journey waxes and wanes for most of us. What follows is a snapshot of where I am, and perhaps a hint of where I may be headed. It is by no means a static or refined truth about my past, but a loose and sloppy rendering of my current sense of self that is supported by the selective recollection of events. So this book has become an exercise in shaping my mnemosphere, in gently nudging episodes of memory into a more transparent framework of associations. Conforming to the spirit of the approach we are promoting here, I must continually question the efficacy and validity of the book's organization. Does it accurately reflect how I came to be who I am today, or how I want to be tomorrow?  Does it reveal barriers to nourishment that I still need to address?  Does it unveil new vistas of self that strengthen dimensions of self?  Are my recollections accurate?  Am I perpetuating some unfortunate illusions?  Is the freshly felt experience of these memories positive and supportive?

Within each chapter I attempt to answer some of these questions, and summarize how each semantic container has contributed to my overall sense of self.  Of particular interest to me is how each conglomeration of episodic memory contains a potent duality:  each contributes both to what could be considered a strength or facilitator of nourishment, and what could be considered a weakness or barrier to nourishment.  The direction these life-themes lead us is determined by many things, but one of the more consistent factors is our emotional disposition at any given time.  When we feel positive emotions, our memories support positive conclusions and outcomes.  When we feel negative emotions, those same memories undermine our strength, effectiveness and well-being.  So we will also explore how I have encouraged, accepted and integrated the most upbeat and constructive interpretations of various memories.  Those instances where I have not been able to do this will also become evident, and these are of course equally instructive.

In the final section of the book, we'll explore some exercises and resources for the five core AMR practices.  As I'll often reiterate, these practices are standalone methods of strengthening connections within all regions of our mnemosphere.  They offer us a means of consciously reshaping every aspect of our self-concept.  We need only stretch our mental, emotional, spiritual and physical muscles to allow the energy of our awareness the freedom and power required to heal and transform itself.

## CHAPTER ONE: FREEDOM & ADVENTURE

When I was just a few months old, my parents packed up the Chevy and drove cross-country from Hartford, Connecticut to Eugene, Oregon, where my father would pursue his professorial career and my mother would study art. This would be a stressful choice for a newly married couple. There were the rigorous demands of University life, the isolation from family and friends back East, the relationship problems native to their youth and inexperience, and of course their disparate personalities and idiosyncrasies. Add to this the constant stress over finances from trying to survive on my father's meager teaching salary, and it's really no surprise the powder keg exploded so quickly. In just over a year my parents were divorced.

My mother – rather abruptly and decisively as both my parents report it – decided to be a single parent, putting herself through school while struggling to make ends meet at home. In today's world this has become less of an anomaly, but in 1967 the resources available to families in our situation were limited. The stigma attached to a young woman with a two-year-old in tow and no wedding ring was a palpable thing. Even in a place like Eugene, Oregon, which had already fully embraced the best and worst of sixties counterculture at that time, our integration into the surrounding social fabric was extremely difficult. Not that my mother didn't try to gain acceptance, or that we didn't have friends or fun times, but our financial and social status, combined with my mother's mercurial personality, often left us stranded and alone in a sea of cultural revolution. We weren't a traditional family and my mother didn't embrace free love and drugs, so it often felt like we were on the outside looking in.

We moved frequently in those first few years. Mainly within Eugene but eventually landing among the coastal dunes of Florence. I would visit my father on weekends, but he was busily building a new life for himself with a new wife who, in turn, had a daughter of her own. So on the one hand, my mother was preoccupied with school, work and a few brave attempts to catch a new breadwinner and make meaningful social connections. On the other, my father and his new wife had very little bandwidth for a highly energetic boy, and what little energy was available was expended managing the incessant conflict between Shelly, my new step-sister, and me. I'll return to these dynamics later on, but for now the main point is that, from age three on, in one household I learned how to entertain myself, and in the other I learned to act out to get attention from others. In both cases, there wasn't much adult supervision and, for the most part, I enjoyed a generously unfettered and self-directed existence.

## Trees, Bicycles & Sand Dunes

From all accounts of the folks who observed me at that time, I was an unstoppable force of nature once I achieved upright mobility. I would walk or run everywhere, clambering or jumping over anything in my path, always seeking the new vista around the next corner or beyond the next fence.  This exploration was not completely solitary, as I was often accompanied by whatever stray dog my mother had adopted at the time. But it was otherwise entirely independent.  Somehow, after hours of crawling under hedges, racing through backyards and clambering up into trees, I would find my way back home.  Whatever adult happened to be responsible for me during these intervals often had little idea of how far I had roamed, or the spirit of carefree trespass I was employing, and everyone but my mother usually discounted my tales of those wide-ranging adventures as the fanciful musings of an imaginative child.  I couldn't really climb over the backyard fence at my age, they reasoned, so I must have remained safely where they had left me in the yard or my room; I must have escaped only in my mind, then torn my clothes, scratched my skin and collected a bug bites and ticks by some other means.

Many of my earliest memories involve being up in a tree.  I don't know when I first discovered their friendly help, but I fell quickly in love with the feel of bark under my fingers, the smell of green leaves and tangy sap, and the unparalleled avenue to freedom they provided.  If a fence had no hand-holds, I could climb a nearby tree, crawl past the top of the fence on a sturdy limb, and drop down on the other side.  If older kids were teasing or chasing me, I could quickly climb up out-of-reach and wait until they got bored of throwing rocks at me.  If a new babysitter was being unreasonable, I could hide from her among the dense foliage of the uppermost branches until she made a panicked call to my mom. Trees were a safe haven, a causeway, a spy platform, a titillating tight rope, a miracle.

My tree-born antics generated enough of a reputation among the neighborhood kids that one day they decided to come to me for help.  Or at least that's what I thought.  Two of the older boys spied me in my front yard and ran over all agitated and out-of-breath.  "You gotta help Jimmy!" they declared, pointing urgently up the street.  "He's stuck.  He can't get down!"  One of them laughed breathlessly.

"What'ya mean?" I asked, staring where they pointed.

"Up there – in the tree!" They began running and pointing, calling back "C'mon! C'mon!" So I raced after them, feeling proud that they deferred to my tree climbing skills.

The boys led me to the base of one of the smaller maples that lined our street. "There, see?" they cried, still pointing. "Right up there!" It was late summer, still warm enough to make shade welcome, and the maple leaves were just beginning to hint yellow around the edges. I peered up into the green but couldn't see anything.

"Where?" I asked.

The boys were exasperated now. "Right there! Hey Jimmy...Jimmy!" But there was no answer. There was an eagerness in their urgency, but I didn't recognize what that meant. I was only four. I studied the tree for a minute and found my route, then began to climb. "Yeah!" one of the boys yelled. "Get him!" The other boy sniggered. Once I got past the first leaves, Jimmy did come into view. Though we were about the same age, he was smaller and frailer, and I was surprised to see him this far off the ground. How had he even gotten up here? He was huddled near the trunk, waving wildly. I climbed nearer. "Hey Jimmy," I said. He looked at me quickly and away again, his face streaked with tears. "What're you doin'?" And then I heard them. The gentle hum of bees echoing off the leaves. He wasn't waving, he was batting the bees away. "Don't do that!" I yelled at him. "Stop, Jimmy!" But he couldn't stop, and with a short, terrified sob his flailing became more frantic. "You're gonna make'em more angry," I started to say, and then a good-sized rock flew up between us, clearly thrown by one of the boys below.

There are some memories so distinct that they seem to convey incredible detail. The smell of leafy life, the gentle warmth of bark, the sturdy spring of a branch giving under a child's weight, the sickening thud of a rock smashing into a beehive, the rising panic as countless angry yellow blurs expand to swirl through every vacant bit of air. Without a thought I dropped to the ground and ran, putting Jimmy's waling cries quickly behind me. I could hear the bees chasing after, and I veered wildly out into the street, behind a parked car, back up the opposite sidewalk, through some bushes, ducking and weaving and scurrying anywhere to escape them.

The older boys were nowhere to be seen. A man poked his head out the front door of a nearby house and looked bewilderedly up and down the street. "Over there!" I yelled. "In the tree!" I pointed, and the man's gaze found the bee swarm with a worried look. Jimmy's muffled cries had turned to piercing shrieks. Then I ran until I couldn't hear Jimmy anymore.

I don't have a clear memory of what happened after that. Just a vague recollection of a neighborhood boy who'd been badly stung by a swarm of bees and rushed to the hospital. "Be careful, honey," my mother warned me when she heard.

"If you swat them it makes them angry," I fervently agreed. Out of guilt, or fear, or an instinctive need to distance myself from the experience, I never told anyone what had happened that day.

§

Trees continued to be an important element of childhood freedom, right up until I learned to ride a bike. Later on, they would become a portal to other worlds of adventure as well, from exploring J.R.R. Tolkein's Ent-filled imaginings in my early teens, to long hikes among the towering cedars of the North Cascades in my twenties, to devotional rituals among oak groves during my early forties. Even the tree-evoking surname I was born with – which I have since changed – opened doors for me. It translates roughly as "acorn man," and held just the right level of ancestral ambiguity to allow me access to disparate ethnic groups throughout my childhood. Some people assumed it was German, other people assumed it was Jewish, so I was embraced at different times by both groups. Of course, my name also awoke prejudices and even overt hatred as members of each group assumed it belonged to the other. All of these experiences would help spur insights into the nature of people's beliefs and emotional patterns later on. So my fascination with and affection for trees has persisted over the decades, and I have often sought out their company whenever I desired inspiration, advice or insight into the human condition.

Then, when I was five, a new discovery introduced me to another avenue of freedom. I already understood bicycles in a practical sense. My mother had routinely schlepped me off to school on the back of her own three-speed, and I had seen other kids riding around the neighborhood, but I had assumed that the privilege of ownership belonged to other people – adults and kids from families who could afford such things – and thus it generated very little interest for me. I think this is something many poor people can relate to. Sometimes a person in poverty might wonder what it would be like to have this or that option in life, but the question is quickly dismissed because those options are simply out-of-reach, and it's time to consider what it possible instead. In fact I did not learn to question the normalcy of many conditions of my upbringing until I was a bit older, after I had spent time with other families and friends. But when I was five, not having a bicycle seemed quite natural.

Then, one fall afternoon, one of my mother's frequent and usually short-term boyfriends, Elliot, asked me if I would like to learn how to ride a bike. It was a revelation. "Yes!" I promptly declared.

"Do you think it will be okay with your mom?" he asked.

I nodded emphatically. "She…she promised I could," I fibbed.

There are a couple of important tidbits to note here. The first is that my mother was not terribly discriminating in whom she allowed to babysit me. It might be the perpetually stoned hippies who lived next door to us, or a brand new boyfriend, or a distracted and stressed-out girlfriend of hers, or the parents of one of my school buddies. Mom often made summary judgments about people which were hasty and incomplete. Eventually she did find a regular babysitter, Darlene, with whom I had a whole new set of adventures. But all too often these random supervisors would for some reason defer to me regarding decisions that were sometimes routine – such as what would I like to eat – or more momentous, such as whether I would like to learn to ride a bike. Perhaps it was an indication of the times, or the inexperience of my babysitters, or my mom's questionable choices in the people she trusted, but nearly all of these folks relied on my judgment instead of their own. And so, to gain the greatest advantage in these situations, I would claim confident knowledge of my mother's opinions in various matters concerning me. As a result, I could usually enlist the aid of these companions in whatever adventures I invented in the moment.

And so it came to be that I found myself racing down a sidewalk on Elliot's ten-speed – a bicycle that was of course much too large for me. At first Elliott ran beside me to keep me balanced, but I quickly gained speed and left him behind. The wind rushing against my face, the sidewalk flowing away beneath me like water, and the end of that sidewalk racing towards me as I approached the intersecting street. I had learned from painful experience to be careful at intersections, and my squeals of delight abruptly quieted. "Use the brakes!" Elliott was yelling after me – but his voice seemed far away. What were brakes? I stared down at the bike, then back at the oncoming street. I was going faster than I ever had on my own. It was incredibly exciting. I didn't want to stop, but I knew that I had to. Not far ahead of me, a middle-aged woman was running across the approaching intersection toward me, waving her arms and yelling.

I don't know how I came the decision I made, but it seemed like the only option at the time. There was low wall on my right, a retaining wall for one of the lush yards in that part of Eugene, and I leaned into it. The front tire skidded against the wall and my right side struck hard, bouncing me off the concrete…but I was determined. I leaned in again and turned the handlebars, bouncing and sliding and grinding to a slower and slower speed until I was a yard or two from the corner. Then the middle-aged woman was suddenly there, startling me, grabbing the handlebars and bracing me to a halt. In a tone I would encounter often from adults during those early years, she cried, "What do you think you're doing?!" More from the pain blossoming along my side than the condemnation in her tone, I loudly began to cry.

"It's okay," said Elliott, catching up with us. "I let him," he panted. "I shouldn't have let him go like that."

The woman gave Elliott a stern look, rolled her eyes, handed the handlebars over to him, and strode off. I gazed down at my stinging scrapes, and my crying increased. Elliott tried to lighten the mood, declaring, "Hey, you did pretty good!" He smiled at me, though I could feel the edge of concern and perhaps a little frustration in his voice. "Hey, c'mon. You did great! A real champ for your first time." Eventually, he calmed me down enough to get me off the bike and into a slow walk home. When we reached the top of the hill, I wiped the remnants of tears from my face, looked back down at the course of my wild ride, then up at Elliott.

"Let's do it again!" I said, beaming at him with anticipation.

Elliott chuckled. "I don't think that's a good idea," he said. This prompted a new course of tears, but Elliott could not be persuaded to change his mind.

§

My relationship with bicycles would endure just as long as my relationship with trees. After much begging and pleading, my mom acquiesced to buying a pint-sized single speed wreck-of-a-bike at a tag sale. With the addition of some training wheels, I was able to zoom around the neighborhood for a few days free of incident. That is, until one bright winter morning I failed to account for the effect of morning dew on the grass of our front lawn. Hurtling a full speed off the sidewalk, I applied my brakes only to discover how slippery dewy grass could be. For Elliott, bless his heart, this would mean my pummeling headlong into his freshly painted bicycle, parked carefully in the morning sun on the concrete walkway to our front door. He had painted it bright green, and as I approached it at startling speed, I remember thinking about the color of the paint, and how angry everyone would be that I messed it up. But that was not what evoked the look of horror on my mother's face as I stumbled up the steps and into the house. No, it was more the sheet of blood from the gash in my forehead, streaming like a hot shower down my face and soaking my shirt.

My mother, convinced that I would never learn how to properly stop my bike, banned my riding for a time, pointedly reminding me whenever I challenged her decision of my frighteningly bloodied head, the twelve stitches required to close up my scalp, and the exorbitant doctor's bill.

But I was hooked, and in years after that, after we had left Oregon, I would be back in the saddle, jumping off of home-made ramps in parking lots, racing along dirt trails in the woods, experimenting with the laws of physics, and generally having a blast. From my banana-seat three-speed Columbia with a sissy bar when I was eight to my trusty Puch ten-speed street bike when I was thirteen, all of my bicycles provided me endless hours of entertainment, thrill-seeking, physical exertion, much needed escape from any drama at home, and a desperately desired sense of freedom.

Throughout my teen years, I would become more serious in my cycling aspirations, commuting to and from school ten miles a day, taking long rides into the countryside, racing cars on city streets, and ultimately touring across Germany and France when I was sixteen. Bicycles would spark my interest in mechanics and design, maintaining and repairing things to achieve optimum performance, and increasing my physical endurance and strength for their own sake. Bicycles would help me bond with my German step-grandfather as we explored the intricacies of using just the right tool for just the right repair job. And I would rely upon bikes for transportation to work whenever I was without a car, just as my mother had in our time in Eugene. But of course I continued to encounter risks along with the exhilaration and expansion of skills and scope. I would wreck three bikes beyond repair, my body somehow emerging unscathed from each incident. I would be beaten with a fan belt – by an angry Frenchman leaning out of his panel van – for running a red light on my Puch near Lyon. I would even be hit by a car, fly through the air head-first some forty feet, and land inches from a telephone pole. But through it all I was committed to my freedom, and to the amazing bipedal machines that made that freedom possible.

I still have a bicycle, of course. A Diamondback mountain bike. At low tide I can ride it along the sea-firmed beach here in San Diego. I can take it into the mountains to explore roads to rough to drive and trails too long to hike in one afternoon. I can run a quick errand to the store. I'm not the daredevil I once was, and all those years of riding have bent, compressed, stiffened and otherwise altered my body in unanticipated ways, so I'm not quite as spry a cyclist as I once was. I also can't quite match the steady 30 mph my adolescent thighs could sustain for miles on end. But the experience of freedom through hard work is the same as it always was. When I ride, I am under my own physical power, relying on my own judgment, and free to explore whatever comes my way without a care in the world. Carefree, that is, as long as I remember how to use the brakes.

§

During the last couple of years my mother and I lived in Oregon, bicycles were not only on the banned list, but also an impractical option. We had moved to a tiny beach house in Florence, on an unmaintained sand road, next to huge sand dunes and just a brief hike to the sandy edge of the sea. This landscape was barely walkable, let alone bikeable, and so most of my days were spent wandering the coast and dunes on foot for hours at a time. Endless sand. Endless sunshine. Endless new discoveries. Endless solitude with no one but my canine pals as companions. I was six years old then, soon to turn seven, and the question forming in any parent's mind at this point might be: why wasn't I in school?

School presented many difficulties for me as a youngster. In part, all those years of running around unattended had conditioned me to be much more active and self-directed than mainstream schooling could readily accommodate. My reflexive independence and adventurous curiosity were simply not an appropriate match for ordered rows of cold, hard desks and the stern taskmaster approach to teaching that still lingered from a previous era. Add to this that I had not adapted well to my parents' divorce, or to their subsequent hostility towards each other, or to the mood swings and angry outbursts they both meted out in their separate households over the following years. All of this resulted in a high-energy, emotionally turbulent little rebel with scant appreciation for structure or authority. Consequently, public school was a disaster.

As my mother tells it, she eventually had to pick me up from class in the middle of the day at the insistence of the Florence grade school administrator. At the end of his proverbial rope, my teacher had disciplined me for misbehaving by putting a diaper on over my pants and ordering me to stand on his desk in the front of the room. I have no distinct memory of this, only a pulsing echo of shame over something that happened at that school, amplified by my mother being summoned to take me home so early in the day. This is mom's recounting from years ago, and although she can be creative with her recollections at times, she has always been convinced this really happened. Regardless of the sordid details, letters from my mother to her mother from those weeks explain that the school advised I should stay home until I was better prepared for the rigors of mainstream education.

To her credit, my mother didn't leave my learning entirely to the dunes after that. She taught me the alphabet and how to count fairly high. I remember one incident involving dinner peas I had spread evenly around my plate to hide the fact that I was not eating them. My mother laughed and made me count the peas, eat some, and count them again to demonstrate the principle of subtraction. She would read to me, or tell me stories before bedtime, or sing quiet lullabies to me to help me sleep. On a few occasions she was able to get Darlene, my babysitter from Eugene, to watch me, and this augmented my education with teen magazines, local gossip and watching Darlene interact with her friends. But most days I was on my own for hours at a time, just as I had been in Eugene, wandering the dunes alone or with my dog Puma, a malamute who seemed to enjoy my company as much as I did his.

And so it came to pass that I learned many unusual things that a six-year-old is usually not privy to. For example, how to shoot a thirty-ought-six. For what I discovered in my wanderings was that the dunes weren't entirely abandoned. Here and there a someone had hermited themselves  away in a driftwood-adorned shed, old canvas tent or broken down camper. One such loner was Mike, a greasy-haired twenty-something fellow in grimy old army fatigues and a blue bandana. He liked to hunker down amid the tall beach grass and shoot at things with a really big rifle. I had watched him from a distance for three days before working up the courage to approach his dilapidated shack. When I finally did present myself, he was cleaning his gun, a gleaming steel weapon larger than life, and we both found ourselves shy and vaguely startled. Given my voracious curiosity, however, that didn't last long.

"Why do you shoot that?" I asked.

"This?" Mike looked down at the weapon. "I don't shoot it. Just keep it handy."

I scrunched up my face and said, "That's not true. I saw you shoot it."

Mike looked around quickly, clearly nervous. "Where're your folks?"

"My mom's at work."

"What about your Dad?"

I shrugged.

"So you're out wandering by yourself then," Mike said.

"Not always. Sometimes Puma comes with me. Sometimes Sundance."

Mike took a moment to adjust his bandana. "Puma and Sundance, huh? They your – "

 "Dogs. Good dogs." I said proudly.

"Right." Mike seemed to relax. He looked at his gun again. "Mostly just rabbits."

"You shoot rabbits?" I was incredulous. "How come?"

Mike hesitated. "Well, a man's gotta eat."

"Oh." Despite the fact that I had never heard of such a thing, it made complete sense to me. A long silence as Mike returned to cleaning his gun. "Can I shoot it?" I asked.

"What?" Mike seemed startled again.

"Can I shoot your gun?"

"Hell no!"

"How come?"

Mike looked around again. "Where do you live, kid?"

I pointed over my right shoulder. "Back there. It's a ways."

Mike considered, his head tilting to one side. I noticed his eyes were a pale, piercing blue. "Can you hear me shooting from where you live?"

I shook my head. "Huh-uh. I walked a long way before I heard."

Mike looked off into the distance, then back at me. "Well, what would your folks think of me letting me shoot a gun?"

"My mom has a gun," I lied. "She let me shoot it once."

"Oh yeah?" Mike leaned forward with interest. "What kind of gun?"

"I dunno. Smaller than that."

Mike laughed. "Well all right, then." He shook his head and laughed again. "Let me show you how it's done."

Mike wiped the gun down one last time and sauntered past a driftwood log lying nearby. Several yards beyond the log an assortment of rusty cans and heavy plastic bottles were strewn about the sand. Every one was riddled with pushed-in holes. Mike used these to construct three jagged pyramids in the sand, then returned to the log and beckoned me over. I moved close, excited by the prospect of really shooting something. Mike smelled strongly of unwashed hair and salty ocean, and I saw now how worn is clothes were. "First, just watch what I do," he said. Getting down on one knee, Mike took a shiny cartridge from his pocket, bolted it home, released the safety, and fired. The noise was huge. A tin can soared into the air and out of sight beyond distant mounds if sand, and the sharp smell of gunpowder wafted across my face.

"Whoa!" I yelled. "That's cool!" My ears stung a little from the noise, but I didn't care.

Mike grinned. "Now you try." He balanced the rifle on the driftwood log and had me kneel down behind it. "Hold it just like that. That's right. Now put your other hand here. Yeah. How does it feel?"

"Heavy!" I said truthfully.

"Yep. It's a big rifle. Thirty-ought-six. You can take down big game with one of these."

"Big what?"

"Big…moose. Elk. Bear."

"Have you ever shot a bear?"

Mike mumbled something incomprehensible. I looked up to see him frowning. "Now look at what your shooting at. Just pick a can."

"Okay."

"Good, now hold it steady. Good. Now pull the trigger."

I pulled. Nothing happened. "What's wrong?"

Mike was grinning. "Well, there's no round in the chamber, is there."

"Oh." I looked at Mike expectantly. He sighed. "You're sure your mom's okay with this?"

"Yeah!" I was really excited now.

Mike took a slow breath and drew one of the long casings from his pocket. "These got a lot of kick. You know what that means?"

"Uh…"

"It means the gun will buck you right off your feet."

"Is that why I'm kneeling down?"

Mike grinned and nodded. His teeth were very yellow. "Yep. That – and the weight of it would topple you right over anyways." And, slowly so that I could watch how he did it, he loaded the bullet into the gun. "Now…see this button here? That's the safety. Repeat after me: 'If it's red, you're dead.'"

"If it's red…you're dead?"

"That's right. It means the gun's ready to fire. So…are you ready?"

For the first time, I felt my excitement shift slightly toward apprehension. I nodded.

He clicked off the safety. "So…steady. Aim…aim right at the can. That's good. Now fire. Go ahead, pull the trigg – "

Concussive pain through my shoulder and a face full of sand. I lay on my side staring odd angles at the sky. My head rang with the rifle's report. "Owe!" I yelled.

"Yep! Hurts like a somnabitch, don't it?"

I scrambled to my feet to find Mike brushing sand off his rifle. I was nervous about how things had gone, but he looked pleased. "Take a look," he said.

One of the pyramids was gone. Scattered to the winds. "I did that?"

"Seems like you did," he said, grinning. "A regular Davy Crockett."

I rubbed my shoulder and looked at the ground.

"You'll sprout a nice bruise, there," he said. Then his tone became worried again. "Probably shouldn't tell your mom how you got it."

"Okay." I agreed easily. I looked at the scattered cans. "Do you really shoot rabbits with that gun?"

Mike nodded. I didn't know how to feel about that. So much power hurled at a tiny little rabbit? "A man's gotta eat," I said quietly.

Mike cleared his throat. "You best be gettin' along home. What's your name, anyway?"

"Todd," I said.

"Well, Todd, I'm Mike, and it looks like I need to get started cleaning my rifle again." He walked back to his shack. It seemed like he expected something from me that I wasn't giving him.

"Thanks!" I said at last. "It hurt but it was fun." I smiled.

"'Welcome. Come by anytime. Maybe bring your mom next time you're here. We'll go and shoot something for her." Mike smiled to himself.

"Okay. Thanks Mike!"

He nodded and I turned and ran, eager to share my exhilaration with the rolling dunes.

Within a few months my mother quit the job that had moved us to Florence, a pattern that would be repeated many times over the ensuing years. There was always some dramatic reason why she had to leave a position – perceived sexual harassment, scheming coworkers, the work environment making her physically ill...something. By her own admission, not long after their divorce, when my father asked her why her beautiful hands had suddenly become so swollen and contorted, my mother said condemningly: "Well, Bill, it's because now I have to *work*." She was actually suffering from an acute onset of arthritis, but she had made her point. My mother always laughs when she tells that story, and perhaps the incident sheds light on why she could never keep a job for long. So we spent our last few weeks at the beach together in our quaint little home among the dunes as she prepared to explain why I now had to go live with my father. I never saw Mike again, but like so many experiences from that time, he has remained with me all these years.

§

Later on there would be many other memories that reinforced these patterns of freedom and adventure, often the result of a decidedly inclusive parenting style on the part of both of my parents. My mother encouraged me to learn how downhill skiing in the hills of Vermont, which led to all sorts of crazy stunts for a young boy who really didn't know what he was doing, but who nevertheless loved the sense of barely-controlled speed. She also let one of her boyfriends take me on a speeding motorcycle ride, where I instinctively tried to stand up on the bike as it leaned low into a corner, almost causing a nasty crash. Mom had me tag along with her to Renaissance fairs in the Oregon woods as well, where naked women sported huge boa constrictors and the air was heavy with incense and cannabis. And although she did warn me at the time that it was illegal trespass, we also teamed up on antique hunts in abandoned farmsteads well off the beaten track.

My father had different interests, but the same stubborn commitment to including me in almost everything. He brought be along with him to parties and singing circles with his adult friends, even if no other children were present. He insisted I go rough camping with him, go swimming in forbidden reservoirs, and go fishing on private property. He always encouraged me to participate in adult conversations, no matter how unfamiliar or technical the topic. When he trained with his friend Dan in the Northfield river race, I would sit in the center of the Grumman canoe and frantically bail out whitewater that splashed in over the gunwale. On other canoe trips I would be sent to scout the river ahead, or retrieve gear that had jettisoned after an unexpected waterfall upended us into the ice-cold water. And of course he brought me with him to his work as well, letting me play with his hi-tech gadgets or participate in his research.

Both of my parents received a lot of flack from other adults – especially other parents – who felt I didn't belong in many of these situations. But both of my folks stood firm; this was probably the most consistent parenting characteristic they shared. And so it should be no surprise that I felt comfortable riding my bike on thirty-mile trips when I was eleven. Or participating in an Outward Bound experience with a dozen other kids in the Green and White Mountains when I was twelve. Or sneaking out at night to meet a girlfriend in the woods at age thirteen, then sneaking her back to my room. When I was sixteen, my father dropped my friend Eric and I off in Orleans, France for a multi-week bicycle trip. With only a rudimentary knowledge of the language, some questionable maps and an old nylon tent, we wound through the Massif Central region down to the beach town of Montalivet, then finished up in Lyons. There were also countless solo explorations of Frankfurt and other European cities in my final years living in Germany, and many harrowing risks as I snapped brazen photos in seedy neighborhoods. And there were a hundred other experiences where an uninhibited impulse to explore the unknown led to amazing, delightful, exhilarating and unmistakably life-affirming experiences. Each of them, I feel, was fueled by my earliest encounters with freedom and adventure.

## What Freedom Has Come to Mean

What can be extrapolated from such a tiny smattering of ingredients? A surprisingly rich pudding of information. Consider what I learned about freedom and adventure. My exploration of trees taught me that I could operate outside of people's expectations – I could do things other kids couldn't. I gained special knowledge and ability. I had fun. I created safety for myself. I was empowered. I grew stronger physically and mentally. All of this because I had the freedom to explore and experiment, to push my limits and assert my will, to boldly go where no other child I knew had ever gone. Then bicycles added more spice and substance to this mix, amplifying my sense of self-sufficiency, the freedom to explore, a slowly proven competence to navigate unknowns and strengthen other skills. And the dunes? Yet another test in that stage of my identity formation. A new landscape, completely foreign, where I was deprived of the two previous tools that had enabled my freedom. Without trees or bicycles, I was still able to feel at home in an undiscovered country, still able to investigate and experiment without fear, still able to create a niche for myself in a foreign ecology, still able to learn and grow in relative isolation. And so my unconscious began to abstract a guiding principle out of these disparate experiences: that the freedom to explore resulted in learning, strength, joy and mastery; that having a sense of adventure and the courage to follow through on it would unveil all the treasures of the world.

This had a profound impact on my later development. It allowed me to be bold and fearless in the face of many new situations, even those with a high level of risk. It encouraged me to be curious rather than reticent, interested rather than disengaged, ambitious rather than passive, persistent rather than defeated. For example, my choice to move from Frankfurt, Germany to Seattle, Washington on my own at age eighteen, without any contacts or real plan of action. Or to hike the North Cascades mid-winter alone, or travel around the U.S. in my camper, or take trips overseas to places I had never been. To start my own technology consulting business, or sing folk songs in bars, or try to get my writing published. To exit the comforts and established routines of Seattle, move to San Diego, and begin a new career. It is from this well I have likely drawn much of my energy to set and achieve goals throughout my life.

But there have been downsides as well. For instance, I have never navigated rigid or hierarchical structure very successfully, or been readily compliant with the status quo, or easily tolerated unchanging routines. I lean more towards impatience than acceptance in stressful situations, and I am always looking for new actions to take and new horizons to explore. Sometimes I dream too large, or underestimate the impossible, or drive myself too hard, or am too reckless. Sometimes I create stress in the lives of those I love when I create change for change's sake. And quite often my eagerness to inquire and explore have set me apart from my peers to such a degree that I have had trouble fitting in.

So the plus-and-minus columns continue to be populated by my well-schooled impulse toward freedom and adventure. On the one hand, I am passionate about new frontiers of mind, place, spirit and emotional experience; I love new experiences. On the other, I rail against most any kind of blind conformity, I bristle at any hint of inflexible rules, and I just can't buy into any system of ideas or beliefs without first experimenting on my own. The advantage of being able to take initiative is coupled with the disadvantage of questioning or resisting someone else's initiative. I lead easily but follow poorly. All of these are at least in part a natural outgrowth of those early experiences. Perhaps I was genetically predisposed to such propensities as well, but my early environments encouraged them to flourish.

As to how I value these aspects of myself, I am pleased to be courageous in the face of the unknown; it has become a much appreciated component of my identity. I am also content with accomplishments that resulted from my adventurous impulses, and am delighted with the kindred spirits I have encountered over the years who would rather take an exploratory risk than suppress their curiosity. But I am saddened that I could not complete college, or easily conform to team-centered structures, or learn before age forty how to constrain my focus or be content with certain achievements. Aside from a few high-quality friendships that were compatible with these adventurous tendencies, the necessity of freedom and exploration has tended to isolate me from others, and interrupt my sense of equanimity.

As I look back at my memories in this category, I can likewise view them in either a positive or negative light. I can celebrate the excitement of new vistas and discoveries, or I can mourn the loss of certain kinds of relationships and belonging. Yes, I have often taken the road less traveled, and the experience was that much more beautiful and intense because of the solitude. But no, I do not thrive in extended isolation, and would rather rejoice regularly with the smiling faces of those I love. So how does this bifurcation inform my identity? Am I a mountain man and explorer, destined to wander the wilderness in search of things few others have seen? Or am I a loner, an outcast, a marginalized fringe element of society, forever on the outside looking in?

These are the sorts of distinctions we routinely encounter while integrating experiences or re-integrating memories. As we will see through examination of other memories with different emotional content, the dichotomy of such choices is inescapable regardless of the experience. Every strength has its weakness; every asset has its deficit; every bright facet of self has its shadow. But if this is true, how can we create harmony within? How can we strengthen a healthy self-concept in the face of such contradictions?

One way is to ignore the contradiction and suppress the distasteful side of each memory pattern. If we filter all our memories through warm, fuzzy, rose-colored glasses, won't that help us be peaceful and whole? As has been observed by many psychologists, the human mind seems to have adopted this method as a default survival mechanism, at least when dealing with traumatic events or dissonant material. Unfortunately, over time, the suppressed aspects of a memory tend to reassert themselves in unpleasant ways, continually challenging our incomplete self-concept until, under periods of stress or during reactivation of unpleasant associations, our various coping mechanisms begin to break down.

Another straightforward method is to embrace both sides of any contradiction as a balanced whole. In other words, to recognize that every deficit also has its asset; every shadow has a bright side; every weakness supplies a strength. If that is true, then we can begin to accept the darker side of our experiences, and intellectually reconcile the seemingly oppositional aspects of our past. But this, too, is really only a half-measure. Like the wounds of a lovers' quarrel that resurface in the heat of fresh argument, our mental balancing act is easily vanquished by strong emotions. Even if our belief is strong, our equilibrium will ultimately unravel under stress, and we will devalue whatever we still consider to be negative.

In order to fully harmonize the contradictions of memory, something more radical and compelling is required. We need to summon a unifying force from the very depths of our being, a force that is more powerful than intellect and more enduring than the theoretical acceptance of abstract beliefs. Even then, in order to be effective, that force must be fully felt, in the present, in a continuous way. It must become the framework through which we view all memory, all facets of being, and all aspects of experience. For the moment we create any exemption – an unpleasant reality we wish to exclude from the clear light of day – we create a tear in the protective fabric of our lives through which darkness, fear, pain, guilt and self-loathing can easily flow back in to fill us up.

What is this unifying force? What will allow us to easily accept and integrate our interior dichotomies? It begins as a specific quality of empathy, a gentle cradling of our experiences in non-judgmental quiet. Then it grows in strength to embrace those experiences with a brimming fullness of compassionate attention. And at long last, with much practice at nurturing our compassionate momentum and letting it override any incessantly negative valuations, we can finally let go of the fear and hurt we have invested in the downside of any memory or facet of self. In effect, we fall in love with our own incompleteness. To be clear, this is not the sort of love that glorifies imperfections, indulges weaknesses or rewards missteps, nor is it a passive kind of love that waits patiently and watches silently from a distance. It is instead active, passionate, engaged and inexhaustible, lavishing boisterous affection on every corner of our being for no other reason than that they are part of us. And although that affection often shines the harsh light of honest awareness on those darkest and most uncomfortable corners of self, perhaps even instigating harsh and uncomfortable interactions with our past, it cares for those facets deeply, joyfully and skillfully. Once firmly established, this love will never abandon any part of us, no matter how deep in shadow.

How do we accomplish this? I will tell you how I did, and how I have seen many others do the same: in short, it can reliably be achieved simply by practicing the tools in our AMR toolbox in some combination that works well for us. *Neutral awareness, gratitude and compassionate affection, therapeutic breathing, cognitive restructuring* and *reinforcement and accountability* are the key to surrounding and supporting any memory with positive emotions. And it is through those positive emotions that we can first accept, then appreciate, then enthusiastically integrate the dichotomies of our past experiences. In my case, neutral awareness allowed me to carefully consider aspects of my childhood that were at first very difficult to look at – aspects that I had preferred to avoid entirely in the past. Therapeutic breathing then helped me ride out any turbulent, intense or negative emotions that arose whenever I brought certain memories to the surface. Gratitude and compassionate affection practices then allowed me relax my rejection of unpleasant memories – that is, of unpleasant parts of myself – so that I could eventually tentatively accept and even compassionately embrace them as part of my interior heritage. Cognitive restructuring helped me interrupt antagonistic patterns of thought and emotion, so that I could invoke such compassion without doubt, guilt, fear or pain. And various forms of reinforcement and accountability helped me continually integrate all of these benefits into a new way of being.

Does this process of acceptance, appreciation and integration always occur in the same manner? For different types of memories – or even the same types of memories for different people – the process can unfold in unique ways. Perhaps gratitude for the positive characteristics of an important person in our past helps us soften negative feelings about them, after which we can examine their contribution to our lives in neutral awareness. Perhaps therapeutic breathing allows us to access memories we have repressed, at which point we must apply neutral awareness to maintain equilibrium. And so forth. There is no set sequence of applying these tools to each memory, which is why it is so important to learn all of them, and to practice each one regularly, in order to exercise and strengthen conscious interplay between each region of our mnemosphere.

## Applying AMR

Let's take a look at some of the gradual introduction and repositioning of episodic patterns that ended up in the "adventure and freedom" semantic container. All of those fun times I had climbing in trees in Eugene, Oregon assembled themselves into a semantic theme we could call "trees are a special kind of fun." This happened quite early on, as there were very few mitigating or contradictory experiences – no serious injuries or negative consequences that resulted from climbing trees – with which to construct competing themes. The conclusions I then drew from my tree faring experiences about the nature of freedom and adventure came later, but were well-seated in my self-concept by age twelve. Any time I spent running, role-playing and exploring in the forest fed more supportive material into that family of experiences. I remember reading J.R.R. Tolkien's biography at about that age and being delighted that he too had a special affinity for trees, and I thought I understood why I had so enjoyed his descriptions of forests and Ents. So even my escape into fantasy literature and identification with its author reinforced my conclusions about trees being a special kind of fun.

Memories relating to bicycles assembled themselves quite similarly, as did wandering the sand dunes of Florence. But as I at some point began to identify a similar resonance among these experiences – a similar felt sense of adventure and freedom – other metathemes began to appear. For example, the idea that I might only be able to enjoy freedom and adventure when I was alone, or that its availability was somehow dependent on an unintended alienation from my peers, or my inability to navigate more structured environments like elementary school. This is how the dichotomies of any container begin to develop, and how disappointment and dissonance can creep into our self-concept. By age thirteen, I was fairly certain that enjoying the outdoors, feeling truly free, and adventuring into the unknown were an integral part of me. I was equally certain that this same part of me required I remain outside of established institutions of social conformance, avoid close relationships with others, and eschew societal expectations in general.

It is easy to observe how various metastructures of being were influenced by such experiences. My narrative self absorbed these lessons as both apparent limitations and ways to self-actuate. My governing beliefs about what freedom and adventure looked like, the importance of contact with nature, how relationships functioned, etc. My somatic memory of trusting my own body, running among sand dunes, hopping along tree branches, screaming down a steep hill on my bike, or breathing in the bright spice of salt air and the heavy musk of tree sap. The emotional disposition of excitement, anticipation, exhilaration and accomplishment that was associated with all of these components of my memory field. Even the spiritual ground of connecting with the natural world was facilitated here. So all these conclusions about myself and the world around me assembled themselves into complex, interdependent structures. They contributed to the bedrock upon which my personality was built.

So how did I go about moderating my conclusions later on, especially those that did not serve my navigation of society particularly well? Remember that all components of the mnemosphere share the same characteristics. One of those is the energy level of the data being stored. All that is required to reshape the content of a given container – and indeed even to shift that content into a new container – is to change the energy levels of that content in a targeted way. In other words, to change the emphasis or priority of the material. How is this accomplished? Primarily through two things: our level of mental focus on chosen aspects of that material, and our corresponding levels of emotional saturation associated with those aspects. If I concentrate on the felt expansiveness of being that always has been and continues to be facilitated by time spent among trees, on a bicycle or out among huge sand dunes, and in fact regularly duplicate or evoke that correlation, then I will fortify the energy of those components of my memory field.

This is achieved through some or all of the five core AMR practices. For example, I can regularly summon intense gratitude for trees, bicycles, sand dunes and all the positive associations they evoke. I can recall well-remembered visions of my adventures in nature while breathing slowly, deeply and evenly, and thereby stimulate and support deep connections with my inner life and the natural world. In these ways I keep the episodic memories that support positive conclusions about freedom and adventure in active, high-priority status. That is, by consciously giving them energy, I encourage their ascendancy in each region of my mnemosphere.

This positive energization is not the complete picture, however. For other, more antagonistic conclusions may still be present, waiting in the wings of my unconscious substrata. In fact, they may be just as energized as they always have been, even though I haven't consciously focused on them. So our goal must also be to change the energy levels of the more negative material as well. This time I might use neutral awareness to first disassociate the felt sense of loneliness, sadness or rejection from any of my experiences with trees, bicycles and sand dunes. Then I might use cognitive restructuring techniques to challenge the idea that my sense of adventure and freedom is somehow linked to social isolation; although one may have coincided with the other on occasion, they do not strictly *equate* each other. Thus I gradually de-link negative associations among the themes and metathemes within this container, reducing their energy level to standby or, ultimately, inactive status.

Of course this is just a brief sketch of one way to approach reorganizing these particular episodic patterns. It does roughly reflect my own efforts, followed by other reinforcing actions. For example, over time I began including more and more friends in my bicycles trips, hiking, skiing and camping, thus providing my mnemosphere with additional supportive material that diluted previous dichotomies regarding freedom and adventure. Yet were I not to address the underlying tensions of this semantic container, I might inadvertently sabotage such efforts, or color them with ancillary failures and disappointments. And so this is part of how AMR works: we energize all memories and current behaviors that support our most constructive and valued themes and metathemes, while at the same time diffusing anything that might erode what we cherish. And by doing this, a positive contributor to our overall identity is encouraged to thrive.

Eric and our bikes at one of many bucolic campsites on our trip through southern France

In terms of reinforcing language, I tend to frame all freedom and adventure in terms of their positive benefits. All such past experiences are moments of excitement and liberation, and all future plans that include elements of freedom and adventure are happy imperatives. Even when relating some of the more harrowing close calls, I describe them in terms of what I learned, the novelty of the experience, and with little regret. For example, when sharing mountaineering tales where I was in real danger from avalanche, weather, injury, altitude, hypothermia, deep crevasses, slippery pinnacles or large predatory animals, I do so with a genuine joy of accomplishment that I survived such dangers. And the same is true of the times I was mugged in Paris, or the many times I've lost control of my bicycle on a steep grade, or the time my Toyota Corolla floated downstream when I attempted to cross a river with it. I take a certain pride in my recklessness, in my willingness to take risks for the sake of discovering something about the world or about myself. Of course all of these stories also afford ample opportunity for humility as well, encouraging me to have a good, hard, long laugh about my own silliness.

What has been the enduring result of applying AMR to my own freedom and adventure memory patterns? I do still associate personal freedom and opportunity for adventure with solitary pursuits, but I am not as invested in my own sense of separateness or isolation. That is, I no longer strongly identify with loneliness, being out-of-step with my fellows, or standing on the outside looking in. I no longer feel sorry for my inadequacies or depressed about the consequences of past choices regarding my self-actuation within this semantic container, because right now, in this moment, I can truly and deeply love this aspect of self in all its frailty and imperfection. I can neither forcefully reject nor passively accept what has happened to me or how it has influenced me, but instead lovingly embrace the reality of how I came to be, selectively emphasizing what I feel to be the crème-de-la-crème of my experiences in this group of memories. This has taken years – in some cases decades – of committed effort. In the case of particularly dramatic or traumatic life events, their impact on my equilibrium and self-concept may never completely attenuate. But that impact can be softened, molded and directed in the most constructive ways possible.

Once this shift begins, once the ball starts rolling in a positive direction for one or more patterns of memory, a great weight is lifted from our mind, heart, body and spirit – from our entire being. And, if the conviction is genuine, one of the sensations that soon follows is a strong desire to heal what is broken in those patterns of self, right whatever and whoever has been wronged, and diligently continue along this course of transformation. But this desire does not stem from of egoism, narcissism, guilt, fear or a sense of duty – we began leaving those types of motivation behind the moment we embraced more compassionate practices – but rather because love joyfully demands it of us. This transition can't be faked, it must be felt…and that takes time. In this vein, what begins with the five core practices of AMR is sustained over time by those same practices, often expanding into new forms or subtler nuances of effort.

In my own inner workings, are there still vestiges of doubt about my insistence on liberty? Do I sometimes regret the forcefulness of my adventurous spirit? Have I sometimes needed to moderate my passion for exploration? Do I ever feel isolated or alone? Of course. Just like everyone else, I am a work in progress; sometimes I still misjudge the slipperiness of dewy grass. But my metastructures of being – my integrative buffer, emotional disposition, somatic memory, narrative self, governing beliefs, unconscious substrata and spiritual ground – have been modified by the conscious rearrangement and selective energization of episodic memory. And that modification continues to provide an avenue to peaceful reconciliation and integration of my inner dichotomies.

So this is a beginning to our journey through the mnemosphere. Just one door to open or close as needed, carefully examining whatever has been stored in this particular room within the house of self. And that brings up one final point before we move on to the next chapter: that each room, each semantic container, is only one small fraction of who we are. It is almost always counterproductive to observe one facet of our being and assume it is somehow our essence, our primary mode of operation, the dominant contributor to our personality, or in any way independent of other facets of self. In my case, there are other memory patterns that create natural counterbalances to my freedom-seeking proclivities, and I try to engage in different flavors of conscious self-nourishment so that no dimension of self is neglected for long. If I allowed any one component of my identity to dominate me, I would undoubtedly create new tensions and challenges for myself. So the way we group specific autobiographical memories under one thematic heading may indicate the importance that heading has in our overall self-concept, but it is not the entirety of our self-concept – it is merely a temporary prioritization that orders the mnemosphere into productive patterns.

Likewise, even our episodic memories are not static or complete in and of themselves, but amalgams of data dynamically reassembled to support each region of our memory field as needed. They are supportive structures, selectively called upon to validate our emotional disposition, or reinforce our governing beliefs, or prop up our narrative self. The same events can mean entirely different things depending on the context of their association-of-the-moment, conforming to whatever dominates our conscious and unconscious mind. By any definition, they are no more real than any fantasy of our imagination. That said, the fantasies of our imagination are very powerful things, especially when we focus most or all of our attention on any particular one, so we should treat them with great care.

## CHAPTER TWO: SAFETY & FEAR

In natural contrast to a spirit of adventure are the boundaries of our actions and will. Early on in my life, experiences evoking fear greatly informed such boundaries. Fear wasn't the only moderator of my wildly curious and often brazen impulses, but without its influence I can imagine some of my behaviors evolving very differently, and perhaps along unhealthy or even sociopathic lines. So in one way I value experiences of fear as important mentors in my early development. In another I wonder how injurious it was for my youthful being to be subjected to those extreme and terrifying situations. Once again we encounter a striking dichotomy regarding what we might conclude from episodic patterns in our lives.

There is one place and time in my childhood where the largest cluster of fear-evoking events seems to have occurred. When I was eight years old my mother and I moved into in a shoddy apartment complex off of Hilliard Street in Manchester, Connecticut, just a stone's throw the from the Hockanum River. There were five huge buildings clustered around a wide, circular drive, each crammed full of narrow, two-story townhouse-style apartments. Everything was painted a dark, foreboding brown that blended into the surrounding trees in summer and fall, then hulked over the black asphalt driveway during the leafless winter and early spring. It should be noted here that my first taste of the East Coast was living a year in my father's home in Amherst, Massachusetts, and I will return to that time for other tales. But soon I was living with my mother again, and my stay in Manchester would be the last I would live with her, creating a natural bookend to our time together as a family.

There are different qualities of fear, of course, ranging from just enough scary to get the heart racing with excitement, to the terror and panic of a life-threatening crisis, to the gut-souring anticipation of dire consequences…and countless other varieties.  Our years in the Manchester townhouse offered me nearly every one imaginable, in varying degrees and durations, and at surprisingly constant pitch.  I have a lot of scary memories to choose from.  As an added burden – a sort of amplification factor – there weren't a lot of positive emotions to mitigate those fears; instead, there seemed an endless parade of antagonisms.  As I consider those tumultuous years, I feel a persisting sense of relief that they are long past.

I should emphasize that up until this point in my life, I hadn't experienced much consequential fear.  In fact, my reckless sense of adventure had landed me in situations where I probably should have felt afraid, but didn't, perhaps because I was ignorant of the real danger.  In those earliest years, in nearly every one of my memories, I  am like a wild cub of some ferocious animal, always in motion – climbing, running, jumping, swinging – always making noise, always making messes or breaking things, always pushing my own limits and the limits of patience in everyone around me.  To say that I had a lot of energy as a child is akin to saying the sun is bright or mountains are big.

The freedom and adventure of the previous chapter is an appropriate preamble to contextualize the frightening events of our Manchester townhouse.  A wild and fearless boy who feels he has graduated from the school of the wild is now thrust into chaotic city life, and he is unprepared for complex social dynamics and interactions with much more dangerous animals than any to be found in the great outdoors.  Here a whole new set of challenges would present themselves, and instead of emerging victorious and empowered, I would stumble and fail time after time.

## Nightmares

There were plenty of things to haunt my sleep.  My mother recounts my waking her often during that time, my night terrors launching me out of my bed and up the stairs to her room.  This happened so frequently that she finally told me to stay in my bed, no matter what, and wake her only if there was a stranger sneaking around the house, the overwhelming smell of smoke, or something equally emergent. So night after night I would wake, whimpering and frightened, into the semi-darkness of my brooding room. I did have things to ease my terror, of course. The comforting warmth of our pet beagle, Sodacracker, who invariably curled up beside me on the bed; the blue-white glow of my night light to keep shadows at bay; whatever toy I had stashed under my pillow (usually a current favorite from among my Matchbox car collection, which I called "maxboxes"); and a fraying monkey doll made of white-toed brown socks and cracked black buttons that I tucked neatly under one arm while I slept.

Amid this safe cradle of familiar things, I would stare through the open door of my bedroom, listening for a slow, creaking step on the stairs. Or I would peek over the covers out my bedroom window to make sure nothing was swooping down out of the sky to get me. A few years earlier, when I contracted chicken pox and my mother was forced yet again to leave me unattended in our Eugene home, I entertained myself by trying to find something intelligible to watch on T.V. Most of the shows were inaccessible to my five-year-old sensibilities, until I stumbled across something called *Dark Shadows*. Although the plot and dialogue were nearly as incomprehensible as the other daytime programming, this one had scary music. And scary settings. And people doing scary things to each other. And things that weren't people doing scary things to people. Before I finally turned off the TV in a fit of fright (I think I even unplugged it from the wall), I had absorbed a lifetime's worth of nightmarish scenarios to feed my hyperactive imagination. So whenever I required some image to match the fear that I felt upon waking, my impressions of *Dark Shadows* were happy to supply one.

Which is why, on one such still and dark night, when I awoke to spy something slowly creeping into view from below my window, I was sure I knew what to expect. A cloaked and grinning vampire that smelled of dust. Or an angry ghost. Or a homicidal relative. And if they were really going to drift eerily through my window, surely this warranted waking my mother. I clenched the covers and readied my scream. But when IT came fully into view, I was entirely frozen with terror. I couldn't scream. I couldn't move any part of my body, not even my eyes, repulsed and riveted as I was. I couldn't even breathe. For just feet away from the foot of my bed, completely filling one of my bedroom window panes, was a giant, malevolently glowing...vanilla wafer.

It hovered, and I waited. I beheld the enlarged texture of its cookie surface, sliding past my window like a rough boulder floating in space. I trembled at its magnificent size and worried over its intent. What did it want? What was it going to do next? As I watched and wondered, I could swear the window was slowly inching open, and the strong scent of lemony vanilla abruptly wafted across my bed. Sodacracker raised her head and, sensing something was amiss, wined softly. How could I save her? How could I save myself? Then, as if to prompt me into action, the vanilla wafer lumbered gently against the glass with a soft scraping sound.

Somehow I was out of bed with Sodacracker gathered in my arms, running up the stairs, crying out "Mom! Mom! Mom!" in a frantic whisper-yell. And she was there in her bedroom doorway, pulling her flower-print robe about her, sleepy irritation vanishing as she saw the terror on my face and the dog in my grasp.

"What is it? What is it honey?!"

"My window! Climbing in my window!"

And as if she had practiced this moment a thousand times, my mother promptly reached back through her door, grabbed the leather blackjack from her nightstand, and headed bravely down the stairs. I trailed slowly after, "Mom!" I called, trying to warn her. She waved me back. She had training. She had tried to become a policewoman that very year, studying for the written entrance exam and passing it, only to fail on the physical. She did everything they demanded of her – carried her own weight for fifty yards, hauled herself over a wall, executed dozens of push-ups and sit-ups – until they had her run hurdles around a track. That had hurt too much, she said. They hadn't let her wear a bra. If she wanted to do a man's job, she had to dress like a man, they said, and men didn't wear bras. So they made her take it off. After the fifth or six hurdle the painful shock of her breasts slamming downward was too much to bear. So she had cried herself off of the field to the whistles and hoots of the other candidates and come home sad and defeated. But now, bravely facing an intruder in our home, it was her moment to shine.

She turned on the lights. I waited long moments as she disappeared into my room, then ran in after her. My mother stood staring at the windows, blackjack still held high at the ready. "There's nobody here," she said flatly. She went to the windows and peered out. "Nobody, Todd." She lowered the weapon and turned to me.

"It was there, mom! I swear!" I pointed out into the darkness. "It was huge!"

"What was huge?"

"The cookie! The...vanilla wafer. It was this big!" I held my arms wide. "And the window was opening and it was coming through – "

"I have to sleep!" She said accusingly. "I have to go to work. Don't you understand that?!" She pointed the blackjack at me, then stalked from the room.

"But...I really saw it!" From her tone I knew I was on thin ice now, but this was important. She had to know.

Mom stopped on the stairs, looked down at the blackjack in her hand, then over at me. I must have been quite a sight – tears streaming down my face, dog still clutched in my grip, sincerity gushing from my whole being. And in one of the miraculous blink-of-an-eye mood changes she was capable of, my mother suddenly smiled at me, then grinned, then laughed.

"Mom!"

"Oh, honey..." She set her weapon on the stairs and came back into my room, arms wide. I stepped into her embrace with a huge relief. Sodacracker's warm, wet tongue began happily licking both our faces. "You really saw a giant vanilla wafer?" She asked, still laughing.

"Yes! It was outside, floating! And then the window opened and I could smell it! I swear, mom! I *swear*." And in response she laughed again, and Sodacracker licked at us, and the world was set right.

After that night, for some inexplicable reason, I was no longer visited by night terrors. In the full light of day, perhaps the utter absurdity of a predatory vanilla wafer – no matter how huge and real it had seemed in the dark – had shaken my imagination free of those extreme and irrational fears. I could suddenly laugh about them, something I had not been able to do before. Thus the wafer dream became, in the sense of how fear affected my life, a rite of passage. However, I could no longer savor a box of vanilla wafers as I once had. In fact, even the smell of them still ties my stomach into knots, and, on those rare occasions when I risk a taste, the feel of their finely bumped surface on my tongue sends chills to the very core of my soul.

## Seeking Acceptance

There are a whole host of fears and anxieties wrapped up in my search for acceptance as a child. Fear that I would not be part of a cohesive group, and thus be vulnerable in some way. Fear that I would not be appreciated, that I had nothing of value to add. Fear that I would be misunderstood, that I could not be heard, that my thoughts and feelings would remain muted to the world. Fear that I would never understand others or how to navigate social situations, and thus suffer endless embarrassment and disconnection. Fear that I would not get my needs met. Fear that I would not be loved. Fear that life would become one painful rejection after another.

So it is in this context that I tried repeatedly but unsuccessfully to find my place in the undecipherable hierarchy of school playgrounds, community sports teams and neighborhood gangs while living at Hilliard Street. Having had so little socialization up to this point, it is not surprising that I lacked the skills to find my way through complex cultural contexts. What is surprising is the level of anxiety these interactions produced. I wanted to be part of the game, I wanted to be liked, I wanted my mother to be proud, I wanted all the things any eight-year-old boy wants out of life. And when, as a stranger in a strange land, I repeatedly failed to gain any sort of social foothold in these situations, I began to doubt my place in the world.

A life of and dunes, trees, half-wild dogs and even wilder adults gave me ample confidence in some city situations. I was good with the neighborhood canines, though they always seemed surprised – and a little put off – that I didn't back down at their showy growls and snapping teeth. The odd or cantankerous loner humans who lived nearby were likewise easy to manage. And, thank goodness, the dense deciduous forest surrounding our apartment complex made me feel much more at home as well. But a kickball or T-ball game? I had no idea how to play, or what to expect, or how to behave, and so despite my natural athleticism I was quickly demoted to last-picked, we-really-don't-want-you-here status.

There were some positive experiences every now-and-then. Hitting a home run with bases loaded. Successfully diving for a high fly ball and getting my picture in the local paper. Accidentally kicking a kick-ball into the face of one of the least-liked bullies in the neighborhood. But these brief flashes of success were as mysterious to me as the sea of rejection in which they occurred. Why did catching that baseball win so much praise? Why was everyone grinning at me when I hit the bully in the face? Why was winning so important and losing so painful for these kids? Why did their parents care so much about the outcome? And why was everyone so disappointed when I couldn't duplicate some random feat over and over again? All of this became confusing and anxiety-producing torture.

The same sorts of dramas played out at school, of course. Here it was tetherball, elimination, and various playground antics. My first year at Waddell Elementary in Manchester was the last year they segregated the playground by gender. A tall, black cyclone fence divided the playground in half, and both boys and girls were discouraged from lingering near the fence or interacting with anyone on the other side. Of course, this made absolutely no sense to me at all. And, given my inability to fit in with my male peers, I would often interact with girls through the fence – and one in particular. Her name was Brooke, and I thought she was the prettiest girl I had ever seen. Here silky red hair, blue eyes and faint but plentiful freckles had me entranced from the first day of school, and despite her own concern about us getting caught in the act, she seemed more than happy to joke, tease and flirt through the black diamonds of the slowly rusting fence.

We were warned repeatedly to cease and desist this outrageous behavior, of course, but the playground monitors had more than their hands full with the bullying, fights, pranks and general mayhem on the boy's half of the playground.  As soon as I could disentangle myself from some boyish plot, I would gaze longingly toward the girl's side of the fence – which had its own unique quality of noisy disorder – until I found Brooke.  I think this was my first big crush…though I had no idea at the time what was happening to me.  What I did know was that all those anxious feelings clustered around wanting to be accepted and liked were now amplified tenfold.  And for the first time, to my shock and elation, someone seemed to like me back!

I was teased mercilessly for my affections, of course.  The older boys made lewd comments and jeered, which provoked a couple of my first all-out fights on that playground.  Other boys my age shrugged off my interest in Brooke with mild disdain – how could I be consorting with *the enemy* like that?  Other girls reliably rolled their eyes at the whole situation.  But I found I could put up with all of this if it meant I could spend more time with Brooke.  In fact, I generally became a calmer human being because of her.  Where previously I had raged back at the teacher whenever I was whacked with the edge of a rule for staring out the window, I could now calmly return to work with little more than a self-righteous glare.  Where I had repeatedly provoked my classmates into rebellious adventures in the classroom and the hallways – leading by my example of disregarding various rules – I now went quietly about my schoolwork as if it were a recurring dream.

Of course, every one of the social variables I was just beginning to understand changed once the school day came to an end.  The bravado of playground bullies evaporated.  Contained and compliant girls suddenly became rebellious and bossy.  Jeering peers abruptly became more friendly.  And the normally shy but inviting Brooke boldly asked me to walk her home.  It's difficult to comprehend in today's world, but this was a time when elementary students routinely walked to and from school, had plentiful time to get into all sorts of trouble without parental supervision, and were generally on their own reconnaissance from the end of school until dinner time. So of course I said I would walk Brooke home.

It was a short walk – her house was only a few blocks from school – but it was the longest walk of my life up until then. I could be relaxed and friendly with a playground fence between us, but now, as we slowly sauntered down the street, she wanted to hold my hand. Again I had no idea what to say, or how to act, or what to expect. Despite my discomfort and insecurity, her warm, delicate fingers were a wonderful gift. So we walked in silence, smiling furtively at each other, until we reached her house.

It was a hot spring afternoon, a muggy promise of a sweltering summer, and Brooke pulled us to a stop as we neared her front door.

"It's that one," she pointed to a white, two-story traditional with a green roof. "C'mon...let's go this way." She let go my hand and ran off between two houses. I followed eagerly. In a moment we came to a set of steps leading to her back door. "Stay here," she whispered, then ran inside. In a few moments she returned, nervously straightening her dress and glancing over her shoulder. "We can't go in right now. Let's go up here – it's my favorite place." With speedy spryness, Brooke clambered onto a structure adjoining the back stairs – a shed, perhaps, or a garage. I was so surprised by her athletics I followed without question. We settled next to each other on the warm shingles amid the smells of hot tar, old paint and freshly cut grass.

"Why can't we go inside?" I asked, squinting through the hot sun at her.

"Sshh!" She warned. "We're not supposed to be up here." She looked back at the house. "It's my secret place."

"Oh," I said. There was a long pause. We both fidgeted and looked anywhere but at each other.

"You won't tell anyone?" Brooke asked abruptly.

"What? No."

"Promise?" She looked worried.

I shrugged. "Why would I tell? It's your secret place."

She shook her head. "That's not...I'd get in trouble. If you told. Even at school or anything." She was looking at me earnestly now.

"Okay. I won't tell." I said. She seemed satisfied.

We sat a few minutes longer. I was finally starting to relax. Being alone with Brooke was very exciting, but I was finding my level. I glanced over at her to find her biting her lip and looking down at her feet. After a moment, she frowned.

"What's wrong?" I asked.

She sighed and looked away. "Aren't you going to kiss me?" A smile touched the corners of her mouth.

My heart stopped. I couldn't breathe. What had she just asked me? "Wh...what?"

The frown returned. "It's no big deal," she said. "Nobody will see us, and I...I've done it before." She looked over at me now, her bright blue eyes searching mine. My heart had started beating again, very fast.

"You have?" Was all I could think to say.

"Well..." she hesitated, "just girls. For practice. You're the first boy." Brooke blushed. Her freckles reversed into tiny constellations.

I was lost. So entirely and completely lost. Ocean beaches and treetops had not prepared me for this. I had never kissed anyone but my mother and grandmother. I didn't know what this kiss was supposed to be. What was the protocol? I don't know how Brooke interpreted my stunned hesitation, but she leaned over and kissed me anyway. It was full on the mouth, a scorching summer day in early spring, a world turned upside down on coarse roof shingles.

When she pulled away, I saw her eyes were closed. She was smiling. In a instant those lovely blue eyes would open again. They would open and look at me and…what then? I touched my mouth as a fresh panic surged through me. I rose quickly and leapt off the roof.

"What are you doing?" Brooke called after me. But I was already scrambling away across the lawn. "Hey!" she cried. I paused and turned. I was all adrenaline and jumbled emotions. I cast about for an excuse. Brooke was standing now, hands on hips, a fierce look on her face I had never seen before. My panic deepened.

"I…I have to go! My mom…."

Brooke gaped at me. "You didn't…." She shook her head and huffed exasperation. Unconsciously, I touched my mouth again, and her expression melted into worry. She leaned forward, reaching a restraining hand toward me, her pale, lovely fingers splayed wide. "Don't tell anyone!" She pleaded.

"I won't," I said numbly, then spun and ran.

§

Anyone who has struggled to fit in knows some of what I felt in those years; my pattern of memories seems less about rejection, however, and more about incompatibility. My mother and I were not emotionally compatible. My wild sense of play was not compatible with most other children's. The confining rules of public school were incompatible with my habits and nature. My social responses were incompatible with the expectations of my peers. So when, upon returning to school the next week, I was informed by my teachers that I was no longer permitted to interact with Brooke at all, a final puzzle piece clicked into place. Just as Brooke had feared, someone had seen us…someone had told. So even exploring the most calming, interesting and exciting aspect of my social life was now forbidden to me. What I wanted was incompatible with what would be. I was, therefore, fundamentally incompatible with human society as a whole. It was a clear and obvious a conclusion that any eight-year-old would come to.

Predictably, I acted out what was now a clearly identified role. All of my preoccupied self-restraint evaporated and I refused to follow any more rules. Regarding anything. Not sitting still or remaining silent in class, not getting permission to go to the bathroom, not respecting what teachers asked me to do. And whenever another kid or adult attempted to correct my missteps, I pushed back…hard. I defied teachers. I snuck into forbidden areas of the school – the janitorial closet, the nurse's office, the girl's bathroom (it had pink tile, to my surprise), the playground when it wasn't recess, and so on. Somehow along the way I broke a water fountain when some older kids wouldn't let me drink from it. Then I got into screaming match with my Third Grade teacher after she swatted me with the metal edge of her ruler one time too many. She tried to grab me and haul me out of the classroom, but I ran, dodging between desks and shocked students. Eventually, when the other kids started laughing at the chase, the teacher gave up trying to remove me and removed all the other kids from the classroom instead. "Go ahead and leave!" I yelled, "And don't come back!" I then barricaded myself alone in the room, pushing all the desks up against the door.

Understandably, that was my last week at Waddell Elementary, and my mother was yet again placed in the situation of trying to find somewhere for me to belong during the day. I bounced around among a few more incompatible educational options until at last I landed in a public program for kids with learning disabilities. Autism, retardation, hyperactivity, obsessive-compulsive disorder – a whole rainbow of challenges was represented there among kids of all ages. And, for once, I felt I almost fit in. Not that these children interacted with me much – I don't remember a single coherent conversation with a peer during that time – but they were all misfits like me. I felt vaguely comforted, and although I still acted out, constantly challenging rules and authority, I calmed down a bit. However, after a few weeks of playing with foam blocks, swinging on the swings and attempting to engage someone other than an adult supervisor in tetherball, I became so bored by the limited routine it felt like a kind of prison to me. At first, I begged my mother to take me out of the school. Eventually, I just refused to go anymore.

In the end, all of those fundamental fears woven into my lack of acceptance were repeatedly confirmed. My mother carted me around to several different doctors, including one highly recommended psychiatrist, none of whom knew what to do with me. In a desperate last ditch effort to preserve my mother's sanity, one of the docs prescribed Ritalin. That didn't work very well, and instead of calming me down the drug had me – quite literally – bouncing off the walls of my bedroom all night long while yelling at the top of my lungs. So when my mother tearfully explained that I would need to go away for a while, to a hospital where they would try to understand what was wrong with me, I completely understood the necessity. I even looked forward to it with some eagerness…maybe they could fix me, and everything in our world would be set right again.

## Murderous Intent

Like most misfits, I was an easy target for bullies. I seemed to attract endless flack from older boys – and even some older girls – for things I said, for things I did, for being different. Most of these situations were fairly easy to short circuit. I learned very early, around five or six, that striking back swiftly and bitingly usually shocked the more casual bullies into leaving me alone. The more aggressive bullies, those with a vested interest in their social status, or those with a darker, meaner constitution, would sometimes require more protracted persuasion. In some cases, things got physical. Out of instinct at first, and then out of more calculated consideration, I learned that the best solution was usually to issue a preemptive challenge. They should meet me in some neutral place, without any spectators or groupies, for a one-on-one to settle accounts. Always suspicious, but equally fearful of being perceived as cowards, the bullies would either agree to the challenge, or dismiss me as not worth the bother. Even the ones who accepted the challenge seldom showed up, and when they did, they were tentative, disinterested in fighting, and much more willing to talk. Almost always a few years my senior, the bullies were often embarrassed to fight someone half their size, and on some level I think they respected my courage to confront them alone.  And because we met alone on neutral turf, there were no lackeys to impress and no face to lose.  After such challenges, I was generally ignored – usually on the condition that I not reveal what really happened during our climactic tête-à-tête.  After that, we had a tacit agreement to pointedly and respectfully avoid each other.

Of course, this didn't mean I wasn't nervous or fearful during these confrontations.  Sometimes I was terrified.  But I steeled myself to put on a brave face because it had helped me survive over and over again.  But of course there were also situations where this strategy did not work. There likely always have been and always will be people in this world who are addicted to having power over others, who take a perverse joy in inflicting pain, and who would rather violently annihilate any opposition than talk their way through a conflict or back down in any way.  And, unfortunately for me, one of these people happened to live in house just north of the apartments on Hilliard Street.

A short hike through the woods surrounding my home brought me to a little red two-story house set back a bit from the road.  Although I had been near the property many times – it bordered the old lady's raspberry brambles I was so often pilfering, as well as many of my favorite paths through the woods – I had never had reason to discover who lived there. One wintry afternoon, I found myself taking a leisurely stroll along the path to the red house.  As I approached, I saw a thin line of smoke rising gently from a shed behind the main building.  Curious, I drifted closer. Everything was quiet.  No birds, no cars on the road, no creaking of ice-laden branches.  Then, out of the stillness, a loud metallic bang echoed through the trees.  My hair stood on end and I almost turned back, but some part of me had to know where that smoke was coming from.  As the quiet returned, I edged toward the shed.

The door to the shed stood wide, and as I approached I could see a fire there with a shadowy form moving quickly around it.  As my eyes adjusted, I discovered a boy my own age, with greasy blond hair and a green down jacket, holding a long pair of metals tongs over the flames.  I was so surprised I made no attempt to hide myself, but just stood and stared.  After a moment or two, I felt the boy staring back out of the dim interior.  "Who are *you*?" he asked gruffly.  His voice was deep for his age.

"I live back there," I pointed. "What 'r you doin'?"

"None of your business," said the boy. But he said it quietly, almost reflexively, with most of his attention still centered on the fire and the tongs he held over it.

I strode into the shed.

"Hey!" said the boy, "don't block the light!"

I quickly stepped aside. Cold sunlight fell on his work and an acrid, stinging smell assaulted my nostrils. "Can I watch?" I asked. I was intrigued.

The boy shrugged. "I don't care."

We stood that way a few moments, staring at the contents of a small cast-iron cup he held in the tongs. Something silvery was swirling in it. The boy smiled and pulled the cup out of the flames. "Watch this," he said, grinning. Moving quickly to a nearby workbench, he carefully poured the contents of the cup through the hole in the top of a strangely shaped metal block. "Can't spill any...burns like a sum'nabitch." Emptying the cup, he chuckled. "Now's the hardest part." He set the tongs and cup aside.

"What's hard?" I asked.

The boy stared at the metal block and rubbed his hands together eagerly. "Waiting!"

"For what? What is it?" I was dying to know.

"You'll see."

The block sat on the bench, holding us captive. With the fire so close behind us, it was uncomfortably warm. The smoke and stink stung my eyes. "I'm Todd," I said to fill the silence.

"Ha. That's funny," he said.

"What?"

He looked up at me. His eyes were fierce and bright. Too bright. Crazy bright. "I dunno." He looked away. "I'm Tom."

"Is this your house?" I asked.

Tom snorted. "I sneak into other people's sheds and make bullets all the time."

"Bullets?"

Tom frowned at himself. "Yeah." He seemed to tense.

"Cool."

Seconds passed. "Okay!" Tom was suddenly alive with excitement again. "Get back a little." He waved me away.

I stepped around the fire and watched as Tom handled the metal cube with a thick rag. In a moment he popped it open and a large gray bullet thudded onto the workbench. Tom laughed. "Look at that, huh?"

"Can I touch it?"

"I dunno." Tom said frankly. "I bet it's still hot."

"Let's see!" I was there beside him and we began tossing the lead slug back-and-forth with our bare hands. We cackled and pranced, pretending the bullet was much hotter than it really was, until the game got old. "Can you make another one?" I asked.

"Sure," Tom said confidently. "Look…this is how."

It was the beginning of the first real friendship I would have in Connecticut. We began hanging out after school, showing off our plastic soldier and odds-and-ends collections to each other, exploring the surrounding countryside and plundering each others' kitchens for snacks whenever we thought our parents weren't looking. He was the only other boy I had ever met who was as adventurous as I. In fact, we tended to take risks together that neither of us would have attempted on our own. We found our way across the Hockanum river, plundering its mysteries. We dug an old wagon wheel from the riverbank – one later identified as vintage mid-eighteen hundreds. We crawled inside an old textile mill, squirming through narrow shafts and low spillways until one of us got scraped up so bad we had to go home. On one occasion, a rusty metal ladder gave way under me and I fell some fifteen feet, ricocheting off the brick walls into the boggy muck below. Tom helped me peel off my ruined shirt and wet the deep gouges in my back with not-so-medicinal Hockanum river water. After hiding the injury from my mom for two days, the infection became bad enough that I had to beg for her ministrations along with forgiveness.

I don't ever remember meeting Tom's folks while we were friends. He always seemed mildly ashamed of them whenever I asked about them, and he was sure that he, not they, was the one to greet me at the door whenever I stopped by. I did meet his older brother, Eric, and the experience left quite an impression. Tom and I were in the kitchen of his house, preparing to head out on some adventure or other, when Eric appeared in doorway to the living room. He was an impossibly tall and lanky teenager with a piercing gaze and rough, scraggly features.

"Hey, who's this?!" Eric demanded.

"I'm Todd," I began, stepping forward despite the sudden chill in the room.

"I didn't ask *you*," Eric said menacingly, "I asked little pussy here." What's 'a matter? Pussy got your tongue?!" Eric laughed gratingly, without humor, until he began to cough.

"Just a kid I know," Tom mumbled at the floor.

"*Just a kid I know*," Eric mimicked. He sounded like a bad parody of a schoolyard bully. "You gonna go out to the shed and poke each other? Huh, *little faggot*?"

I was stunned.  Not because I hadn't heard taunting language like this before, but because from the look of them they were obviously brothers, and because Tom was so clearly afraid.  He wouldn't look up.  Wouldn't run.  He just stood there, waiting for things to end.  He had such energy and spirit inside him most of the time, and it was being smothered with fear.  I felt rage bubbling up inside me.  "We're just going down to the river," I said flatly.

"I said *shut the fuck up!*  I ain't talkin' to you."  Eric raised a menacing backhand in my direction.  I glared at him.

"Don't!"  Tom yelled.  "Just leave us alone!"  It burst out of him so forcefully I was stunned.  Eric seemed surprised, too.  He turned a sly grin on his brother.

"Oh!  So *that's* how it's gonna be, huh?"  In two quick strides he was across the kitchen, flat-handing Tom in the face and neck, then shoving him to the floor.  The violence that followed was so casual, so extreme, I was too shocked to move or say anything.  When Eric was satisfied, he stepped over his brother and out the back door, laughing as he went.  "I better not see you around here anymore, little shit."  He called back over his shoulder.  "It's not good for my little brother."  The door slammed behind him.

I went to Tom's side to help him up.

"Get away from me!"  he yelled, fighting back tears as he hoisted himself off the floor.  "Just…go home."  And he ran from the room.

§

This wasn't the end of our friendship, but it did result in our outings being less frequent and our strategies for meeting or being seen by Eric a bit more circumspect.  When I asked Tom about what happened, he said Eric hadn't always been like that, just lately.  Something was wrong with him.  He was sick.  He kept getting into trouble.  And so like any other kids we shrugged off the past and made plans for the present.

Then, on a warm spring day, I was sitting in a grassy area out in front of our townhouse, whittling away at a piece of tree bark, when I spied Eric crouched beside one of the buildings nearby. He was peering around the corner of the building, watching something intently, and I followed his gaze to a shiny black Lincoln pulling through the parking lot. The car stopped a few feet away from where I sat, and middle-aged man in a dark suit got out. I recognized him as someone who visited here often. The man opened the trunk of the car and retrieved something, closed the trunk, and walked over to the door of the nearest townhouse to disappear inside.

Eric was fast for his size. He sped over to the car and had the trunk open in moments, digging quickly through its contents. Heaving a small gray suitcase from its depths, Eric quietly closed the trunk again and began casually to walk away. That was when he noticed me. He glanced over his shoulder to where the man had gone, then squinted angrily in my direction. "You don't tell anyone what you saw. Understand?"

Something in his tone – something flat and sharp and ugly – made me nod without question.

"You tell anyone, and you're dead," he warned, pointing at me. And then he was gone, around the building and out of sight.

A few minutes later the man in the dark suit reappeared and returned to the trunk of his car. He stared inside for a long time, blinking, then looked around the parking lot. His gaze flicked across me then back again. He walked over. "Hi there," he said nervously, "Did you see anyone take something out of my car?" The man didn't look very happy, but Eric could still be within earshot, or watching from somewhere in the trees.

"Huh-uh," I said, and returned to my whittling. The man stood over me, fidgeting and glancing around the parking lot, and then strode back into the nearby townhouse.

My tree bark was pretty much whittled down to a nub by then, so I went back inside my own home to get a glass of water. By the time I thought to look out the window of my room – a view that overlooked the spot where all of this occurred – the glossy black Lincoln was surrounded by two sedans and a police cruiser. A handful of serious-looking men in dark suits stood nearby, deep in conversation.

There are moments when we all must weigh one fear against another and make a choice to act. My mother would be angry if I talked to strangers. Eric would be angry if I ratted him out. I already didn't like police from the visits they had made to our home in the past. But something important was going on and I needed to find out what. So I ran down to the parking lot and sidled up along one of the men in suits to listen.

"…probably thousands," said the man who owned the Lincoln. He was leaning against his car now, sweating profusely. He looked pale.

"Jeez, Doc. You should be more careful," said a dark-haired man in a grey suit. He was holding a small pad of paper and taking notes. He reminded me of the "Just the facts, ma'am" guy on Dragnet, but fatter.

"I know, I know. I was only gone for a minute. The thing is, I don't usually carry that much with me."

The Dragnet guy shook his head and scribbled. "Huh. And nobody saw anything?"

"Nobody's volunteered," the Doc said quickly. "You'd think they would notice all of this…." He gestured to the police cruiser.

"Maybe," said Dragnet, "This neighborhood… ."

"Yeah," the Doc grimaced. "Sorry guys." There was something wrong with the way he was acting, but I didn't understand what.

And I made my choice. "Mister?" I said to Dragnet. He seemed intent on his note-taking. "Mister?" I pulled at his jacket.

"Well hello there," said Dragnet, looking down at me.

"I saw Eric take that suitcase from his trunk."  I paused, screwed up my courage, and asked, "Was it important?"

Dragnet was startled into a laugh.  "Well, that all depends…."

"He didn't see anything," said the Doc.  "I asked him right afterwards."

"What do you mean?"  Dragnet was suddenly more alert and focused.

I started to object but the Doc spoke right over me.  "He was sitting in the grass right here next to the car – "

"I did to!" I finally managed.

"Okay, okay," Dragnet chuckled.  "Why don't we go over here and talk."  As Dragnet led me to the other side of the parking lot, I glanced at the Doc and noticed he wasn't just hot and sweaty, he seemed scared.  He watched me steadily until one of the other men in suits distracted him with questions.

"That man's scared," I observed reflexively.  "Is he in trouble?"

Dragnet started, then smiled.  "Huh.  Well, he just lost something very valuable.  Very important.  Maybe you can help us find it?"

"Okay," I said.  I pointed off through the trees.  "Eric lives in the red house through the woods.  I'm friends with his brother."

Dragnet scribbled away.  "Oh?  And what's his brother's name?"

"Tom," I said.  "He didn't do anything.  Eric is pretty mean."

Dragnet nodded.  "And what's your name there, Buck-o?"

"Todd.  I live here."  I pointed to our apartment.

"And you saw…Eric, you said?"  He was acting as if he didn't know who Eric was, but I had a sense that he was pretending.

"Uh-huh.  He took the suitcase…"

"Now when you say suitcase, about how big was it?"

"Really small," I said.

"Was it a briefcase?"

I shrugged.  I didn't know what a 'briefcase' was.

"Okay.  And he ran off through the woods?  Back towards his house?"

"Yeah, I guess."

Dragnet looked toward the trees, then said, "Can you wait here a minute?  Just have a seat on those steps there, and I'll be right back."

I sat and waited, dividing my attention between the men in suits and the grayness beneath the trees.  My fears had receded into a growing excitement.  After a minute, one of the sedans started up and sped out of the parking lot.  Dragnet got into the other car and was talking on its radio.  After what seemed like a long time, Dragnet got out of his car and strode back over to me, this time with a younger, equally suited gentleman in tow.

"Listen, Todd.  Do you think Eric could have gone somewhere else besides his house?"

I thought about it.  Then it hit me.  Of course!  Tom had shown them to me on one of our adventure down by the river.  "I know a place where Eric hides stuff." I said.  "It's a secret, though."  I remembered Tom's clear warning.

"Well, we like secrets," said Dragnet.  He smiled at the other man.

"What's your name?"  I asked boldly.

Dragnet nodded.   "I'm Lieutenant Sheffield, and this is Detective Grange."

"You're cops?"

"Officers of the law," the younger Grange corrected me.

The older Sheffield chuckled. "Yep. We catch bad guys."

"Okay. I can show you where to go."

Sheffield held up a restraining hand. "I think it would be better if you described it to us, then we'll go there on our own."

I considered. "It's down by the river. But you'll never find them. Holes in the ground that go way back...under the trees and everything. They're hidden."

The two men looked at each other. "How far is it?" Sheffield asked.

I shrugged, frowning. "A ways?"

Grange shook his head. Sheffield sighed. He gestured down the hill behind the apartments, toward the Hockanum river. "Lead on."

I spent the better part of that afternoon leading the two men through my favorite stomping grounds. I felt important, but I was also nervous. What if Eric was there, hiding? What if he found out what I had done? But we trudged onward, and they muddied their suits and shoes crawling into the holes Eric had dug, emerging with grins and jokes I didn't understand – jokes about soiled clothes and wives doing their laundry and finally getting proof of what they'd always suspected. Jokes about hot afternoons being led around through the wilderness by an eight-year-old. Jokes about hiding places and something called "paraphernalia," and how Eric had dug himself a far deeper hole than he realized today.

Eventually we found our way back to the apartment complex. My mother had come home in the meantime and was beside herself with worry about my whereabouts, but the muddy policemen explained what fun we'd all had together and everyone had a good laugh. It wasn't until later that night, until the darkness rose up to swallow my room and I could stare down at the still, shadowy parking lot, that I realized the danger I had put myself in. I didn't sleep well that night, but I also knew what I had to do. I had to meet the bully on his own ground and show him that I wasn't afraid. I had to go visit my friend Tom.

§

The next day was Saturday, bright and warm and eager. As soon as I was finished with breakfast and my chores, I told mom I was going outside to play. I didn't want her to worry, so I didn't elaborate further. As soon as I stepped out my door I could feel the weight of what lay ahead descend upon me.

I walked slowly through the woods to Tom's house. I stopped frequently, listening to the animals and insects making their way into Spring. I was nervous but resolute, swallowing my fear but eager to get this over with. Soon I stood outside of Tom's front door. I knocked softly and waited. At first I didn't hear anything. Then, as I leaned around the entryway toward the living room window, I heard someone crying. Was it Tom? Was he in trouble? I didn't know what to do. Maybe I should get help. Maybe I should barge in and try to stop what was happening. I knocked again, louder this time, and abruptly the crying stopped. I thought there were footsteps inside the house, and then silence. I waited. Nothing. On some impulse – curiosity, concern, stupid courage, or some combination of all of these – I tried the front door. It opened easily and I stepped inside.

Glancing into the living room I found Tom. He was tied securely to a chair with thick gray rope. His mouth was gagged with a sock and tears streamed down his face. He was shaking his head furiously, looking toward the kitchen, then shaking his head again. Those bright blue eyes told me everything I didn't want to know about what had happened to him. I ran to him and began untying him as quickly as I could, but he kept shaking his head, his arms, his legs…almost as if he was trying to fight me off. The knots were too tight for me to loosen. I ripped the gag from his mouth.

"Get out of here!" he whispered. "He'll be back any minute. He's gonna…he's gonna…"

"What did he do to you?" I asked worriedly.

"It don't matter. I'll be…okay. You gotta get out of here. If he finds you here I don't know what he'll do. He's crazy. Crazy…." New tears welled up to replace the drying ones. I saw the marks now, the welts on his neck, the swelling in his face.

"I'll get help…" I said. "I'll – "

The back door creaked open. Footsteps.

"Go go go!" Tom mouthed silently.

I ran for the front door, but even as I did so, I sensed a shadow appearing behind me in the living room.

"Run!" Tom screeched.

I had always been fast, but I knew Eric was probably faster. By the time I reached the woods at a full sprint the sound of his pursuit was already closing on me. Impossibly, I ran even faster, careening over the roots, rocks and fallen branches of the trail, hoping something would cause Eric to stumble or slow. I was only a half dozen strides ahead of him now. I realized had to do something drastic. Face him, crazy and all? I knew deep down in my bones that would be a mistake. At a turn in the trail I spied a thicket of raspberry brambles over dense ivy and dove in, wiggling myself frantically beneath the green, heedless of thorns and clinging to hope. Running footsteps skidded to a halt and I heard Eric's fast and furious panting. I froze, too scared to breathe. I could see him through the leaves. Saw the wildness of his bared teeth, his clenched fists, the hunting knife in his hand. Saw deep, black pools of violence in his eyes – violence that could not be stopped and knew no boundaries. Saw tears of rage that streamed into his open mouth.

"I'm gonna KILL you, you fucking *bastard!*" He bellowed, shaking his fisted knife in the air. He ran further down the path and then returned, still searching. For an instant I thought his crazed gaze found me among the thorns, but then his eyes shifted. "What the fuck are *you* looking at, bitch?!" I didn't dare move, but I heard another sound now. Something thudded softly on the ground just a few feet away. I was incoherent with fear, the only thought remaining a simple plea: *please no*. Eric's breathing slowed, his features softened and the knife dropped slowly to his side. He turned and walked casually back towards his house, never glancing back.

I finally took a breath and looked behind me. A bent, elderly woman with long white hair and a beige dress stood still as stone on her lawn, an easy reach away on the other side of the raspberries. These were her raspberry plants, the ones I had so often plundered because she'd been mean to me in the past. And now she stared silently at me, just stared without expression, leaning heavily on the cane she so often used to threaten kids away from her prized fruit.

"Thank you," I gasped, and took off down the path toward home. She called after me, but her voice was like the shallow scratches all over my skin, the twigs in my hair, the smell of leafy earth in my nostrils – all a streaking blur that had to be cast off and left behind.

There were calls to police and a few days of worry until Eric was finally apprehended and brought to trial. Whatever happened to Tom and his family I don't know – or I've forgotten – but my mother forbade me from visiting their house again, and I don't recall Tom never appearing at my door after that. I am grateful to him for almost certainly saving me from serious harm. I seldom trespassed that section of woods afterwards, having resolved out of a sense of gratitude and duty to leave the old lady her raspberries and some semblance of peace.

What did I learn from this? The limits of my own courage, certainly, and the value of mortal fear that results in meaningful action. Fear could preserve life, teach valuable lessons and instigate maturity. Up until that point in my life, I think I had resented fear as a boyish weakness, as a limitation of my capacities and creative thought. Now I understood that fear could be healthy, sometimes even necessary. I also understood something I had never fully realized about certain people: that they cannot always be reasoned with, or confronted when they were in the wrong, or beaten at their game of bullying. The look I had seen on Eric's face was an abrupt education about the dangerous wild animal residing within every human being. I would encounter that look again over the years. In a number of bullies who never had anyone stand up to them before. On the face of a mentally unstable Big Brother I taunted past his breaking point. In a neo-Nazi who thought I was a young Jewish kid and stalked me for an entire summer. In a crowd of Germans protesting against the American military's presence in Frankfurt when I was living there. And in each of these cases there was no way to reason, no way to soften the wrath or the threat of real physical harm. If I had not learned what it meant to quit the field and run, to find safe haven, to know for certain when my well-being was irrevocably threatened and to choose survival over pride, I surely would have been brutalized…or worse. As it is, so far, I have escaped with my skin – and a healthy self-preservational fear reflex – intact.

## The Enduring Lessons of Fear

There are countless other fearful moments that plagued my youth, but all of them fit neatly into three categories. Either they were creative but irrational fears like my nightmares, fears about not meeting someone's expectations or fitting in with my peers, or fears about my safety or survival. In one category, I learned the importance of responding quickly to fear in dangerous situations, and thereby securing my own well-being with proactive effort. In another, I learned how to dismiss fears that had no rational basis, were degrading my equanimity and paralyzed my ability to respond constructively. And in the third category, I learned that I had to work much harder than most kids to satisfy other people's expectations or fit in, and that my failure to do so resulted in painful rejection and isolation. In all three categories, I came to accept that I would never be safe and secure without prodigious vigilance and effort. As a result, I have struggled with persistent anxiety and the stress of readiness throughout most of my life, especially with respect to complex social interactions.

It is important to note here that without repeated experiences reinforcing these lessons throughout my early years, I would have not reached such firm conclusions. Had I found some niche where my life experiences and personal attributes were regularly appreciated, my anxieties around acceptance and approval would likely have softened. If I had not been exposed to dangerous situations over and over again, my heightened anxiety and reflex to take self-protective action would probably have attenuated. If I had not observed the negative consequences of my own irrational fears many times over, I might not have learned how to let go of them. Easily observable repeating patterns are what made these experiences so formative. And the fact that the patterns repeated while living in the households of both parents, while interacting with different groups of kids in different contexts, and even amid different living environments in different parts of the country, all amplified an inferred universality of my experience. As with so much of our learning in this area, it seems understanding moves from specific to general and back to specific again.

Various pluses and minuses grew from these lessons as well, and persist in my current sense of self. On the one hand, I can quickly identify irrational fears in myself and others and empathize with the past patterns that produced them. On the other, I have a reflexive impatience and intolerance for ideas and actions – issuing from myself or others – that are governed by nonsensical fears or a propensity for emotional drama. On the one hand, my quick reaction to dangerous situations has preserved my own well-being and the well-being of others many times over the years. On the other, my tendency to take control in threatening situations has sometimes undermined those in formal positions of authority, or diluted a victim's sense of sovereignty regarding their own well-being, or caused people who believed it was their responsibility to be helpful or protective to feel disempowered. On the one hand, I have been able to let go of my attachment to acceptance or approval and thereby achieve surprising results in many disciplines. On the other, I have also sabotaged my well-being by creating conflict and dissonance in many of my most important relationships, mainly as a perverse re-actuation of the rejection I experienced earlier in life.

Once again, there is that persistent dichotomy inherent to episodic patterns. All patterns of memory create patterns of self that can alternately support us and help us achieve great things, or tear our world apart in obvious or subtle ways. When we focus on the positive outcomes of our internalized lessons, we can feel good about ourselves and the world; we can begin to see that learning as a strength and an asset. When we focus on the unproductive outcomes of our inner patterns, we begin to see those facets as negatives, as weaknesses that undermine our wellness and success in life. And yet both of these extremes are part of us. Every pattern has at least two sides, and to completely reject either positive or negative is to view ourselves incompletely and unrealistically. In fact, by acknowledging and honoring both sides of our internal dichotomies, we create a dialectic, instructive tension that enhances our self-nourishment and well-being. As we come to recognize the intrinsic value of this tension, it is that much easier to develop compassionate affection for every aspect of self and successfully integrate them into a whole.

## Applying AMR

As with freedom and adventure in the first chapter, to fully embrace the fear-based dichotomies of who I am, I had to develop an unconditional empathy and compassion for each one – to lovingly appreciate both constructive and destructive potentials. For me, this began and ended with gratitude practice; the stronger my ability to summon gratitude, the more elective any destructive fear and anxiety responses became. Cognitive restructuring methods have also had a profound impact on this semantic container, ameliorating the negative influence of certain fears by challenging underlying assumptions and beliefs I held about myself. I have also introduced some of the more challenging episodic content into neutral awareness, so that I could evaluate what occurred from many different angles, and with many possible explanations. And for particularly intense, overwhelming or irrational fears, therapeutic breathing has provided a much-needed relaxation effect, which in turn allowed me to begin managing those fearful reactions more effectively.

Let's examine the application of AMR to one particularly potent generalization that arose from my early experiences of fear: I became fairly certain that I would never be safe and that my environment would never be calm, no matter what assurances others made or what precautions I took. Any illusion of serenity or safety would swiftly be overtaken by my own fearful imaginings, or the hostile intent of others, or my own inability to conform to social expectations. What energized this generalization? A majority of outcomes in vivid memories from a formative time. But many conditions have changed since that time. I am no longer in elementary school. I no longer live with my mother. I have learned many social skills that help me integrate with my peers better than I did early on. I don't live near bullies who routinely target me. And so on. And as I pointedly remind myself of these changes in environmental conditions, the energy of past outcomes begins to dissipate. It is no longer so pertinent to the present, can be disconnected from broader generalizations, and eventually drifts towards my integrative buffer. This is how we can begin to apply cognitive restructuring to specific fears.

And as I de-energized the assumptions behind my fears, I concurrently energized expectations of more positive conditions and outcomes. I actively chose work environments where compassion and cooperation were highly valued. I sought out friendships and social communities where I could feel safe and appreciated. And of course a more overall positive emotional disposition was facilitated with ongoing meditations on compassion and gratitude. As a final reinforcement to my sense of safety, I also regularly engaged in neutral awareness practice, which by its nature softens the edges of both fear and the situational stimuli that provoke fear and anxiety. All the while, I still allowed enough of my autobiographical memory into my daily life to provide some level of caution, proactive planning and prudence regarding my own well-being, so that positive aspects of fear remained energized as well.

However we arrive there, once we recognize that all of our strengths and weaknesses emanate from the same set of tendencies and learned responses, we can begin to relax our struggle to elevate some of them while suppressing others. For every component of our self-concept that evokes discomfort or loathing, there is another side to that component that can bring us joy, contentment and admiration. And for every strength that inspires pride and confidence, there is an aspect to that strength that can cause us debilitating harm. Human characteristics are never one-dimensional, and fear is no different.

So even as I learned to chuckle over irrational night terrors, I also came to respect and appreciate the importance of fear in my life. To understand what I am truly afraid of helps untangle my most complex emotions and motivations. Using language that explores those fears without amplifying them, without making myself a victim, or blaming anyone else, or amping up my anxiety, has also aided management of this challenging semantic container. To feel compassion for myself when I am afraid, and to feel affection for the role fear plays in my life, are what allow me to identify, discuss and process my fears in the most discerning and constructive ways possible. I have learned that any kind of fear, in any sort of situation, is almost always instructive – so why not pay attention? Why not try to understand the nature of my fears? Why not name them aloud to diffuse their power? Why not empathize with fear responses, and explore them carefully and lovingly…without letting them take control?

Over time, as I revisit my most fearful memories through the lens of compassionate attention and neutral awareness, I can begin to transform the most unsavory and difficult moments into tales of wonder and awe, and sometimes even joy. And once I can do that with patterns of the past, I can begin to do the same in real-time, in the patterns of the present. I can convert fear into either equanimity or exhilaration and excited anticipation right now. In fact, the more capably I hold my most fearful moments in the gentle hands of gratitude, compassion and neutral awareness, the more I can create the same healthy responses – self-preservational, action-oriented, creative, interdependent and relational responses – out of love and calm instead of fear.

A byproduct of this process is that some episodic memories that once primarily inhabited the "safety and fear" semantic container actually shifted into other containers as their primary habitat. It is of course common for the same events to support multiple themes and metathemes, but there is almost always a main emphasis. For example, when at age ten I donned skis and pointed them down a hill in Vermont, I ended up wedged up to my waist upside down in a snowdrift for over an hour, which in turn led to soaking my ski pants with my own urine because I could not free myself. Not only had I been terrified by my out-of-control descent – during which I startled several other skiers and even toppled a first aid tent – but I was deeply ashamed of my wet and stinky clothes and the loss of one of my ski poles. But later, as my mother and I recounted the story to friends and family, I was able to appreciate the humor in it that everyone else so easily found in the story. After that, each successive skiing experience tended to settle into the "freedom and adventure" container, with any fearful elements translating into excitement and exhilaration. In the same way, the AMR tools and steps often shift entire metathemes and all supportive structures from one semantic container into another, either temporarily or, with ongoing practice, permanently.

In full disclosure, however, some of my greatest failures over the years have been the result of my inability to manage my fears. Whenever I am physically tired, emotionally raw or spiritually depleted, I am particularly susceptible to having my fears and anxieties get the better of me. I will assume the worst of the people in my life, I will anticipate rejection and proactively isolate myself, I will seek ways to insulate myself from perceived harm, and maneuver myself out of relationships that evoke feelings of vulnerability. I might overreact to a perceived threat to my safety or the safety of those I love, and so on. And of course these were the routine survival reflexes of my youth, when fear taught me that people were unpredictable, that being accepted and fitting in wasn't part of my experience, that my own imagination could create horrific apparitions out of thin air, and that action was sometimes all that remained to preserve life. Vestiges of these operating assumptions persisted into my late teens and early twenties, only slowly relaxing through gradual maturity, successful interdependent relationships with others, nonthreatening environments and a lot of skilled therapy. These many years later, some of these reflexes linger, uninvited guests in my house of self; I am always surprised, chagrined and humbled when they rear their terrified heads. But in response, I continue with my core practices and I try to be forgiving of my fears…and not overly frightened by them.

## CHAPTER THREE: SHADES OF PAIN

As we saw in Chapter One, pain is another natural boundary to youthful exuberance. It teaches us the limits of our capacities in bold, irrefutable strokes. And it endures in memory as few other events can. In concert with fear, pain sets our experiences in bold relief, defining wise from foolish, right from wrong and good from bad like sharp, biting phrases carved in stone. We carry that stone with us wherever we go. There is no escaping its constant heft in the back of our minds, the continual chafing against our conscience in every new situation we encounter, and the sharp relief of each chiseled letter as we grope through past events for guidance in the present.

For me, nearly all distinct memories of pain fall into three categories or semantic types: the surprise of abrupt physical pain; the enduring discomfort of shame; and the sharp ache of deprivation and loss. These are first and foremost physical, emotional and mental types of pain, but give the right context they may also become spiritual pain. And when any experience or memory is layered with pain in many dimensions at once, the consequences can be devastating. The resulting associations, no matter how I question or approach them, tend to remain rigid and strongly directive, insisting I pay attention. They threaten to define my relationship with the world and the inherent limitations of my self-concept. Beyond natural or constructive boundaries of self, they have the potential to shackle my heart, mind, body and spirit with raw and lasting injury.

Grouping these various shades of pain into one semantic container becomes a particularly potent force in my mnemosphere, and managing that container becomes a critical aspect of my well-being. How will I allow this force to shape my identity? How will I manage deeply seated reflexes in my psyche that were formed through pain? Of all episodes in memory, it seems that those including pain are the most challenging to reorganize. With patience and consistent application of AMR, however, it is possible to claim victory here as well.

## *My Mother's Unpredictability*

My mother has experienced extreme mood swings all the years I have known her, but what made these difficult to witness during my early childhood was their unpredictability. One moment she would be smiling and jovial, the next raging and violent, the next inconsolably distraught – each without apparent explanation or provocation. The severity of her responses has likewise been impossible to anticipate, but almost always disproportionate to whatever seemed to be triggering the change. Her emotional shifts were not always directed at me, of course. Our pets would often receive scolding and rough treatment, or be party to her sudden fits of sobbing – as did neighbors, friends and other relatives. In most cases, her outbursts were severe but brief, quickly reverting to a more amiable affect, with her dogged insistence that nothing of import had occurred.

For all but the most thick-skinned and committed parties, these hysterics were thoroughly alienating. To her credit, my mother did seem to be able to conceal or defer the strongest of her emotions in certain situations, such as with authority figures like police officers, social workers, doctors or her boss at work – and with anyone else she suspected held more power than she did in a given situation. This allowed her to navigate society and survive in a sometimes hostile and equally unpredictable world, but it also meant that those perceived as weaker or dependent received the brunt of her instability.

As an almost daily occurrence during the time I lived with my mother, examples are too numerous to really mean anything. That is, a certain level of immunity to the severity of her dysfunction was provided by its regularity – its subjective normalcy. Children tend to adapt to their environment and learn to accept whatever chaos or instability permeates their lives.  In the midst of turmoil, they must learn how to survive and get their needs met.  So I adapted to my mother's random outbursts by leaving the room whenever she became intensely sad or frustrated, learning how to quickly apologize for any wrong she may have perceived, half-heartedly resisting any violence that came my way, and then continuing calmly with whatever I had been doing before the outburst occurred.  In one of her frequent letters to my grandmother when I was about six, my mom confesses: "I see how the dog reacts when I yell at Todd and how much it must hurt him."  I think part of the reason she could not recognize the impact she had was because, over time, I had learned to react as little as possible.

That said, there are some extreme cases that rise easily to the surface of memory and persist as stark moments of pain in the vast web of self that memory perpetuates.  One of the clearest occurred in our infamous Manchester town home.  We had had a rare, pleasant day together, and I had gone to bed happy and relaxed for the first time in weeks, falling quickly into a deep, dreamless sleep.  At some point in the small hours of the night, I was awoken by sharp, fiery pain.  Someone was violently yanking me out of bed by my hair.  I cried out, floundered and fell, and as I was dragged swiftly across the rug I tried to catch a glimpse of my assailant in the dark.  "Stop!  Stop!  Please stop!"  I whimpered, trying to catch my breath between shrieks of pain, groping for the hands that held my scalp with such brutal strength.  As I was pulled headfirst down the carpeted stairs, I found the smooth, delicate knuckles of my captor's fist, and through my panic I knew then that calling for my mother's help would be futile.

Then there was light.  Brilliant, painful brightness in a field of blinding white. As my mother's fists shook me and her most grating, hateful voice screamed into my ear, the whiteness took shape.  Without warning my face was inches from clear water and the curving walls of a toilet bowl.

"Does this look CLEAN to you?  *Does it?!*"  I knew that tone.  It was the wounded, accusing hysteria that lay beyond any attempts at reason or explanation.

*"Please, mom!"*

"You said you *cleaned this* today!  You told me you CLEANED the bathroom!  And it's NOT clean!  Is it?  *Is it?"* She forced my face deeper into the bowl, shaking me violently back-and-forth until my head banged repeatedly against the glossy porcelain.

"No!  I'm sorry mom!  *I'm sorry!"* I was crying earnestly now.

*"You don't do anything I tell you to do..."* Her grip tightened, pulling my hair out by its roots.

"I tried, mom!  I'm sorry!" I sobbed.

*"YOU DID THIS ON PURPOSE!"* Her voice was a screech now, crazed with hurt and accusation.

"No, mom, I..." Words were muffled as my face slapped porcelain again.

"Clean it up!  *Clean it up NOW!"* she screamed, shaking harder still. And, as abruptly as it had begun, it was over.  Her hands let me go and I fell sideways against the wall.  Angry steps retreated back to her room. "Right now!"  She called back, and there were hot, angry tears in her voice.

I sat crying for a few moments, listening warily for returning footsteps. Then I looked around the bathroom until I located my salvation.  I grabbed the toilet brush and began to scrub.  I couldn't see what part of the toilet wasn't clean, but I scrubbed away anyway.  Maybe it smelled funny?  Mom was always sensitive to smells.  I scrubbed and sniffed and rubbed my head.   Somehow I would make it right, I would make everything clean.  I would be a good boy.  At eight years old, I had learned in the countless episodes of my mother's volatility that she would eventually forgive me, and say she was sorry, and hug me and love me so that we could have a few more days of peace and contentment before the storm broke over us again.  I just needed to try a little harder until then.

§

Of course it is not my responsibility to apologize for someone else's actions, but to balance out this account I think it is important to explore all the possible dynamics at work here. There was the stress and strain of single parenting in the early 1970s. There was my youthful energy, independence and rebelliousness that would challenge any parent. There was my mother's loneliness and her frustration with work. And there were her underlying mental health issues. Although she has never been formally diagnosed, mom admits to hearing voices for most of her life – from her adolescence up until menopause. Voices that accused and berated her. Voices that encouraged her to feel suspicious, isolated and afraid, and with whom she had boisterous, spiteful arguments whenever she thought no one was listening. And despite her efforts to conceal it, her instability was nonetheless well known. When my father first spied mom's slim, lithe figure across a crowded college cafeteria and asked a friend about her, the friend replied: "Which one? Oh, her. That's Susan. Everyone calls her Crazy Susan."

Anyone who has a friend or family member with a personality disorder or serious mental illness knows that the demands of parenting are often simply beyond them. As much as they love their children, as much as they yearn to be a good provider and a stable, caring influence, they simply can't. Schizophrenia, if that is indeed what my mother suffered for so many years, is particularly debilitating. Add to this that, in nearly all of her letters to her mother and father over the years, mom was fixated on her own needs not being met, her constant feelings of abandonment and betrayal, and the pervasive unfairness of a world she felt was just too difficult to navigate on her own. In one Christmas missive when I was four, mom complained bitterly that I was receiving more gifts than she was every year. In other letters around that time she despaired that her sister, Donna, was receiving preferential treatment "just like she always does" – in the form of the money, clothes, gifts and emotional support my mother always craved from her parents. Clearly, her ability to mother me with any consistency was crippled by her own mental illness, her insecurities and these unhappy relationships.

Just as I have over the years, my mom has turned to poetry to work through intense or tangled feelings. To offer insight into her struggles, consider this poem she wrote about a lover in Eugene, Oregon:

### The Ashes' Glow

How shall we survive
If love is just –
A sparkle of sunlight
on the sand
A driftwood fire in the rain –

And when the wind and cold
drive us inside
do we just settle
for a presto fire
confined by bricks,
the security
of nine to five?

When those
last few grains of sand
have sifted through the hourglass,
Will we look back
in wonder
at the ashes' glow?

And much later, after returning to Manchester, Connecticut, my mom penned this poem about her sister Donna:

### Family-Ties

It wasn't so bad this time,
the loss seemed more like a gain;
Remembering the strained moments –
Holidays heavy with past resentments –
or completely empty.

How the hell did I sustain
those fragments of family-ties
all these years?
I tried so hard;

To ignore the insults,
bury the hurt.

"I don't come to visit
because I hate your guts!"
were her last words.
That made it easy –
to untie the knot in my stomach,
loosen my expectations
and face the fact:

"a cracked jug just don't hold no water."

Even with a better understanding of her experiences and suffering, neither my mother nor I are freed from the painful consequences of so much violence and hurt.  The pain involved in stories from my childhood is of course not only physical.  There is the pain of betrayal of trust in a parent's protection and love, and loss of reliance in the safety of a hearth and home undermined by fear.  There is the pain of shame and lowered self-esteem, of reviling myself for not being a good enough son to avoid my mother's wrath.  There is the grief over the irrational conclusion that because I could not live up to my mother's expectations, she would send me away to live with my father as she had done before. And there is the pain of acting out my shame, fear and confusion in other relationships at that time.

Because of my mother's volatility, nearly all of the cats and dogs we kept eventually became neurotic, fearful or aggressive no matter how sweet their initial disposition.  Animals, like children, will adapt to almost any situation.  But, unlike humans, they lack the ability to challenge or question the patterns of emotional pain that accumulate within their scolded hearts and beaten bodies, and so they lash out indiscriminately and fearfully at the world until, by my mother's reasoning, they have to be put down or sent away.  I, too, lashed out at my surroundings.  I imitated my mother's fury, rebelled against societal expectations and authority, and disrupted social situations with inappropriate behavior. As already noted, I was expelled from elementary school, bounced from one special needs program to another, then placed in a psychiatric facility for evaluation.  Finally, at age ten, my mother sent me away to live with my father in a heart-wracking affirmation of my own self-loathing.


## The Bouncing Baby Boy

Loss is a powerful emotional force, regardless of its cause. Perhaps some children feel secure enough – or are materially spoiled enough – not to care when their contact with toys, friends, homes, parents or other family members is abruptly cut off. For me, as I struggled to connect with the world around me, it seemed that I could never rely on the accessibility of any possession, relationship, routine or physical space for very long before it was taken away, and this repeating theme planted a dull ache of grief within me that continued to grow throughout most of my life. It was as if the lesson of impermanence and temporal variability were being drummed into my psyche during those earliest years, with the cycle of attachment and loss becoming a central tenet of my existence.

We had very little money when I was small. My mother's letters from that time are filled with requests for basic necessities and worry over finances. But somehow we survived, sometimes on public assistance, sometimes on the charity of relatives or friends, and sometimes through austere sacrifices. When, at age three, my one and only favorite toy, a yellow Tonka dump truck, was stolen from our front yard, I was beside myself with outrage and confusion. Of course, at three years old, I took it personally. Why would someone take the only material thing I cared about? Why would they want to hurt me like that? Why did they hate me so much? It was a feeling that would be reiterated many times as other favorite possessions would be stolen by poorer kids, brazenly wrenched from my grasp by older kids asserting their authority, or broken and disfigured by jealous playmates. On the few occasions when I decided to imitate this behavior and take what others valued for myself, I could never get away with it – I was always found out shortly thereafter, and always punished. What did this mean, then? Was I not supposed to call anything my own? Was I supposed to stop caring about material things?

Along similar lines, the friendships I made when I was young were also short-lived. As we moved often, or I was pulled out of school, or my mother behaved irrationally around someone's parents, my tentative connections with other kids were severed. On one occasion, when I was five, my mother left me to play with a neighbor boy, David, for one long, sunny Saturday. In my excitement, I wanted to show David my style of adventurous exploration, and led him on a three-hour expedition into a wooded mountain park a few blocks from his house. His parents, having no idea where we had wandered off to, were frantic. By the time we returned, my mother had already arrived to retrieve me. "We went exploring!" I proudly declared. David's mother was hysterical and quickly herded her son out of sight. David's father was furious.

"How could you do such a thing, Todd? We had no idea where you were!" he said angrily.

"But I knew where we were..." I started to explain.

My mother's laughter interrupted me. "That's just how he is," she said, smiling and trying to lighten the mood. "I'm sorry he scared everyone, but David's home safe and sound and everything's fine."

"I don't want him anywhere near my son. Not ever again." The father said with finality.

Mom's smile faded. "Come on, honey," she said, taking my hand. "These people don't understand." And we left.

So my own behavior inadvertently sabotaged attempts at lasting friendship as well. I would use vocabulary other kids didn't understand, or tell incredible stories they didn't believe, or behave in ways that seemed disrespectful to the rules and etiquette established by their parents or older siblings. So aside from the intense relationship I developed with my step-sister, Shelly, I wasn't able to establish close bonds with kids my age until my early teens. And I think this reinforced conclusions I had drawn from other experiences: I must not be likeable; I must not be normal; there must be something horribly wrong with me that made people around me evaporate so quickly; I would never be accepted; I would never fit in. And, of course, all friendships and connections must by nature be temporary and fleeting.

Now add to this bitter soup one final ingredient:  my bouncing back and forth between my father's and mother's households.  Sometimes for just a few months, and sometimes for a year or more, I would abruptly find myself living in a new home, with new rules, new parameters of authority and new relational dynamics.  Between age two and ten, I would be moved back-and-forth seven times without any cogent explanation.  At age thirteen I would even live with a kind-hearted foster family for a year, then join my father and his new wife in Germany. Sometimes these moves would be across town, sometimes a few hours away in a neighboring state, sometimes across the U.S. from one coast to the other, and ultimately across the Atlantic ocean.  And what did this game of badminton unintentionally communicate to an insecure young boy?  I wasn't wanted anywhere.  I didn't belong anywhere.  I wasn't loveable or even likeable.  I was a painful burden.  I was a pain.  And because of these deficits in myself, I became certain that even my most important relationships would never last for long.

And thus we arrive at the quintessential valuation that created an enduring force in my own development:  to never be sure if I was loveable or loved, to question the very existence of love or being loved as a valid experience, transmuted the events of loss, perceived abandonment and grief into fundamental beliefs.  The belief that people and relationships are not important.  The belief that no one had my interests at heart.  The belief that other people's actions are generally selfish or self-serving.  The belief that as long as I never become vulnerable, never open myself to connections with others, I can avoid being hurt.  As I approached adolescence, these were my guiding sentiments.  If not for subsequent life experiences that contradicted these assumptions, I likely would have hardened myself still further to the world, closing off all channels of connection that risked additional pain. Well into my adulthood, the currents of sorrow, disappointment and hurt would course beneath my thoughts, emotions and actions to sabotage my happiness and well-being.

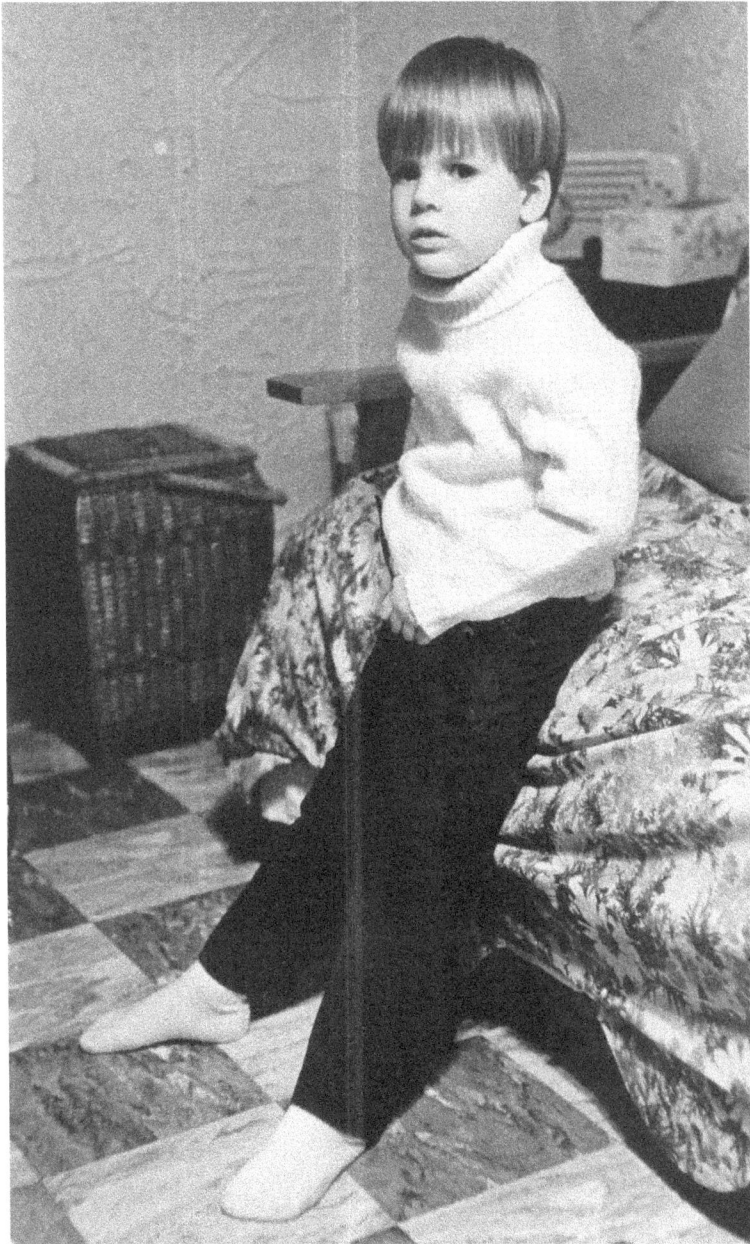

At about age four in our Eugene, Oregon home

### *A Body Cries Out*

Separate from pain that is clearly inflicted from without by others, there were also physical pains that were self-inflicted. I was a sturdy tyke when I was little, tall for my age with a wiry strength from tree climbing, and a quickness from running freely and racing with dogs all the time. But I had my share of accidents. Falls and scrapes, sprains and cuts. When I was five I watched my step-sister Shelly hanging upside down by the crook of her knees in a tree beside my father's house in Eugene. It was pretty high up but it looked like a lot of fun. The two of us were the same age and always competing with each other – mostly my trying to keep up with her sharp mind, and her trying to keep up with my spry physicality. In this case, though, she was doing something in a tree – a place I of course considered to be my domain – that I had never even contemplated before.

I quickly scrambled up the tree and out onto the same sturdy limb. Shelly was always wise and insightful for her age, and warned me not to try what she had been doing so effortlessly. "You'll fall," she warned.

"No I won't!" I rashly declared, and so she made room for me out on the branch.

Imitating her as best I could, I hooked the back of my legs over the branch and swung backwards and down. I immediately fell head-first onto our driveway. Miraculously, I didn't break my neck, but my head hit hard enough to start me howling. My step-sister quickly clambered down to where I lay, looking worriedly back at the house. "Ssh! We'll get in trouble!"

"You should'a told me!" I accused.

"I did! C'mon, get up." She grabbed my arm and helped me sit, then her eyes went wide. Instantly she was up and running toward the front door. "Mom! Mom!" She disappeared inside the house, the screen door slamming behind her.

I stayed sitting there, my head throbbing, and I reached up to probe my wounds – they must be pretty bad to scare Shelly that way. But instead of the bloody mess I expected, I found a short, splintery board. Just sitting there on top of my head. I tried to pull it off, but it wouldn't move. Then I really started to cry.

My father did not engage himself much in my upbringing during those years. He was busy teaching college and entertaining his new wife, Mary, and whenever he was home the two of them tended either to be drinking alcohol, yelling at each other, or locking us kids outside so the newlyweds could "take a nap." As a result, almost all of my interactions with him – and certainly all of my enduring memories of him during those weekends and summers in Eugene – involved corporeal discipline for something I had done wrong, or stern instruction on what I ought to be doing to avoid getting in trouble again. Even when he was absent, my step-mother, Mary, was adept at leveraging my father's authority with the classic phrases: "Just wait till your father gets home" and "you're father's going to hear about this." Consequently, whenever my father appeared on the scene, I reflexively felt fear and a strong need to explain myself.

Now, on this warm summer day, sitting on the stinging-hot pavement and holding my throbbing head, I watched the screen door open and my father appear.

"I didn't do it!" I cried.

"Jesus Christ," he said with alarm. He threw his lit cigarette on the ground and in a few quick strides stood over me.

"How the hell...?" he began.

"The tree," I said, pointing.

He glanced up. "You fell out of the fucking tree? *On your head?*"

I tried to nod, but he was already gripping the board with both hands. He yanked once, lifting my entire body off the ground. "Holy shit," he said. Instead of just irritation, there was fear in his voice now. "Hold still!"   He braced my head between his knees and yanked again.   The board pulled free and he stepped away.  We both looked at the two rusty nails sticking out of the board.  "Jesus fucking..." he muttered.

"Were those in my head?" I asked, gently rubbing my scalp.

My dad ignored the question and strolled to the metal trash can beside the driveway.  With a loud clang the board was quickly out of sight. Then he turned to look at me.  "Are you bleeding?"  I patted my hair and my hand came away with only a hint of blood.  I showed it to him. "Don't go up in that tree again," he said firmly, then walked back into the house, picking up his discarded cigarette along the way.

For a few minutes I was left by myself.  I heard raised voices inside the house and stood quietly, probing the top of my head and staring at my fingers.  Then my step-sister reappeared, angrily wiping tears from her face.  With hands on her hips in a perfect imitation of her mother's ire, she leveled a squinting frown at me and said, "Now I can't climb up in the tree, either!"

"Why?" I asked.

"Because you hurt yourself!" she huffed.

"That's not fair," I said fervently.

"No," she agreed, her features quieting a bit.

Then I had an idea.  I smiled at her, ran to the tree and started to climb.

"Todd, don't!" she whisper-yelled, glancing furtively back through the front door. Then she ran over to the tree. "*Get down!*" she hissed.

I grinned at her, shimmied out along the branch, and slowly – and much more carefully this time – lowered myself to hang from the branch by the backs of my knees.  I giggled down at her and the distress on her face slowly broke into a smile.   It would not be the last of our secret rebellions.

And this is why, as you can imagine, I ended up injuring myself with some frequency. Although I never broke any bones, I did experience a lot of physical pain throughout my early life. And when I wasn't unintentionally inflicting pain on myself, I could reliably earn a sturdy spanking from my step-mom, or a belt-whipping from my father, or a solid back-hand from my mother. So, as a means of enforcing boundaries for my actions, physical pain became a fairly casual companion in my daily life. It should come as little surprise then that, as I began at an early age to experience a more chronic pain, first in my abdomen, and then in my back and chest, that on some level I dismissed it as the natural consequences of my wild and self-destructive behavior.

On another level, however, I also learned that physical pain could be used to win attention from others. Sometimes I would use it to impress my peers, and sometimes to garner sympathy from adults. I would routinely invite other kids to arm wrestle me, punch me in the stomach, or otherwise challenge me physically, just to prove how strong and tough I was. I would throw a handful of heavy rocks straight up into the air to scare off kids who were gathering around me, further impressing them when some of the rocks hit me in the head. Some kids saw me as particularly tough, and others as particularly crazy, but I nevertheless carved out a special place for myself in the social order this way. In the first months of sporadic elementary school attendance, my regular injuries also became a ticket out of the uncomfortable social pressures of the classroom, and I could take refuge in the nurse's office. Sometimes my mother even came to pick me up from school. Once, when I was five, my mother sought to dissuade me from melting Crayola crayons in the space heater of our home (one of my favorite activities at that age) by holding my hand against a hot burner of our kitchen stove. I then took great pleasure marching around the neighborhood to show everyone the spiral burns on my palm. "Look, my mom did this!" I would declare with pride. I was almost tempted to melt some more crayons, just so she would do it again.

With some members of my family, my self-injuring behaviors didn't always reap the sort of attention I desired. But I still tried. I would stick my foot in the front tire of my bicycle while racing down a hill, just to see what would happen. Or I would leap from my skateboard to see test how quickly the skin grinding off my arms and legs would bring me to a stop.  In response to these attempts, my father frowned, called me an idiot, then took away my bicycle and skateboard. When I was around seven I challenged some neighborhood kids to a contest:  by tying one end of a rope around my neck, and the other around the seat of their bike, I would attempt to hold them in place with my neck as they tried to pedal away.  Unfortunately, I used a simple slip knot on my end of the rope, so even though I did hold my ground for a few heartbeats, I also succeeded in choking myself.  This attempt was made in the driveway of my maternal grandparents in Manchester, Connecticut.   So when I ambled inside to show off the ring of burst capillaries around the base of my throat, my grandmother Rita said flatly:  "I saw everything, Todd. The whole time.  What you did was the stupidest thing I've ever seen in my entire life.  Someone ought to wring your neck, but you've already don it yourself!"

Over time, these patterns of physical pain left their imprint on my personality.  I have learned to tolerate a fairly high level of physical discomfort, pushing myself hard in many physical hobbies like hiking, skiing and swimming.  In sports like tennis, basketball and ultimate Frisbee, I generally measure the sincerity of my efforts not through racking up points, but through the seriousness of my injuries.  For many years, my chronic stomach pain perpetuated more formal attention from healthcare providers, and until it began to really interfere with my quality of life in my thirties, the condition was yet another badge of strength and courage in the face of calamity.  In other words, whether through deliberate effort, disposition or circumstance, my body – my somatic memory – became a repository for various proofs that I either deserved to be in pain, that pain was somehow inevitable, or that pain was a useful tool in my navigation of relationships and society.  Pain became an affirmation of being alive, an opportunity to have a slight edge of control in unpredictable situations, and a confirmation that I was, in fact, undeserving of my parents' love.  It became an integral part of my identity.

### Shamed into Goodness

My fiery constitution and early experiences made me almost immune to the more common types of embarrassment. As I quickly learned how different I was from other kids, any words or actions that were awkward or made me stand out affirmed who I was rather than inducing shyness or discomfort. My mother's outgoing personality and unpredictable responses also made me relatively thick-skinned to the judgment of others – they were always judging or rejecting my mother and me, so what did it matter? I had also schooled myself to remain calm in the face of mom's frequent tantrums, so that, too, disconnected me from feelings of humiliation I might otherwise experience. I had encountered a lot of cruelty in other kids over time – from name-calling to hurtful pranks to outright beatings. I think young children have a finely tuned radar for identifying anyone new, strange, different or otherwise out-of-place in their world, and most have learned from their parents to be fearful and aggressive towards outsiders or the unknown. So on the whole, my exposure to public ridicule and ostracizing was fairly fast and furious, and callousness and indifference seemed more the norm than the exception.

At the other end of the spectrum were my father's rigid parental prescriptions for acceptable behavior, as well as a demonstrated commitment to his own ethical sensibilities. He wanted to do right by people, and felt bad when he failed; and I think it was this well-developed conscience that at least in part caused him to retreat into alcohol. So although he was harsh and dictatorial about his rules, he provided some much-needed moral consistency in my life. With his clear standards of behavior and reliable meting out of consequences, I encountered a well-reasoned moral structure that was either absent or unpredictably flexible when I lived with my mom. With his expectations and example as the backdrop for my choices, the mysteries of right and wrong began to clarify themselves in my childhood worldview. His rigidity became my moral anchor in an otherwise relativistic storm. With my mother, I might have fears about getting caught doing something of which she didn't approve, but with my father, I learned how to feel ashamed of doing something that was in itself morally questionable.

There are some critical distinctions to be explored here.  As a preteen, I was rebellious towards authority, including my father's, and yet I somehow held on to a strong sense of right and wrong.  Some things became very black-and-white.  My adventurous nature made me non-conformist, but my sense of moral rectitude led me not only to edit my own behavior but also pass strong judgments on others.  I routinely defended weaker kids I thought were being bullied, stood up to adults and children I thought were doing something reprehensible, and felt deep and abiding shame about mistakes I made.  In other words, I became a law unto myself.  I felt responsible for my own actions and even for correcting the actions of others, but I resisted any authority or accountability I perceived to be outside of my own judgment and control.

This is important because it frames nearly all of my experiences of shame as being internally and independently generated, rather than induced by the condemnation or ridicule of others.  My conclusions about what was right or wrong were certainly strongly influenced by society, parents and peers, but my harshest judgments and sense of accountability came from within, not from without.  To some degree, I think this explains why certain memories replay themselves so forcefully at times.  It seems that I allow my memories to beat me up because I have always beaten myself up; I have always held myself to stringent and difficult standards of conduct in certain areas.

Which brings us to some of the shameful experiences themselves.

When I was eight, I stole a pink marble from the daughter of one of my mother's friends.  It was the girl's most cherished possession, a sphere of pink quartz that glittered in the sun.  She would not even let me hold it or touch it, it was so precious to her.  I could only gaze upon it longingly and marvel at its beauty.  As we were about to leave their house, I snuck back into the girl's room, found her marble bag, and quickly snatched up the pink marble.  I didn't intend to keep it long, but I thought it was unfair that she wouldn't let me play with it or hold it.  I thought she was being mean.  So I set out to teach her a lesson and enjoy the pleasure of which she had deprived me.

As soon as we got home, I rushed up to my room and fished the marble out of my pocket. I held it up in the sunlight and gazed in wonder at the endless refractions of light. It was so warm in my hand, so alive with sparkling shadows, that began to wonder if it was more than just a marble. Was it magical? Could it change my luck? Could it make a person happy or sad? If I gazed into its depths, would I see a world unfold there, like when Horton heard a Who? If it was magical, maybe I shouldn't have taken it. Maybe that's why the girl didn't want me to hold it. Maybe it was part of her somehow. I felt the first small pangs of guilt over what I had done.

Our phone began to ring. Was that my mother's friend calling to ask about the marble? I looked around my room for the best place to hide it, and spied the tin box where I kept some of my collected treasures. I ran over to the box and grabbed it off the top of my dresser. The lid slipped open as I lifted it down, and I fumbled to keep the box's contents from spilling out all over the floor. In the process I dropped the magical pink marble. I lunged after it, meaning to catch the marble but only swatting it hard as it fell. If it had landed on the carpet I'm sure all would have been well. But instead it ricocheted off the dresser with a loud smack and angled into the wooden baseboard, where it shattered into countless pieces. I stared down at the pink fragments in horror. What had I done? What had I destroyed?

I heard my mother end her phone call and come up the stairs. I sat on my bed and stared at my hands, holding my breath. Mom continued up the stairs to her room. Nothing happened. I began to breathe again and beheld my handiwork. There was nothing beautiful or magical about the marble anymore. Numbly, I cleaned up the pink fragments, put them inside a fresh sock, and hid the sock back inside the dresser drawer.

Days passed. No call came. No accusations. But I was miserable. What began as seeds of guilt grew into remorse, and remorse flowered into shame. But I couldn't bring myself to tell my mom. I didn't know how she would react. I felt I should make things right, but I had no idea how that could be done. Then, perhaps a week later, I stumbled upon an idea. After quickly rummaging through my room, I grabbed what I needed and ran downstairs.

"Mom?"

"Yes, honey?" She was sitting on the living room couch, sipping a glass of grappa.

"I found this today." I held up my favorite blue glass marble. "I think it belongs to that girl."

"What girl?"

"The girl we went to see?"

My mother thought for a second. "You mean Marla's daughter?"

"Yes!"

Mom looked at me. "Did you steal that? You *did*, didn't you?" She wasn't happy.

"No, no. I put it in my pocket when we were playing. I just found it!"

My mother frowned, then wagged her finger at me. "If you're lying...."

"I'm not! Here!" I thrust the marble into her hand. "I just wanted to give it back to her." And I turned and ran.

We didn't speak of the marble again for a couple of days. Then my mother cornered me in my room. "Todd, Marla says her daughter is missing a pink marble, not a blue one. Do you know anything about that?" She was being casual, but whenever my mother addressed me by my given name, I knew things had gotten serious. I had to tread carefully.

I chose the easier course. "No...it's the blue one. That's hers. But I'll look if you want."

"You didn't take a pink marble?"

"Huh-uh," I said, shaking my head and looking at her beseechingly.

"Okay, if that's what you say," she said doubtfully. She turned to leave.

"Doesn't she want the blue one?" I thought to ask.

Mom continued down the steps. "If that's the only one we have, that's the one I'll give her," she called back, reproach in her tone. I could tell she wasn't convinced, but I was too ashamed to admit the truth.

This wasn't the only time I had engaged in this sort of retaliatory theft. When the purveyor of a local tractor trailer repair shop chased me out of his truck yard with threats of violence, I took revenge by sneaking back that night and stealing all the keys and fire extinguishers out of the cabs of all the trucks. I was just curious about the trucks, I reasoned, and hadn't been doing anything wrong, so what right did he have to chase me and threaten me? Eventually, my mother found the keys in the drawer of my desk, and when she asked me about them, I proudly told her the whole story. The fire extinguishers, which I hid in the woods, were discovered by the neighborhood kids, who rapidly proceeded to empty them all over each other in a grand battle in the woods. When an elderly neighbor threatened me with her cane because I was walking too close to the raspberry bushes in her yard, I snuck back the next day and ate as many raspberries as I could. And so on. Anytime I felt slighted or wrongly accused, I would instinctively fulfill the lowest possible expectations of my accuser by finding some devious way to lash out at them.

But in the marble incident, I had crossed an unexpected line. The outcome had not been what I anticipated. The "punishment" had accidentally become too severe for the perceived offense. I had not balanced the scales, I had broken them. I felt such regret about that pink marble, such persistent shame, that it actually affected how I behaved after that. Instead of deviousness, I shifted to confrontation. When other kids blamed me for something they had done, I would furiously confront them no matter how much older or bigger they were. When teachers at school accused me of exaggerating or lying about some experience I was sharing with the class, I would become so enraged they had to clear the classroom. When an adult talked down to me or was somehow dismissive in their attitude towards me, I would loudly declare they were doing so. Once, when a dentist tried to convince my mom that I needed braces to correct my overbite, he kept ignoring my questions and objections. I didn't want braces, and he wasn't listening. So I stood between him and my mother, pointed a finger at him accusingly, and declared, "All those bad things you keep saying about my teeth won't happen for a long, long time!" It shut him down. Thus, instead of spiteful, passive-aggressive sneakiness as retaliation, I chose boisterous, self-righteous anger instead. For a while, standing up for myself seemed to work pretty well. Right up until I got my first paying job in a hierarchical workplace.

§

There are, of course, other experiences of shame that helped form my sense of right and wrong. There was the time around age eleven when a friend and I hurled a huge chunk of icy snow onto the windshield of a passing car, only to observe with horror the same car pull into my driveway just down the street. When I sheepishly returned home a few hours later, my father didn't confront me directly, but instead recalled how frightened his coworker had been during the incident. He explained how large chunks of ice could damage a windshield, how they could cause an accident when a driver overreacted, and, finally, how they could morbidly embarrass a passenger who knew it was his own son who had delivered the frigid missile. I was mortified, and stood dripping in the entryway staring at my mitted hands, fully expecting a severe and likely corporeal punishment. I couldn't deny my obvious involvement. But instead of being kicked, whipped or thrown down the stairs to my basement room as was the usual course, my father simply said, "That was a really, really dumb thing to do." And then he went into the living room, leaving me to stew in my stupidity and humiliation.

Much later, when I was fourteen, I was caught trying to ride free on the Strassenbahn in Frankfurt, Germany. The streetcars at that time ran on an honor system, where riders were expected to purchase a ticket from a kiosk at one of the stations without threat of their purchase ever being confirmed. They did do spot checks on the trains occasionally, but it had only happened to me once, and that time I had a ticket. In fact, I had always bought a ticket when I first started using the Strassenbahn. But as a forgetful teenager, I neglected to bring cash with me or to buy a ticket before stepping onto the streetcar more and more frequently. So I got lazy, and I got caught.

The train slowly rolled to a stop in the middle of nowhere, between two stations. Then a dozen plain-clothed inspectors rose from their seats to demand tickets, and I had none. Apparently, they didn't cuff offenders or haul them straight of the train. Two of the inspectors just stood next to me until the end of the line, while all the other riders stared disgustedly to one side of me or above my head. It felt like an endless public caning. Then the inspectors, hands firmly on each of my arms, led me off the train to a waiting police cruiser. At that point, the Polizei gave me a choice. I could pay the fine right then, or they would issue a citation. As I didn't have the two-hundred-and-forty Deutschmark that was required, I opted for the citation. This required I present my I.D., which, unfortunately, I had also forgotten.

In the early eighties, all U.S. citizens were required to carry their passports on their person at all times in West Germany. So my lack of proper identification was actually a further offense of the law. In order to avoid being placed in a holding facility, the Polizei would have to escort me to my home to verify my identity. So that's what they did, in plain view of our entire neighborhood. Adding an extra layer of humiliation to the experience, I had not cleaned my room for weeks. It was filthy, and smelly, and cramped, and the two officers watched with grimacing distaste as I dug through my sordid belongings for my passport. Thankfully, my dad, his wife and her parents were not home at the time. It was, after all, their house…and their reputation…that I was degrading.

Once I showed the Polizei my passport, they took down the relevant information and left, promising that a citation would arrive in the mail in a few weeks. When it did, my step-grandfather, Joachim, opened it. I had given him a vague sketch of the situation, just the bare essentials, and told him that as soon as the citation arrived in the mail, I would take care of it. I actually had no idea how I would take care of it, other than begging my father for the money, but I trusted Joachim to alert me when the envelope arrived. He didn't. Instead, he paid the fine himself. He said nothing to me about it, nor to anyone else. It was only a few weeks later when I asked him if the letter had arrived that he said, not quite looking up from his work, "Well yes. I paid it already."

I thanked him profusely, promising to pay him back, and he waved me off dismissively, not saying another word. He never mentioned it again. I was confused and humbled. Joachim had shown nothing but kindness during my stay in his home. I had not spoken a lick of German when I arrived from the U.S., a petulant and uncooperative teenager pining for the friends and familiarity I'd left behind, and he had patiently helped me adjust to my new life. During our daily walks he would help me with my German and tell me stories of his life – how it was before the war, how he had fought and been captured near the coast of France, how he had met his wife, a Dutch nurse, when he returned to Germany after the war ended. He let me use his workshop to rebuild my bicycle and build all manner of contraptions out of his carefully accumulated odds and ends. He even let me write a paper for German class about his stay in an American prisoner of war camp. And this was how I repaid him. By breaking the law and letting him pay the fine. Perhaps he anticipated the fruits his stoic response would yield, for in my shame I strove mightily never to put him in that situation again.

If I reach back further into my earliest childhood, the rooms of memory darken as I search for ignominy. There are experiences there – I can sense them like a muffled argument behind closed doors – but they remain inaccessible to my conscious awareness. Perhaps they are repressed, though hypnotherapy and other approaches have not brought them successfully into the foreground. There were also the fleeting episodes of superficial embarrassment that all children have. Such as the time when I was three when one of the older neighborhood kids persuaded me to eat dog crap. Or the time at age four when I asked the first black man I had ever seen if could rub his skin, because I didn't believe he was really black. But these other experiences do not appear to have left a lasting mark on me – at least none that I can easily identify. Although they surely influenced my development in some way, and likely had a common-sense impact on later decisions (I never ate dog crap again or challenged the color of a person's skin), they did not create patterns that were reinforced over and over as part of my evolving identity.  Unlike the shame-filled memories that continue to hold a sting of regret, these superficial moments merely offer opportunities for chagrined laughter.

## What Pains Me Now

Much of the time, the echoes of pain do not shackle me in obvious ways. Instead, they manifest as inexplicably strong emotional reactions triggered by association – or as equally severe, often ineffective choices in words or actions during circumstances that parallel earlier experiences.  But the strength of painful memory's presence also percolates into conscious awareness.  At times when I am relaxed and inattentive, a vivid memory of pain will suddenly present itself.  Perhaps an embarrassing incident in sixth grade will surface while I'm taking a shower.  Or a memory of childhood abuse will flash before my eyes as I'm driving to a routine destination or talking one of my daily walks. Sometimes the sadness of a childhood deprivation will grip me while cooking dinner.  Without apparent cause, even if my mind drifts into an unspecified or spacey place, the memories of hurt can rush forth to fill my entire imagination.  And such constant reminders cannot help but influence my self-concept in the present.

These persistent, involuntary recollections of personal suffering have motivated me to engage in all sorts of behaviors – some constructive, others less so.  Throwing myself into adrenaline-seeking hobbies, for instance, or escaping into fantasy and science fiction role-playing games, or playing video games for hours on end.  Sometimes pain has prompted a more self-destructive direction, such as adventures into alcohol or unhealthy relationships.  Ultimately, these patterns of memory and escape behavior inspired me to seek healing through therapy, alternative healing arts and introspective meditation.  At the same time, my urgings toward creative self-expression have certainly been fed by this family of experiences as well.  Painful patterns from my past have even prompted me to explore spirituality, for they could accurately be called personal demons, tempting and taunting me without reprieve.  So here again we see various metastructures of being infused with specific frequencies of energy due to repeating autobiographical patterns – and a dichotomy of outcomes and characteristics.

Over the intervening decades since those formative years, there have been plentiful chances to feel various intensities and varieties of pain. The knifing fire of kidney stones. The grief and shame of divorce. The loss of close friends when one of us moved to a new town. A nasty skiing accident. The death of a relative. The end of a hope or dream. The humiliation of trying and failing to explain a traffic violation to a judge. But all of these are really just echoes of earlier experiences. They don't offer new, formative material, only affirmations of patterns that are already known and have already become part of me. The dried husks of physical pain, intense grief and loss, and visceral regret were already inherent to my associative matrix. All new experiences have done is add fresh vitriol to reconstitute and enhance what my mind, body, heart and spirit already intimately know. The question then becomes: how can I best manage that reconstitution so that pain no longer has such a prominent role in my life?

## Applying AMR

After years of working to understand the core material of these memories and the impulses and environments that reconstitute their associations in the present, it is inconceivable that I could ever suppress, avoid or deny what happened to me, or the lasting impact of those experiences on my being. However, it is an equally untenable option to give them more weight than they are due, to consider myself a victim in these experiences, or to seek blame or retribution over what happened in the past. For in both extremes I would empower my shame, loss and pain, energizing it to wreak further havoc in my life and perpetuate more damage and destruction in myself and my relationships. As with other semantic containers and the episodic memories supporting them, this becomes a crucial aspect of my inner and outer dynamic equilibrium: to acknowledge, accept and integrate without enlarging, energizing or empowering negative aspects. As we shall see, though demons do exist, they can be trained and transformed through conscious, compassionate effort. With patience, forbearance and love our most painful memories can become influences for good in the world.

First, I must recognize the same dichotomy exists  as with any another aspect of memory-identity.  Why is this so important?  Because if I restrict myself to viewing painful memories as purely antagonistic and destructive to my well-being, I have very few choices in my identity formation.  I either become a victim of grievous or humiliating circumstances if I don't feel responsible for what happened to me, or I become a terrible person because I am either solely responsible for all that has happened to me or have somehow invited this pain into my life.  The consequences of such self-limiting choices are predictably severe.  I will tend to reenact my suffering over and over again because that is how I see myself.  I will fulfill my self-concept by creating new pain through every choice, in every relationship.  In this perpetually glass-half-empty view, all future shame, grief and physical pain are validations of my impoverished character, my hapless lot in life, my abject unworthiness.

The long-term consequences of cleaving to such conclusions are also predictable.  It is likely I will reinforce my victimhood by choosing abusive people as friends and romantic partners.  Or I might become an abuser or a criminal myself.  Or I might be chronically ill, have a series of injurious accidents, or perhaps even attempt suicide.  I might choose a career, place to live or romantic partnership that punishes me in some way, that restricts or shuts down whole dimensions of my being so that I never fulfill my potential.  I might engineer situations where I lose what is dear to me over and over again.  And whatever suffering I endure will make perfect and ordinary sense to me – no matter how severe it becomes – because I have accepted my own failure and wretchedness as inevitable.  Most of this will occur on an unconscious level and, depending on my self-awareness, I may never question it…no matter how miserable I become.

At the other end of the spectrum, my suffering can also help me become strong and resilient.  I can develop a thick skin that makes me less vulnerable to criticism or hurtful events.  I can perfect a sense of humor and warm personality that disarm those who wish to do me harm and charms those I feel might become a threat.  I can increase my tolerance of physical pain and hardship.  I can remain a bit more detached and aloof from other people – or material things, or the place I live – so that I feel less pain when I am separated from them.  I can develop a street sense about the actions and broadcasted intentions of those around me, so that I can avoid stumbling into harmful situations. I can become more wise and discerning about how to navigate the unhealthy relational dynamics I have experienced before. I can seek out positive, supportive and constructive friendships and community, offering support and healing to myself and others. I can empower myself with careful life planning, healthy emotional boundaries, diligent physical self-care, and other measures to reduce exposure to the many shades of pain and suffering I have previously experienced.

To whatever degree I follow this second path, I draw upon the pain in my past to create a capable, confident and self-reliant identity. And yet, at the same time, I must learn to embrace the painful core material with unconditional love. If not – if I am only trying to escape the pain, or deny its existence, or otherwise minimize it – all such empowerment is just a sham, a thin façade to conceal the memories I am unable to face, let alone embrace. And any such concealment can eventually morph into a disorder – narcissism, egotism, control behavior, paranoia, self-isolation, dissociative identities, etc. Therefore, as with all other memory management, I must learn to consciously integrate all aspects of this potential dichotomy until some sort of equilibrium is achieved.

So I am not a victim, I am not a monster, and I am not destined to perpetuate my own suffering...but neither am I an impervious, all-powerful being who needs no one and no thing, or someone who has completely transcended his past and elevated himself beyond the reach of physical, emotional, mental or spiritual pain. I am none of these extremes, but my identity contains aspects of them all. And this is where AMR tools come in. As I return to those original, formative experiences in neutral awareness, I come to view them from a calm and disinterested distance, entirely without judgment. With particularly volatile memories, I might ride the rapids of intense emotions with therapeutic breathing techniques. Through cognitive restructuring, I challenge self-limiting reflexes and the demeaning conclusions that underlie them. In my gratitude practice, I hold these memories in the strong but delicately cupped hands of compassionate caring. Ultimately, I seek to fall in love with younger me who suffered, and with the brokenness of those who participated in painful past events. I allow my grief to express its depths, my shame to look at itself honestly, my hurt to unfold in the warmth of my own embrace.   I invest consciously in exploring the unconscious assumptions and beliefs that have grown out of my past distress, digging deep to bring everything I can into the full light of day.

Why have I been so committed to this course?   Because those early patterns of experience are imbedded in my current sense of self, they are part of the inescapable reality of who I am.   In purely self-preservational logic, I can neither suppress or ignore them, nor allow them excessive sway over my self-concept.   Therefore, I gently venture forth into the unknown of my inner life, separating the core material of my past from its emotional and mental associations, then providing new, more productive contexts.   One way of looking at this is as an exercise in creative rationalization – I am simply inventing a new lens through which to filter all of my experiences.  For that is precisely what we all did while growing up:   we begged, borrowed an stole whatever imagined meaning or explanation was readily at hand, and plugged that into our burgeoning understanding of ourselves and our environment.   There was no rational structure or priority to that process; it was, in essence, an arbitrary linking of experiences, reactions, observations and generalizations.   The advantage we have as individuating adults is that we can consciously reconstruct that process, drawing upon a larger picture of the world and its interdependencies, with greater maturity and a few more helpful tools than we possessed when we were children.

This is of course an ongoing, iterative process.   As with all memory, some things are easy to accept, integrate and fall in love with, and others are more difficult.  Feeling affection for my German step-grandfather for the shame he provoked in me was relatively easy.   Forgiving myself for depriving a little girl of her most prized possession took a bit longer, as did reconciling myself with the repeated loss of my own cherished connections with people, places and things.   And, for nearly twenty years, feeling anything more than confused, lukewarm affection for my mother was nearly impossible.  I had to traverse a twisted landscape of other emotions first – feelings of revulsion, mistrust, anger and, ultimately, grief.   To begin grieving over a childhood lost to fear, bewilderment and violence softened my other emotions and allowed me to slowly let go of the most acute and damaging hurt.  Eventually, after spending most of my late thirties and early forties in careful exploration and caring for my younger self, I could finally say "I love you, Mom," without it feeling like a half-truth.

All such effort also requires renewal, frequently revisiting our most painful core material in order to check in on our progress. Can I feel, in the present moment, compassionate affection for my younger self during past episodes of abuse or self-injury, or do other reflexives from older emotional patterns reassert themselves? Is there any residual guilt or shame over certain experiences, or am I truly free to be happy with who I am, with what I have become? Have I passed beyond forgiveness to a gentle sweetness of caring acceptance for those who injured me, or do the vestiges of anger, resentment or protective denial still cling to each memory? Can I speak of these incidents using a vocabulary of kind, patient understanding and insight? Can I share the pain of my past with others without feeling sorry for myself or creating new drama in my life? Can I perhaps assist people in processing their own pain without injuring myself or codependently trying to rescue them?

In the present moment, then, pain has come to mean many things to me. It means I have learned to be strong in the face of adversity. It means the generational cycle of abuse can be stopped. It means there are certain types of relationships, situations and environments that I may still associate with pain, and I should be conscious and careful in how I plot a course through them. It means there are clear choices I can make that either invoke or avoid repeated pain. One related consequence is that I have consistently resisted having any children of my own to avoid perpetuating suffering. In one way this could be seen as reinforcing negative conclusions about myself and my past – limiting myself out of fear of instigating more pain, etc. But although some negative associations may have informed this choice, the stronger, more energized theme behind this decision is my fervent desire to serve the good of All with every ounce of my creative effort. My assumption has always been that I would tend to invest in loving relationships with my children above passions of the imagination. Instead, I have achieved a lifestyle that permits me the freedom to write, explore the world with photography, play music, provide counseling and coaching, and nourish my being in every dimension. I have been drawn toward creative self-expression, philosophy, spirituality and the healing arts as ways of processing and transforming my own hurt and helping others do the same.

The losses and dysfunctional episodes of my youth have also helped me better appreciate the quality of my current relationships, the beauty of the places I live, and the value of learning to be content and grateful in times of plenty and times of deprivation. More than anything, I believe the shame, loss and pain of my childhood have helped me learn the most challenging lesson of all: how better to love others with less conditional expectations or needy attachment, while at the same time preserving personal boundaries and a clear sense of self. That is, loving freely and richly with love that isn't earned, without adopting the codependent identities of a victim, rescuer or abuser. Do I still revert to pain-inducing behaviors in certain situations? Certainly, but now I can almost immediately identify what is going on. With every healthy choice I make in this regard, I prove to myself that the pain of my past is not my master, but the servant and collaborator of my consciousness. In what I consider in part to be a validation of AMR, I no longer experience those sudden, unbidden memories of pain and shame with such disturbing frequency, and can welcome them less judgmentally and with more understanding.

## CHAPTER FOUR: FAITH & MYSTERY

When faced with the inexplicable, it is human nature to either question the reality of the experience or invent explanations. Our attempts to explain may range from the reflexive application of traditional cultural memes, to scientific inquiry, to emotionally charged superstitions, to outright rejection of whatever has happened. Is the old wizard who keeps appearing in my dreams an entertaining fiction created by my unconscious? Is he a memory of someone I knew in a past life? Is he a visitor from another plane of existence? An angel? An alien intelligence? A government-funded experiment in mind control? An amalgam created from childhood memories? Is he a message from my ancestors? A projection of my soul's will? Should I pay attention to what the wizard has to share, or should I try to forget all about him and move on with my daily survival?

For a child, there is already so much mystery and wonder in the world that a few more inexplicable experiences do not warrant rigorous evaluation when first encountered. Everything is new and exciting and incredible – and all equally so. It isn't until later, when we begin to learn what is socially permissible and generally accepted that we begin to categorize the wonders and mysteries of life into mundane, questionable, incredible or dismissible pigeonholes. And as we are exposed to more and more phenomena, the frequency of various occurrences begins to separate the unbelievable from the normal for us. The fiftieth full moon tends to be taken for granted much more readily than the first few spectacular moonrises we witness, and so on. As we mature, we tend to become inured to the wonders and mysteries of daily life in this way – unless there is some unexpected deviation from the norm, or we discipline our senses to be more carefully attuned to the moment.

So on the one hand we learn over time what is socially acceptable and manageable as our personal reality, and on the other we slowly shut down our sensitivity to mystery and become dependent on predictable beliefs about our experiences. Both of these things happen even if we hold views that run counter to our culture's dominant memeplexes. It is a matter of pragmatic survival. If we were to maintain a childlike openness and curiosity about everything we encounter, no matter how many times we have encountered it before, our ability to function in this highly mechanized world would quickly be undermined. Of necessity we create habits of mind, heart, body and spirit that allow us relatively swift and efficient navigation of new situations so that we can successfully cooperate and compete with our peers.

It is against this backdrop of the gradual deterioration of wonder that I offer up patterns of memory that evoke faith in mystery. That is, faith that relaxes into unknowns, that sighs gracefully into the inexplicable and ineffable. Faith that it is permissible and acceptable to leave what is not easily explained in its original state. Faith that trusts what cannot be detected, categorized or fully understood as something positive. In one way, this faith keeps a sense of discovery, newness and wonder alive in my consciousness. In another, it allows me to embrace any number of explanations for the incredible things that have happened to me. Do I know for certain what these mysterious events mean? Can I extrapolate from the patterns of memory a clear and decisive idea of what lies behind the wonder in my life? Of course not, as that would defeat the purpose of this mental, emotional and spiritual balancing act. But I can begin to detect, through various disciplines of perception-cognition, a number of plausible possibilities. I can skirt the edges of substantial hints at what might be. And that is enough.

## Miracles, in Retrospect

Our dog Puma appeared one day at our Eugene home when I was five years old. When my mother first saw him, she thought he was a wolf and resisted his friendly overtures. Once she discovered he was a gentle Malamute who took instantly and affectionately to her young son, she welcomed his presence in our lives. He appeared with no collar or tags, so at first mom named him Puta, but that proved problematic for the

Spanish-speakers in our neighborhood. She eventually settled on Puma, and he became a regular signatory of mom's letters to friends and family.

Not only did Puma dislike collars and tags, he didn't much like being inside the house. Leashes were out of the question entirely. In fact, he pretty much came and went as he pleased, and, like me at that time, had little interest in conforming to social expectations of where dog or child were allowed to go. Fences were just interesting challenges. As my mother tells it, Puma and I were inseparable. I had gotten along fine with our other dogs, but there was something special about this relationship. He was my best buddy and partner in adventure.

Puma appeared at an interesting time. As I've alluded to previously, some of the older kids in the neighborhood had been creating much grief and mischief regarding me. They taunted and bullied, played dangerous pranks, and were generally mean-spirited at every opportunity. To fully characterize these boys in one brief stroke, consider the one December afternoon when, while at age three and lost in play on our front lawn, one of them approached me and announced that Santa Claus had died. I was disbelieving at first, then mortified, then inconsolable. When I began to cry the boy laughed and declared he was just joking, that there was nothing to cry about. After all, he said as I sniffed back tears, Santa Claus didn't even exist! But once Puma began to join me outside, the first mysterious blessing of his presence was made evident: these older boys promptly desisted in their shenanigans. I don't remember Puma growling or baring his teeth, just that he settled happily in the grass beside me, nose-on-paws. But that was enough for my former bullies to keep a respectful distance.

At age five I loved to run. I ran everywhere – in the house, outside, through the isles of the grocery store, while we were having a quiet dinner with friends...I was unstoppable. Puma seemed to enjoy running as well, and loped beside me wherever I went, just keeping pace or moving slightly ahead, his pink tongue lolling and glistening in the sunlight. One day, when my mother and I were walking down to the corner store, I ran ahead in gleeful anticipation of a candy treat. Yelling and jumping with excitement, I failed to hear or understand my mother's warnings. "Stop! *Todd stop!* STOP!" So on I ran with Puma at my side, laughing and leaping without a care in the world.

I heard the garbage truck before I saw it, its brakes barking and air horns blaring explosively through the quiet morning. I looked up at all the noise and saw the grill, headlights and huge tires rushing toward me even as I jumped off the curb to cross the street. In mid-leap there was nothing I could do but land right in front of the oncoming truck. Then, just as recognition and dread began to blossom inside me, something huge and heavy slammed against my side, throwing me back onto the sidewalk with enough force to steal my breath. The crushing weight continued and without thinking I pushed back, struggling to rise even as the garbage truck roared past my feet. A low growl enveloped me, and I discovered Puma's snout inches above my face, his teeth bared aggressively while his paws pinned me to the ground.

The previous summer my father and I had arrived at a large gathering in the woods – some sort of music concert – and made our way through the trees. We met a man with a large German Shepherd, a dog that looked just like one mom rescued from the pound in Eugene and had been living with us for over a year. So I reached out to pet the "Nice doggy!" on the head with the flat of my hand. Although the man with the dog lunged to prevent it, the dog was faster, snarling and viciously biting my face. I was more surprised than hurt, but blood began gushing from a cut on my cheek. "Can't you control your damn dog?!" My father yelled. "It's not the dog's fault!" The man retorted. "Teach your kid how to offer his hand first!"

That ended our little outing in the woods, but it also taught me that not all dogs were as gentle and protective as those in my life up until that point. So when Puma, who had never so much as snapped his teeth in my vicinity, snarled at me and pinned me like that, I was horribly distressed. I felt betrayed and hurt and angry, and I struck out with my fists, beating my canine friend about his furry shoulders. Puma didn't fight back, he just sprang away with a quiet whine and hovered just out-of-reach. My mother's arrival ended any further struggle on my part, as she lifted me gruffly by the arm and began yelling. "Didn't you hear me?! Didn't you see that truck?!" Puma began barking as well. It wasn't until much later, when everyone had calmed down, that my mother and I reflected on the miracle that had occurred. Puma had saved my life.

Many times over, Puma demonstrated an uncanny instinct for finding and helping me whenever I was in danger. For a time I thought we had lost Puma altogether. Mom had taken him up into the woods during a trip for firewood, and had somehow left him behind there, miles from town. I was upset, but mom would often tire of animals and give them away without warning, so I accepted the loss. After a few weeks, we packed up all of our belongings and headed out to Florence, where mom had landed a new, better paying job. When we arrived at our little cottage on the beach, a place neither of us had ever been before, there was Puma, sitting serenely on his haunches by the front door. Waiting. Incredible as it sounds, my mother and I just laughed and greeted him warmly, accepting the mystery.

Puma rejoined our family just in time for my unfortunate adventures in first grade. I of course had little interest in school, and certainly not in remaining seated and still inside on a beautiful day at the beach. My mother also recalls several stories of an abusive teacher, horrific pranks and indifferent school administrators. Whatever was happening inside that school, Puma didn't like it. He repeatedly snuck into the building and into my classroom – to the hearty enjoyment of the other kids and fury of the teachers. On those few occasions when the school staff successfully herded Puma out of the halls, he would sit outside my classroom window, barking and howling until the exasperated principle called my mother. I admittedly felt more comfortable with Puma by my side, but that was one of many painful adjustments to institutional life I would have to make that year. This dance went on for some months until the school administrators decided I wasn't yet ready for first grade, and I once again set free to roam the dunes and beaches with my canine pal. Puma was understandably much happier with that situation.

One cold, overcast day, Puma and I found ourselves at the beach once more. In those years, huge rafts of freshly felled timber were floated down the Columbia to be milled. These were big trees, old growth several feet in diameter, and difficult to steer on open water. Occasionally, whole sections would break loose to escape their fate, and instead of houses and tables and chairs, they became vast driftwood playgrounds on the Pacific coast. We had more than our share of these in Florence. The huge logs would slowly accumulate on the sand, pounded into neat, parallel rows by the relentless surf. Often these rafts would stretch out into the ocean hundreds of feet, creating floating islands of splintered wood and slick bark. All a young boy had to do to explore this freshly formed real estate was hop from one log to the next, being very careful not to fall down between them.

Starting with the logs set firmly into the sand, I balanced and hopped, balanced and hopped, until the rolling surges of sloping wood beneath my feet told me I had was afloat on the ocean. I was ecstatic. Waves raged further out to sea, frustrated by the dam of trees, occasionally finding a gap to plume their fury up into the air. Despite my obvious excitement, Puma objected vociferously to my exploration. He remained on terra firma, yipping and prancing, barking more and more frantically the further out I ventured. But I was fascinated by the massive girth of these trees, by their slow rolling, by the stunning force with which they slammed against each other as the remnants of each wave lifted and settled them. And the smell! Kelp and sap and wet bark; high mountains bowing into the sea to take a drink. Squatting on the biggest one yet, staring down the coast at the sluggish roiling of the massive flotilla, that fascination is probably what distracted me from one slightly stronger surge in the waters below.

Not while I was jumping from one log to the next, not during some risky balancing act, but while I sat relaxed to gaze upon this man-made mystery, I slipped and fell down between the massive logs. I can still feel how cold that water was, how bottomless, how silent below the surface. I bobbed and splashed, and the huge logs rolled. They lifted and descended, the timber smacking together like giant baseball bats. Only because the logs were so huge, there was a sizeable triangle beneath where they met, a triangle where a boy's head could poke briefly above the water and not be crushed. When the logs parted again, I tried to find purchase in the splintered wood, protruding knots and remaining chunks of bark, and began a mad scrabble up the side. I slipped and fell back down. I tried again, and had to let go almost immediately as the logs rushed together once more.

All of my excitement was quickly being leached out of me…along with my body heat. I began to shiver. Stinging seawater found its way into my eyes, nose and mouth, my fingers were growing numb, and my arms could barely pull me up out of the cold. I cried for help, a tiny voice amid loud crashes, creaking moans and frothy gurgles. I did not really grasp my predicament, other than suspecting I would be in big trouble for getting my clothes wet. Then a thought occurred to me: maybe I could go under the log! If I could just swim until I found a sandy bottom, then I could stand up! I waited for what I thought would be the right moment, took a deep breath, and felt along the wood beneath the surface of the water.

At precisely that moment, I heard a wild scraping just above my head and looked up. "Puma!" I cried. Ears back, four legs shaking as he scrabbled for surer footing, Puma looked down at me and yipped loudly. "Puma!" I cried again, and with a surge of renewed effort clawed my way upward. Lowering himself with one sharp, high bark, Puma sank his teeth into the shoulder of my jacket and pulled. I grabbed the fur of his neck and scrambled. In moments we were atop the log, Puma licking my face and me hugging him tight to keep us both from falling back into the water. After a second or two to catch our breath, we hopped and careened with crazy speed back along the logs, then jumped to the beach. "Yeah!" I yelled, pumping my fists and dancing in a circle. Puma barked happily, tail wagging, and pranced with me as we circled in the sand.

This stray Malamute, this gray warrior with a mountain lion's strength and a sibling's devotion, was my guide, companion and protector. Why did he appear in my life when he did? How did he know just how to help me out of each dangerous situation? How did he find our new home in Florence before we even arrived there? What bound us so closely that he would risk his own life to save mine? This is the true mystery. Any number of mundane explanations might be reasonable, but to my mind and heart they would be no more accurate than the most outrageous or supernatural. Having experienced the benevolent power of his presence, my adult mind rejects neither his divinity nor the extraordinary capacity of his ordinary dog nature. To my childhood awareness he just was. He was Puma, a free spirit and partner in necessary adventures. A dog, a friend, a teacher.

Puma stoops for a drink while mom and I hang out in the middle of a stream

On several occasions during our stay in Florence, Puma also placed himself between my mother and me when she flew into a rage. I think, on some level, she was a little afraid of his protectiveness. Perhaps that is partly why she gave him to a travelling salesman the following Spring. In her letters, she describes her decision to do this and its consequences. Just as he had been wild and untamable with us, Puma could not be penned up in motel rooms or the inside of a car for long. The salesman called mom to tell her that Puma somehow kept breaking free. Puma also ate the salesman's wallet and all its contents. But the salesman didn't mind; there was something about this dog that made him special, so they kept travelling together until, after a year or so, we lost contact with them both.

## More Encounters with Mystery

As an adult I have explored many different philosophies about what could loosely be called psychic phenomena, each with its own intricate, supportive belief system. From this experience and study, it would be all-too-easy to categorize memories according to my current understanding. As a child, however, I had no such conscious differentiation of sensations, insights or events. There were different qualities of feeling, and different consequences to the choices I made, but not necessarily different explanations or a distinct hierarchy of import. They were all of-a-piece, a natural extension of daily life, and I took most of them in stride without question.

For instance, my mother routinely consulted tea leaves as part of her personal ritual, and she would often ask my opinion of what I saw in the leaves as well. She was quite disciplined about not prejudicing my interpretations with her own, but would let me feel my way through the reading, ask questions, and only after I had reached my own conclusions would she share hers. Despite the fact that many important observations and decisions were made throughout both of our lives in this fashion, the exercise itself was a casual habit, like buttering toast, washing hands or boiling water – a routine and accepted means to an end. The fact that what we saw in the leaves was often confirmed by later events did not seem strange or surprising, either. That, too, was simply part of my burgeoning understanding of how things worked.

I also learned early on that there were certain qualities of dream that set them apart from other nighttime imaginings. These dreams were more vibrant, more detailed, and felt entirely disconnected from my personal experiences. They seemed to fall into two categories. One type of dream was about other people, other places or other times in which I was merely an observer, hovering undetected somewhere in each scene. Whenever I tried to interact with the dreamscape in some way – speak to someone or affect whatever was playing out – the dream would usually end abruptly, or veer off into a more commonplace, self-referential images. In the other of these types of dreams, I fully inhabited someone or something else, but was still caught up in an unfolding situation over which I had only rudimentary influence. In this second type of dream, something fairly dramatic and memorable would usually happen to me.

Over time, I began to realize something about the first type of dream, the "floating observer" variety: that whatever I witnessed in the dream had either already happened somewhere at some time, or would ultimately come to pass. In fact, as early as age thirteen I began keeping a journal of the observer dreams, so that when, months or years later, I would witness or learn about a strikingly similar event, I could compare reality with what I had written down. Those who have lived through this type of experience know the weight on the heart and mind that goes along with realizing such correlations. It is much easier to keep such things to ourselves than to broadcast them, and, in terms of social acceptance, much safer to do so. It is, in fact, almost never beneficial to disclose what we come to know in this way, because even when we do so as a warning or advice, most folks either don't give us much credence, or they quickly forget what has been conveyed. Of course, this begs the question: what is the point of having such dreams, if we can't effectively communicate them or influence outcomes?

To give you a flavor of the second type of dream, I'll relate an experience I had when I was three years old. In my dream, I found myself low to the ground in a dirty, dusty yard. The yard was enclosed by a high wooden fence. Although a bright, yellowy light filled the yard itself, no light penetrated the darkness beyond the top of the fence. I could hear something on the other side of the fence, however. It sounded like a large group of people whispering or crying softly, and there was a layered sort of shuffling or slithering sound, like insects crawling over each other. Curious, I looked around the yard for some way to get over the fence. When I did so, I found I had a glorious peacock tail. I stared at it, then looked down at my body to find I did indeed have a peacock body and wings as well. So I gazed intently at the top of the fence and began to flap my wings. It was difficult to lift myself off the ground. I was heavy. I flapped harder. Slowly and with enormous effort, I began to rise into the air. I was ecstatic, and, drawing near to the top of the fence, eager to see what was on the other side. As I came up level with the top of the fence, I could sense something horrible taking shape on the other side. Something writhing and heaped and revolting in the endless dark. Though the light from the yard did not pierce the black beyond the fence, there were impressions of tangled bodies groping blindly in pain. And so I faltered in my flight and I cried out in my peacock voice. It was a long, shrill call that grew larger and deeper, taking on a life of its own. And along with that call, blasting out of my open beak, a blinding white light radiated like lightening out into the black infinity before me. I awoke distraught, and remained awake and fretful until dawn.

How does a child get his mind and heart around such experiences? He can't. He has to accept them as part of himself, part of the fabric of reality in which he lives, part of being human. What else can he do? Over time, I noticed that it seemed to require the better part of a week to process either of these two types of dreams. Thankfully, neither of them occurred very often. I also found that as I began writing down my dreams, I could forget about them much more quickly. Eventually, I decided to stop keeping a journal, and trained myself straight into forgetting. Today, only rarely does a particularly strong dream break through my defenses.

There is one last kind of encounter with mystery I would like to share. In these memories I interact with someone or something that, in retrospect, seems rather fantastic or alien. On one occasion, when I was about five, my mother, her friends and I were out wandering deep in the Oregon woods, and I was separated from the group for a time. When I returned, my mother asked me if I had gotten lost and I responded testily that no, I wasn't lost, I was playing with a girl in a white dress, out among the trees. How had I found my way back to them, my mother asked? The girl had shown me the way, I replied. On another occasion, when I was about eight, I was standing on a local playground late at night when a light from the sky swooped down and enveloped me, knocking me to the ground. I was frightened and ran home as fast as I could, but I kept returning to the playground each night, hoping it would happen again. I also had recurring dreams where a kindly, white-haired man would show me mechanical drawings on his workroom wall, pointing repeatedly to things, trying to get me to understand, but apparently unable to speak to me. I came to call him "The Wizard."

What is the recurring theme here? What is the unifying pattern? I believe now that theme is simply extrasensory communication and connection. Throughout my youngest years, I would feel intimately connected to certain places, activities, animals or plants in profound ways because of these experiences. Perhaps, because of my unstructured childhood, I was permitted to tune into a capacity that all people have, a type of perception-cognition that is native to most children. Because I was not forced to abandon this capacity through early conformance to cultural institutions, because I was allowed to run free and wild a bit longer than most children in the U.S., it could be that this access or aptitude persisted a bit longer than usual. At least, that is one possibility. Another is that I was just imagining all of this because I spent so much time alone and was desperate for connection. Or perhaps I was actually traumatized by certain experiences, and instead of facing the ugliness of victimization I escaped into supernatural perceptions, suppressing what really happened to me. Whatever the case, the ultimate result is that a sense of mystery about the world around me has persisted undaunted into my adult years, strongly influencing my self-concept and worldview. I continue to accept the extrasensory, the miraculous and the mysterious as routine facets of my life without trying to pin them down in a structured way.


### *The Faith that Remains*

It is difficult to describe in words how these patterns of experience have affected me. I feel deeply connected to the natural world and to what I can only describe as the realm of spirit. That is the language I have learned to use to identify these mysterious relationships and extrasensory perceptions. Much of my life has been spent trying to understand this component of existence. I journeyed far in my searching, immersing myself in Christianity, Hermeticism, Wicca, Hinduism, Sufism and many other spiritual disciplines. I have studied alternative healing modalities like hypnotherapy, Reiki, craniosacral work, chakra tuning, Yoga, traditional Chinese medicine and other approaches that include spiritual, intuitive, somatic or energetic components. I have studied the neurophysiology of spiritual experiences and experimented with psychedelic drugs. I have spent countless hours in prayer and meditation. I have made important decisions throughout my life using different methods of divination. I have performed sacred rituals and felt the distinct presence of spirits, deities and angels. I have relinquished all sense of self into an infinite ground of being. And all of this was driven to some degree by my childhood exposure to mystery.

What has been the cumulative result? Did I find the answers I sought? I do feel blessed in many ways by these explorations, for they helped me let go of many of my questions. However, this does not mean those questions were definitively answered. In fact, I would say that this journey created a simple faith that beings, forces and perceptions beyond my comprehension do exist, and do have roles in our daily lives. What these perceptions, forces or beings really are – what they are named, how they interact with the material plane – I can only speculate upon. But more important than my metaphysical beliefs is the faith the remains when intellect runs out of answers. I hold in my heart a certainty about the reality and vital importance of the spiritual realm, and that is enough. So rather than relying on my dreams for tactical guidance, they serve to remind me of the spiritual realm and its purpose; as it says in the Bhagavad Gita: "Wherever you find strength or beauty or spiritual power, you may be sure these have sprung from the spark of my essence…Just remember that I am, and that I support the entire cosmos with only a fragment of my being."

What this means is that, as part of every moment of every day, I try to consciously honor this dimension of existence. I invoke gratitude and worshipfulness in my heart. I dedicate myself to spiritual edification and growth. I consciously remember and humble myself before that which brings All Things into being. I pray without ceasing and meditate without an agenda. I practice techniques that open doors into what could be called spiritual memory, the collectively shared understanding of the spiritual realm. And though I no longer read tea leaves, I do consult other forms of divination when I desire clarity and wisdom for particularly challenging decisions. In other words, I try to bring spiritual connection into the foreground of my life in conscious ways, while encouraging it to simmer in the background of my unconscious the rest of the time. And, as those who have read my writings on mysticism will recognize, many of the tools used in active memory reorganization are also avenues to spiritual perception-cognition.

Is there a dichotomy inherent to these faith-inducing patterns of self, just as there is for other aspects of identity? Of course there is. On the one hand I can feel empowered by my intuition and spiritual awareness – I can be strengthened by insights that heal, edify and transform. On the other hand, I can lose myself in spiritually-oriented processing and forget about the more mundane aspects of material survival. I could even become so obsessed with the spiritual that I form a debilitating addiction, or open myself too quickly to energies and influences I cannot manage or properly integrate. There have been times when I have suffered from suppressing my spirituality, and times I have suffered from immersing myself so completely in spiritual practice that I neglected other aspects of my life. As with all other dimensions of self, there is a carefully balanced tightrope walk that synthesizes all sides of the equation.

For me it has been relatively easy to appreciate and love these mysterious patterns, as on the whole they have added tremendous value to my life. Like my portentous dreams, I can accept them for what they are, be thankful for them, and honor the Source. Of course, there have been exceptions that were more difficult to integrate. For example, after one particularly intense session of spiritual healing in my thirties, I found my perception broadened in unexpected ways. I was suddenly acutely aware of the suffering of others around me – it seemed I could see, hear, feel and sense all the hidden pain of my fellow human beings. To stand in a checkout line at a grocery store was to be overwhelmed with the unspoken hurt and grief of others, their physical diseases, their barely suppressed rage, their amorous longings and obsessive intentions. For several days I could not venture out in public at all, until I learned how to construct what I suppose would be called psychic boundaries to these perceptions, and realized with great relief that I did not bear personal responsibility for immediately remedying all the ills I perceived.

That said, I have come to believe over time that the essence of spirit is love, and to allow positive spiritual energies to flow freely in my life requires a grounding in affectionate compassion. There is no escaping the mystery all around us, and we can never know everything there is to know, never comprehend all the forces at work in every moment, never fully appreciate the countless interdependencies that support our existence. But we can feel beyond our conscious knowledge. We can intuit much that we do not fully understand. And that is perhaps the most important spiritual takeaway of my childhood encounters with mystery: that I can trust what I do not entirely comprehend, and be carried forward to wonder-filled, edifying, empowering and humbling moments on currents beyond my wildest imagination.

## Applying AMR

The five core practices of AMR can themselves be developed as potent mystic activators, encouraging unfiltered access to the ground of being through an alternate, spiritual perception-cognition. When used appropriately, they are therefore self-reinforcing techniques with respect to faith and mystery. They tend to encourage the discovery and rediscovery of creative, wonder-filled and spiritual connectivity on a daily basis. The more intensely I immerse myself in these practices, the more easily I can identify or contextualize past and present experiences as relating to the mysteries of life, constantly adding renewed focus and episodic material that energizes the themes and metathemes of this semantic container. At this point in time, I don't feel a compelling need to challenge or reorganize the wonders of my childhood, preferring to embrace their ambiguity and ineffability. In fact, I would rather just add new episodes to this particular narrative.

In terms of reinforcing behaviors, I routinely create space in my life for the mysterious and prioritize those encounters in my memory field. Beyond meditation or other introspective disciplines, any time I spend in Nature is integrated into my "faith and mystery" practice, as are high-quality exchanges with friends, regular exposure to the arts and my own creative endeavors. When my emotional disposition is tuned into wonder, awe and gratitude, nearly everything is permeated with spiritual energy. To eat a satisfying meal, sing a boisterous song, hug a loved one, breathe in a salty sea breeze, read an honest poem or laugh at the antics of a beloved pet all create a supportive environment for faith and mystery when viewed through this emotional filter.  And as you can tell from the words I use to describe this aspect of self, I find that unabashedly spiritualizing my language also enriches this dimension.

The more devotedly I journey down the mystic's way, the more every moment of my life comes to represent an underlying mystery and contributes to my sense of faith.  That is, this semantic container expands to include objects, types, themes and metathemes of all other containers.  As this occurs, all metastructures of my being are permeated with the characteristics of faith and mystery.  My governing beliefs, narrative self, somatic memory, unconscious substrata, emotional disposition and spiritual ground all become energized with this particular resonating frequency.   And the longer and stronger the unbroken chain of associations persists, the more effortless its projection into the future.  So my intermediate goals and overall life vision are naturally aligned with this family of experiences as well.   And the more this spiritual orientation is refined and concentrated, the more fractally it represents itself across All that Is, replicating the same beautiful, chaotic symmetry on every scale of existence.

How has all of this worked for me?  Has it facilitated nourishment in multiple dimensions of self?  Has it enriched my life and enhanced my self-concept?  Subjective evaluation is of course colored by emotional disposition, so if I observe that I am joyful and inspired as a result of spiritualizing my existence, this is perhaps too self-referential – after all, someone addicted to a euphoria-inducing drug could claim the same.  But if I can also observe that I have a stronger sense of purpose, or more discernment about choices that are skillfully compassionate,  or  more clarity about where I need to heal and grow, then I can gain a better handle on the positive impact of the current organization of this aspect of self.   And yet, what if my equanimity is shattered by some petty, inconsequential event?  What if some other component of my memory field – such as fear, or anger, or pain, or adventurousness – asserts dominance and undermines my equilibrium to a debilitating extent?  Well, then clearly I have more work to do.  To some degree, such interruptions are part of the natural ebb and flow of existence, and the true measure of balance seems to be how quickly I can recover equilibrium.  I suspect my refinement will be endless.

## CHAPTER FIVE: ANGER & CONFLICT

There are so many shades of anger, most of them either stemming from or resulting in interpersonal conflict. There is the reflexive lashing out in response to physical or emotional pain, flaring brightly but fading quickly. There is a slowly simmering rage over ongoing injustice or abuse, in which we or someone we care about seems to be a helpless victim. There is the anger that blooms from frustration, impatience and exasperation over unmet expectations. There is the anger of meanness – a controlling or manipulative anger through which we seek to empower ourselves by disempowering others. There is a more constructive, protective anger that preserves us when we feel cornered or threatened. There is the anger of superficial retaliation over perceived wrongs, and the more abiding fury grounded in deep resentment, grief or woundedness. And for each of these qualities of anger there are different amplitudes as well, corresponding with different intensities of conflict. The full range of these interior and relational conditions is extraordinary.

Personal and cultural beliefs about anger vary widely as well, as do our individual and collective ability to manage these emotions. To fully appreciate the meaning of anger and conflict patterns in our own life, it is important to consider the influences of our formative environments. What were our family traditions regarding anger and conflict? What examples did we observe in our surrounding culture? Were open expressions of anger and confrontation permitted or taboo? Were we encouraged to contain or internalize our anger, or express it openly?

Were displays of anger only permitted in the privacy of our home, or were they allowed in public as well? How did those around us react to anger and conflict? Were they frightened? Did they laugh? Were they defensive, or were they conciliatory? Did they retreat or shut down in the face of conflict, or did they attack? Did they avoid anger or compassionately engage it? All of these things feed into our understanding of what anger and conflict are for, when they are appropriate, and whether they are ever healthy or helpful.

Anger and conflict in some form were an ever-present feature of my childhood, but their value, meaning and impact shifted from one context to the next. In my mother's home, anger was like a thunderstorm on a sunny day – brief, intense and frightening, but quickly overtaken by the warmth and bright sunlight of her affection. The conflict between my paternal grandparents was more like a festering wound, carefully hidden behind sarcasm and needling criticism, persisting for months and years without ever finding resolution. My father's anger was like the threat of an annihilating singularity, devoid of light, hovering just out of sight and only taking form when he was pushed beyond wit's end. My stepmother favored conflict that was sharply confrontational and spiteful. My step-sister Shelly's anger was quietly retaliatory but extremely rare. And so on in an infinite and fascinating variety of multifaceted examples.

I think more out of bewildered confusion than any well-defined innate tendencies, I was compelled to try on all of these suits of conflict and anger just to see how they fit until, ultimately, I settled on a pattern was distinctly my own. Someone in my life was usually accusing, or yelling, or hitting, or retaliating – I was not always directly involved, but such tumultuous patterns were always playing out nearby. In Amherst, perhaps a neighbor would be chasing his screaming eight-year-old son around the front yard with a riding crop in hand, or the three big brothers down the street would be viciously beating up on each other, or a heated argument would erupt between my father and my step-mom. In Connecticut, there were constant scraps between neighborhood kids, whose parents could likewise be heard screaming and carrying on inside their houses, often to the accompaniment of slamming doors and crashing pots and pans. And of course there were my mother's screaming matches with her own parents, a neighbor, or her imaginary accusers. It was all of-a-piece, and I emulated what I observed to see what would work best for me.

## Recrimination, Revenge & Challenging Goliath

I developed a strong sense of right and wrong at an early age, and that sense was oriented mainly around discovering or discerning someone's intentions. If I was playing kickball and received a solid hit to the back of my head by accident, I was quick to forgive and move on. If however, it became clear that someone was trying to injure me, I would fly into a rage whether they succeeded in hurting me or not. The same was true of injurious intentions directed at others. Whether it was a group of kids bullying someone they thought was weaker, or an adult being hypocritical and controlling, or a stranger of any age brutalizing their pet, the urge to intervene always seems to have been present in me. Perhaps I was born with a propensity for reactive righteousness, or I learned it very early on.

However, how I chose to engage the perceived perpetrators in each situation changed over time; that is, the quality of my anger and conflict responses evolved. What began as yelling and screaming and physically intervening in my preschool years was eventually thwarted by larger kids and adults who had no compunction about back-handing a mouthy five-year-old. I then began calling upon authority figures (i.e. tattling), or threatening to do so, which was surprisingly effective for all but the most recalcitrant cases. For any situation where such threats fell on deaf ears – or where I might actually be on shaky evidentiary ground myself – I began to scheme more devious retaliations. As described in previous chapters, pranks, sabotage, theft and the like created a whole new vocabulary of rectification for the uncooperative. This approach persisted until age eight or so, when I was able to add a few more confrontational responses to my repertoire once more.

That is not to say that I always believed I was in the right. My father reports that I initiated countless fights with my step-sister Shelly when we were little – seemingly out of jealousy – and that I was generally prone to hitting first and lying later. I was also skilled at provoking adults into anger when their only offense was to have some sort of authority over me that I didn't appreciate or want. Creating random conflict was also an effective way to get attention from my parents, who for different reasons were often absorbed with their own issues to such an extent that they felt, to my childhood sensibilities, very disconnected from me.

So by the time I was ten years old, I had a whole bag of anger and conflict tricks to influence others. This was when I moved from Manchester, Connecticut to Amherst, Massachusetts to live with my father. And suddenly all of the variables changed. There was my father's authoritarian parenting style, the new pecking order of the neighborhood kids, and the cultural differences between a liberal and affluent college town and a more conservative, blue collar Manchester. It was also the first opportunity for me to experience an educational environment that was flexible enough to accommodate my wildness and nonconformance, introducing another layer of interactions and relationships for me to navigate. It would become a major turning point in my life.

Amherst's Fort River Elementary had at that time just begun experimenting with a "quad" system of open classrooms, increased teacher collaboration and more diverse student participation, as well as a host of self-directed study tracks for both gifted and challenged kids. This was perhaps inevitable given the population of the Amherst community at the time. There were children from local farming families, there were kids whose parents had multiple PhDs and taught at one of the local colleges or UMass, and there were other kids like me who had diverse cultural and experiential backgrounds that didn't fit easily into a traditional educational system. Because of this stunning diversity, I actually felt more at home than ever before.

I was also frustrated with my situation. A new parenting environment with new structure and expectations was a major adjustment. I was also expected to integrate with a challenging curriculum and a complex social landscape. And, for the first time in my life, I was surrounded by kids who were as well-spoken and curious as I was – and often a lot brighter. Fifth-graders like Jean, who had already plowed through a host of classic literature and was rapidly reading her way into modernity. Or Peter, who adored astronomy and was already gearing up for pre-calculus. Or

Tom, for whom mastering nearly all subjects seemed as easy as breathing. On the physical end of the spectrum, many of the local farm boys were descended from sturdy Polish stock, joyfully engaging in sports like hockey, football and wrestling, and were generally able to overpower me with little effort. In other words, I was now confronted with the unsettling reality that there were people my age who were smarter, stronger, wilder...or all three.

Of course I was also still struggling to catch up from not being in a formal educational environment for most of my childhood. So, in part to act out my frustrations, and in part to carve a distinct identity for myself amid so many extraordinary achievers, I rebelled angrily. In the first months of school, I got into three fights with other students, punched a teacher, demolished half of the student library, hurled outrageous insults at the school nurse and my cello instructor, and repeatedly broke every school rule known and unknown to me. I was full to the brim with self-righteous rage, and expressed it at every turn. I fully expected to be kicked out of Fort River, or at least for my father to discipline me harshly once he found out about everything I had done.

But something magical was happening. Something I had never experienced before that changed the course of my development. I was surrounded by people who not only cared about my well-being, but were also willing to provide the nurturing space and direct, compassionate communication I so craved in a skillful and accepting way. I wanted to challenge Goliath, but Goliath turned out to be a patient, gentle giant who cared only for my welfare and a well-rounded education.

### Challenging the Challenge Reflex

Ann was a small woman, but her office was so tiny it made her look larger than she was. Somehow she had crammed in a couple of bookcases and a large desk, behind which she now sat considering me with a quiet look. Her hair, a frizzy graying mass that seemed likely to rebel at any moment against the hair combs that held it in place, framed a soft, round face.

"Hello, Todd.  My name is Ann."

I looked at the floor.  I was tense, ready to run from the room, but something about this woman's calm manner held me in place.

"What do you do here?"  I looked carefully around the small room for clues.

She smiled.  "I'm a counselor here at the school.  Kids can come and talk to me whenever they want to."

I digested that.  "What do they talk about?"

Ann paused, then asked, "About anything.  What would you like to talk about?"

"I dunno."  I considered, calming down a little.  "What are these books?"

Ann leaned forward, interested.  "All kinds of books.  Some of them are stories.  Some of them are books written for children.  Some of them are books to help me."

I looked at the books, stalling for time.  Then, although I thought I knew the answer to my question, I asked, "What are you gonna do?"

Ann's brow furrowed slightly in puzzlement, and then came understanding.  "Do you mean about your hitting Miss Dalton?"

I nodded, pulling one of the smaller paperback books from the shelf and studying it.  "Yeah."

"What do you think I should do?"

I shrugged.  "I dunno.  Punish me I guess."  I snuck a peek at my counselor to find her face shifting toward sadness.  Tension began to creep back into my limbs.

"Can you...explain to me  why you hit her?"

I looked up, surprised to find real curiosity in Ann's expression. "She grabbed me. She kept saying *go the other way* but I had to go to the bathroom." I felt the fires of rage kindling inside me, but Ann remained calm and inquisitive. "She *grabbed my arm!*" I yelled, trying to impress the outrageousness of this fact upon on Ann.

Ann nodded calmly. "So you hit her?"

"No…*no!*" The fires were burning brighter now. "I pulled back, like this – " I demonstrated yanking my arm from Miss Dalton's grip, "and I ran, but she got in front of me. Right in my way! And *grabbed my arms.*" I was reliving the frustration, my voice getting louder and louder. "*She wouldn't let me go!*"

"And that's when you hit her?" Ann asked quietly.

"No! No no no!" I threw the book I was holding on the floor. When that didn't achieve the response I expected, I began dumping every book I could reach on the ground. Enraged embarrassment for what I had done coursed through me like lava, driving me to empty Ann's entire bookcase.

Ann sat calmly, without expression, and reached into her desk. She took out a pen and began to write on a small white pad. She seemed to be ignoring me completely. I was shocked. It stopped me in my tracks. I stood still and glanced at the door.

Ann looked up from her writing. "Would you like to leave?"

How had she known? I challenged her: "Do you want me to leave?"

She looked surprised, then put down her pen. "I would like it if we could keep talking."

I was confused, off balance. No one had ever reacted to my antics this way before. I felt my anger leech out of me more quickly than it had come. I nodded and looked down at the mess I had made, then looked back at her. My defiance melted and my eyes found the mess on the floor once more.

Ann waited a few moments. She seemed to expect something from me, but I didn't know what. Then I understood. "I'm sorry about the books," I said meekly.

She nodded. "I'm sorry too."

"I'll put them back," I said, grabbing a handful from the floor.

"If you want," she said quietly, watching me.

I quickly picked up more of the books and began stacking them haphazardly on the shelf.

"Do you like books?" she asked.

I nodded. "I like to read. Mrs. Logan won't let me read the books I like in class, but I read them anyway."

Ann smiled faintly. "What kind of books do you like?"

That was easy. "Books about Merlin and King Arthur. My favorite is Mary Stewart's *The Crystal Cave*, it's really good. *Really* good." My excitement was picking up speed, my favorite scenes from the stories I loved dancing through my mind. "Steinbeck wrote one, but he never finished it. It's not bad."

"John Steinbeck wrote a book about King Arthur?" I stopped and squinted over at her. I was used to those kinds of questions. Questions that doubted, that accused, that belittled. But Ann didn't look disbelieving, she seemed just to be asking.

"Uh-huh," I said, continuing to neaten the books on the shelf. "He talks a lot about Arthur and Lancelot and Guinevere. But I think he misses the point."

"Oh? What does he miss?" Again I checked to see if she was mocking me, but again she seemed genuinely interested.

"Arthur does what he thinks is right. He doesn't just…do things because he wants to do them. I don't think Steinbeck understands that."

Ann seemed to be considering this. "Have you read any other books by John Steinbeck?" She asked.

I grinned. "I just finished *The Grapes of Wrath!*" I said conspiratorially. I knew that Mrs. Logan, my homeroom teacher, would really disapprove of that one. Probably because of what happens at the end, in the barn. "I really liked it. It's much better than the other one we read in class."

"In Mrs. Logan's class?"

"Uh-huh. *Of Mice and Men.* It was okay." All the books were now back on the shelf. "I heard her arguing with Ms. Gilman about it."

Ann laughed. "I'm not surprised."

I liked the sound of her laughter. It was…genuine. "I don't think they agree about how to teach stuff," I said.

Ann began to say something, then stopped herself. There was a long pause. I began to fidget. Then she asked, "Todd, can we talk a little more about what happened today, or do you think it will be upsetting for you?"

I blinked. I was feeling relaxed, and that was a rare thing. I felt I might be able to trust her, which was even rarer. "No. That's okay. I won't get upset."

Ann took a breath. "Did you know that Miss Dalton is pregnant?"

I was stunned. I felt sick to my stomach. I shook my head and looked down at my hands, which were already balled into fists. But I had said I wouldn't' get upset. I bit my lip, took a step toward the door, then back. My breathing quickened. "But she's not married!" I blurted.

"She's…engaged," Ann said with the hint of a smile.

"So…she's pregnant. So what?" I countered defiantly.

For the first time, Ann seemed taken aback. But her face quickly smoothed over again. "How do you think Ms. Dalton feels – "

"I don't care!" I didn't mean to hurt Ms. Dalton, I had just lashed out to break free, and she had crouched down on the ground after I hit her, holding herself, while the other teachers rushed me away. Besides, was Ann really telling the truth? I could feel a familiar anxiety rising in me, weaving the muscles in my chest and stomach into rock-hard knots. I took a sideways step towards the door.

Ann let the silence draw out. No one was grabbing me. No one was yelling at me. My breathing began to slow, my muscles relaxed.

"Would you like to talk to Miss Dalton about what happened?" Ann asked very softly.

"No," I said, but there was little conviction behind it. Ann remained still, her hands folded in front of her on the desk, her head tilted slightly to one side. She nodded but said nothing. Suddenly the tension ebbed within me. "Yeah, I guess," I said. I studied my hands again, which seemed to be worrying each other like young puppies. "I…I want to apologize." I glanced up to gauge Ann's reaction.

My counselor's features shifted into something I couldn't read. She cleared her throat. "Would it be okay if I came with you?"

Was Ann offering me her protection? Would she be my ally? Or was she making sure I did what I said I would do? Maybe she didn't trust me. I didn't know what to think, but for the first time in a long time, I wanted to believe that someone had my best interests at heart. "Okay," I said.

She rose from behind the desk. "We can go there now if you like," she said. I nodded and we left her office, walking slowly down the hall back to my classroom. My stomach was still tight, but I could feel the rightness in this. Ann let me lead all the way to the classroom door, then asked me if I could wait in the hall while she went inside. I said yes, but as soon as she disappeared I almost bolted. Somehow, despite the panic reasserting itself in my gut, I stayed put until Ann returned with Miss Dalton. The young teacher kept her distance from he, holding one hand protectively over her stomach. I could see the slight bulge beneath the dark blue fabric now. I could also see the engagement ring on her finger. I hadn't noticed either of those things before. Ann hadn't lied.

"I'm really sorry," I said earnestly, looking up at her with all my courage. "I shouldn't have hit you. I'm really sorry." I held my breath.

Miss Dalton looked down at me softly and opened her mouth to speak. Her eyes began to shine, and she shook her head. "It's…all right," she offered in a whisper, then she turned abruptly and went back into the classroom.

§

And so began a coordinated conspiracy to normalize my interactions in elementary school. Others were enlisted to create options for me whenever I was feeling overwhelmed, threatened, anxious or stressed out. If I needed some time away from the other kids, or a break from the academic rigors of the classroom, I had a free pass to search out certain people. I could go visit with Margie, the quirky, wise-cracking secretary at the front desk. Or I could hang out with Gary, a very low-key Vietnam vet with a dry sense of humor, in the Audio Visual room. Or, if I was really upset, I could meet with Ann, and each week I continued my regular counseling sessions with her. On Fridays I also had the option of spending an hour or so with Mr. Roth, a laid-back hippy with seemingly infinite patience, who would work one-on-one with me on various hobby-like projects. Slowly, in repeated interactions over the school year, I not only had ways of relieving my nervousness over new social dynamics and expectations, but I also began to discover what healthy relationships looked and felt like. It was a revelation for my social and emotional life.

I benefited in many ways from the high-quality interactions at Fort River. From Margie, I learned how to have a more relaxed sense of humor about myself and the world. From Gary, I learned how to operate all kinds of A/V equipment, tricks to fix ailing machinery, how to splice and edit video, how to create stop-action animation with clay, and much more. From Mr. Roth, I received my first instruction in mediation and relaxation techniques, as well as how to remain calm in a crisis. And from Ann I continued to learn constructive ways of resolving conflict and manage my emotions.

At some point during that first year, I decided to build a miniature house out of plywood for Cinnamon and Pepper, the two cats that came with my dad's girlfriend, Kathy. Mr. Roth was eager to help me with the project, and we made quick work of it using power tools I'm not sure would be permitted in today's elementary schools. In any case, we were putting some finishing touches on the house – hammering and screwing things together – when Mr. Roth suddenly paused and said, "Huh. Well, that's interesting." I looked over to see him examining a medium-sized flathead screwdriver, which he had somehow driven clean through the palm of his hand – right up to the handle. He started to pull it out and grimaced in pain. His tanned skin blanched a bit. "I'll be right back," he said tightly. In a few minutes he returned with a thick layer of masking tape wrapped around his hand and a big smile on his face.

"Is it bad?" I asked. "Did it hurt?"

"It'll be fine," he said. "But I don't recommend that particular move."

In another half hour we finished our project, stapling a piece of carpet into the bottom of the house, attaching the roof, and painting "Pepper & Cinnamon" over the door. The house wasn't a big hit with the cats, who wouldn't go near it, let alone inside it. But I will never forget Mr. Roth's reaction to his accidental injury, and the contrast that presented to my previous experience. Anyone else in my life up until that point would have gotten angry or hysterical after injuring themselves, and only calmed down later. They would have yelled and cursed and carried on, and, if I was anywhere nearby, probably taken the lion's share of their frustration out on me.

The audio-visual technician, Gary, and his wife moved into a trailer home just off of Route 9, a mile or two down the road from my house, and I would stop by and visit them even after I left Fort River Elementary for Junior High. When I needed a reference for doing audio-visual work in Junior High, Gary provided it. I also made one of my closest childhood friends, Dean, while working with Gary. Dean was as excited about the A/V tech as I was, and we frequently collaborated on projects together. Whenever I entered Gary's A/V editing room, I could relax into an analytical mode of being that made everything serene, reasonable and intellectually compelling. Machines worked according to specific principles, and as long as you abided by those principles, you could make them do seemingly miraculous things for you. Adding even more value to the experience, I could engage this orderly and reasonable world with a close friend.

At the editing console in the Audio Video room of Fort River Elementary

Margie would become an important part of my life in the years after that. She and her husband Rick would welcome me into their home in a fostering arrangement, mainly so I could finish Junior High while my dad and his new German wife, Jutta, settled in Frankfurt, Germany. I also think Rick and Margie saw this as an opportunity to liberate me from an unhealthy home environment. Margie had a habit of "adopting strays," as Rick put it, and I gratefully fell in with the rest of her pack of oddball adoptees. I spent a year living with these two quirky and wonderful people, learning more about how to have honest, open and nurturing relationships, as well as continually improving my sense of humor under their generous tutelage. I also learned how to fell trees with a chainsaw, optimize a wood-burning furnace, drink hard liquor, testify for the prosecution in a criminal trial, herd baby Dachshunds, and kiss girls – but those are stories I hope to relate at another time.

My counselor Ann continued to provide excellent guidance in the gradual normalization of my social behaviors. If I had any ongoing conflicts with other kids, she arranged to have a wrestling coach show us how to wrestle, then she would referee matches after school to settle the dispute. This fell right in line with my earlier experiences in dealing with bullies *mano a mano*, and I participated eagerly. It was amazing how quickly hostile antagonism could be converted to friendship once the question of who was physically stronger had been fairly settled between two boys. The best of three sequential matches, with no illegal holds or technical violations allowed, ended with clear and unquestionable pins to the mat. I think I lost about as much as I won, but it didn't matter. The sport planted the seeds of restraint and respect in both opponents, and settled any and all lingering scores.

But here's the real conspiratorial kicker in all of these developments at Fort River: my father knew nothing about any of it. At some point, he either gave Ann permission to pursue whatever course she saw fit, or simply remained uninvolved. He has little recollection of how this unfolded, and believes now that he was entirely unaware of most of these events. But Fort River made an immense impression on my growth and understanding. I learned it was all but pointless to become angry around any of these fine people, as it simply did not evoke the negative responses I was accustomed to. My fury in the presence of such calm did not reinforce any of my cherished negativity about myself or affirm anger as an effective tool to keep myself safe in the world…it was just so much wasted energy followed by uncomfortable silence. Once, when I blew up at Gary over some frustration I was feeling in the A/V lab, he was obviously shocked by my behavior, and rapidly got up and walked out of the room. When he came back a minute or two later, he seemed to weigh what he was about to say, then offered: "You know, getting angry really doesn't solve anything. If you want to get angry, that's your business. But I really don't want to be around any of that while your in here. Okay?" It was just one more link in a long series of interactions that proved anger to be a less than useful response to many situations.

Toward the end of my stay at Fort River, I remember one final incident that was particularly instructive. Kids from multiple quads – the integrated classrooms – were lining up for something in the cafeteria. It was a long line, and when some of the older kids I didn't know cut in front of everyone else, I was outraged. "Hey, you can't do that!" I said furiously, stepping out of line to approach them. "Go back to the end of the line!" Both of the boys were big, and although they were surprised by my aggressiveness, they clearly had no intention of moving.

"Shut up," said one of the boys.

"Yeah, weirdo. Get out of here," said the other.

Clearly they didn't know who they were dealing with. I picked up two of the cafeteria chairs and hurled them across the room. They bounced and banged over some empty tables before clattering to the floor. I was surprised how far they made it across the room. "You're nuts!" said one of the boys. I started toward them with fists clenched and the kids around them began to back away.

"What was that?!" A woman's voice boomed nearby. A middle-aged cafeteria lady, in well-worn cap and apron, and with arms as thick as my dad's legs, poked her head out from a doorway. One of the kids pointed in my direction. When the woman's eyes found me her features quieted. "Oh, it's just you," she said, looking away. "Okay everybody, back in line!" Everyone obeyed.

Imagine a young boy whose entire life has been consumed in defending and asserting himself, carving out a niche of survival among bullies and abusers, acting out violently to gain a sense of safety or attention. Now imagine that boy subjected to compassionate acceptance, patient encouragement, and no rewards at all – no negative or positive consequences – for his aggressive behavior. I stood there among my peers as every justification for the anger and conflict driven aspects of my personality melted away. I thought: *Even the cafeteria ladies know what to expect from me. Is this what everyone thinks?* I was chagrined and sad and, probably for the first time, genuinely introspective about my behavior. After that day, I no longer thought of violence the same way. I wanted to change what people thought about me. I desperately wanted to have self-control over those reactive impulses and learn a different way to be.

## Anger's Residue & Taking Responsibility

Today I am generally not a violent person, but the thoughts and impulses from my childhood patterns are still there, hardwired options for any occasion. It would take dozens of hours of counseling over the course of my twenties and thirties to fully unravel the chained associations that prompted angry expressions of my hurt and anxiety. I would have to learn to shed tears of frustration instead of lashing out in rage. I would have to learn to exit provocative situations and go for a long walk rather than stubbornly confront or be confronted. I would have to learn how to be vulnerable in intimate relationships, and then how to be hurt without retaliating. I would have to learn new ways to channel and diffuse my fury if I was not successful in preventing it. I would have to learn a lot.

By age eleven, I had taken the first tentative steps towards managing my anger – and towards mitigating conflict instead of inciting it. One event in particular seemed to capture this fledgling transition. It was during my second summer in Amherst, and involved two other boys, each of whom represented aspects of my own previous anger and conflict responses. On the one side of the spectrum – and the north side of my house – was Jesse, and on the other, south side was Kevin. Kevin was an awkward, geeky sort of kid with thick glasses, a slight build and wispy bond hair. He was obsessed with comic books and insects, and although he was enthusiastic about his interests and highly verbal, some sort of illness or developmental disability made him mentally slow. Jesse was big, brash and aggressive, with dark hair and eyes and an even darker mean streak, and was considerably more thoughtless than he was slow.

I had interacted with both of them frequently over the summer. Jesse had asserted his neighborhood dominance by playing a number of vicious pranks on me. At the height of his efforts, he succeeded in peeing on my face from the top of an abandoned truck in a nearby field. That resulted in my returning to his house later the same afternoon – after a shower and a change of clothes – to settle things once and for all in his front yard. I called him outside, we both got in a punch or two, and then his mother intervened. Which gave me an opportunity to tell her why I was there – what Jesse had done. By the look of fear on his face, and the bright and seething fury on hers, I suddenly found myself feeling sorry for Jesse and the punishment he undoubtedly had in store. After that day, Jesse and I avoided each other, but there were no more pranks…and no more pissing matches.

In many ways, Kevin was the more challenging of the two relationships to manage. He wanted to be friends, but I found him pushy and whiny. During the times we hung out together, he would often become frustrated that I didn't know some necessary bit of information, wouldn't lend him money, or wouldn't go along with some elaborate plan or other. After being stung once too many by his disappointment and accusations, I began to avoid him. As with many such reactions, it was likely the similarity of his own faults to my own that caused my discomfort – in other children's eyes, it was often me who was perceived as pushy, demanding and quickly frustrated.

It was at this well-developed point in both relationships that I discovered Kevin and Jesse in the field next to my house, squaring off for what looked like a fight in the early morning light. It was an uneven contest, to be sure, so I thought I should at least go down and referee, if not help Kevin out of a pickle. By the time I arrived, Jesse was squinting meanness and Kevin was blinking nervously and backing away – frankly I was surprised he hadn't run home already. Though the two boys were the same age, Kevin was a lot shorter and scrawnier than Jesse, and a lot less physical. The morning was cool, the yellowing grass still damp with dew, and low, dusty light angled between the houses.

"What's up?" I asked, as casually as I could.

"None of your beeswax," Jesse said angrily.

At the same time, Kevin yelled: "He stole my lunch money!"

Jesse balled his fists and took a step toward Kevin. I tried to catch his eye and he hesitated. "I didn't steal nothin'," said Jesse. "He jus' tattled to his mom that I did…" Jesse looked at me meaningfully, and I began to understand. Kevin's mom had probably confronted Jesse's mom, landing Jesse a sound beating whether he had really stolen the lunch money or not.

When I turned back to Kevin, he was staring at his feet. "So how do you know it was him?" I asked.

"It was!" He glanced up at me defiantly. I waited for more explanation, but suddenly Kevin was furious with me. "How come you won't help?! Why are you just standing there…?" I was taken aback with his fury, and then I saw it on Kevin's face: that telltale, frustrated look when he wasn't getting his way. So I made my decision.

"Kev, you should give me your glasses." I said.

"Why?" He was defensive, wary.

"Because you might break 'em in the fight."

Kevin's eyes grew big for a moment, then something inside him shifted. The anger evaporated, replaced with a look of resignation. He slowly took his glasses off and handed them to me. I held them carefully and nodded, backing slowly away from the two boys.

Once I made my intentions clear, Jesse didn't hesitate. He rushed Kevin and pushed him forcefully to the ground. "You're a *liar!*" He declared, then he kicked Kevin in the ribs, just twice and without much effort, but it had to hurt. Kevin covered his head with his hands and drew his knees in to protect himself. Jesse made to kick him some more, but hesitated. "You better not try that again, *not ever!*" I was surprised to hear his voice crack, then shocked to see him wipe tears from his face in two angry swipes. Then he turned and, without looking back, stomped off through the grass.

I waited for Kevin to collect himself, sit up, and scrub his own cheeks dry with the sleeve of his T-shirt. Then I walked over and offered his glasses. "I can't *see* anything without these!" He complained. It sounded like he was excusing his inability to fight back, or perhaps accusing me of letting him down, or both. But he took the glasses and, after adjusting them carefully on his face, looked up at me warily. "Thanks," he said.

I felt a little guilty. "You want to get a soda?" I asked. That was something we had done before, up at the corner store by the railroad tracks. We would split a Hershey's chocolate bar and lukewarm Welch's grape soda, sitting in the hot sun. I usually paid for the both of us, but I didn't mind.

Kevin shook his head. "Naw," he said. He stood up, took a slow, deep breath, and began walking toward his house. I watched him for a half-minute, noticing the long grass still stuck to his pants, the way he pushed his glasses up his nose every few steps, and how his feet splayed out when he walked. A stooped and defeated old man in a child's body. Just like Jesse, he didn't look back, and I was left standing in the field alone, vaguely surprised by my own dispassion about what had just happened. The early morning shadows had receded and the earth was warming up in earnest. I went back inside to make myself some breakfast.

§

As with everything else, anger and conflict present dichotomies of positive and negative. In the counseling I have provided others over the years, it has become clear that anger is often a necessary tool in healing and transformation. When a teenager begins to individuate from their parents, there is often a period of rebellious frustration that fuels the formation of a unique identity separate from parental or family identity. In the same way, when we reconstitute interrupted grieving over something we lost long ago, or try to separate ourselves from abusive environments, or try to break free of our own self-injuring patterns, or create boundaries in our lives where we previously had none, anger directed outward is often helpful and even necessary. In these situations, anger infuses positive, healthy efforts with the courage required to put our foot down, stand our ground and follow through.

So there are plenty of situations where anger is useful, and anger should not be dismissed out-of-hand. Eventually, of course, the healing process allows us to move beyond anger to other, more harmonious emotions. Ideally, whatever initially incited our wrath can be embraced with unconditional love – though this is often a long and arduous road, to be sure. In cases of abuse, trauma, deprivation or other marked interruption to well-being, there may be a lifelong progression of reconciliation within and without. But it is possible. Whatever the source of our anger, it can and should be forgiven. Yet the most challenging candidate for our compassionate affection is usually ourselves.

If we remain perpetually angry at ourselves, we have two choices before us: either we can give in to the conviction that we are so flawed that we will always perpetuate our own victimhood, or we can attempt to shift our intentionality in a more empowered direction. That is, we can take responsibility for our own healing and growth. Ironically – especially if we have victimized ourselves for a long time – this may require that we get angry about being angry at ourselves. Eventually we must find a way to break free of all that rage and find a warm and loving place to rest within our innermost being. This transition from anger to affection is no different than, say, first being frustrated with someone we appreciate and cherish and then, because of a foundation of loving relationship with them, being able to forgive them and moving on. We may still confront, we may still clear the air, we may still find ways to improve the dynamics of our connection so that neither party gets hurt in the future, but we don't hold on to our hurt moving forward. If we truly have affection for them, we will learn to let it go.

## *Applying AMR*

From my own patterns of frustration, anger and conflict throughout my early life, and the enduring patterns of those memories, I carried a lot of thinly suppressed rage well into middle age. At different times, that fury was directed either outward or inward, disrupting my relationships with others or my sense of wholeness and contentment within. At one time it grew intense enough that I thought seriously about suicide. How, then, did I learn to appreciate the dichotomies of anger or conflict? How did I integrate them successfully into a balanced self-concept? And how was I able to develop compassionate affection for them?

My own process of integrating anger and conflict in healthy ways has relied on three avenues of introspective effort. The first was coming to understand what my aggressive responses were trying to accomplish; what was it I believed anger and conflict would provide for me? What desires did I feel were being met? Once some of these desires were identified, I could separate them out into healthy, constructive desires and unhealthy, destructive desires. Each of these threads of desire was then treated very differently. In the case of healthy desires – the desire to be loved, to belong, to feel safe, to be appreciated, etc. – I began to look for alternative ways to accomplish these ends, identifying when aggressive responses made sense and when they didn't. In the case of unhealthy desires, I discovered which areas of self were neglected or injured to such a degree that I was seeking out destructive substitutions, and began to more fully nourish those depleted dimensions instead.

I was convinced from my earliest experiences in life that unless I boisterously asserted myself, or created conflict, or misbehaved, or otherwise initiated some sort of aggravated nuisance, I would for the most part be ignored by those whose attention I most sought. From my interactions with neighborhood bullies, I concluded that I had to confront anyone I perceived as unjust to protect myself from harm. I also believed that unless I stepped in to help others, they might be victimized as well. In addition to these governing beliefs, I also was compelled to imitate the anger and conflict I witnessed in others on a daily basis. All of this added up to my reliance on conflict and anger to get certain fundamental, healthy needs met, while also encouraging more unhealthy desires. For example, I developed what I would describe as an addiction to the physiological rush of becoming angry. I also adopted a perverse enjoyment of conflict – I somehow found comfort and reassurance through creating situations where there was crisis. I also developed a strong need to control my environment when I was feeling vulnerable and anxious, especially when I suspected immanent failure or abandonment.

Cognitive restructuring, initially in the form of CBT, helped me identify these internal realities and begin reinventing my governing beliefs about the effectiveness of anger. Therapeutic breathing helped me calm myself when I was experiencing the fears or anxieties that often precipitated anger responses, attenuating strong emotional reflexes that seemed to issue from somatic memory. Gratitude and compassionate affection practices strengthened my resistance to relying on anger as a first response, mainly by conditioning my emotional disposition into a happier, more relaxed and peaceful place. And neutral awareness helped me envision different choices and trajectories of action that more effectively met my needs, while at the same time allowing me to identify areas of nourishment that had been neglected for many years. All of these practices also nourished my most depleted dimensions of self to varying degrees, thereby relaxing my need to compensate with old, unhealthy patterns.

In concert with these efforts, I also began to introduce other positive self-nourishing techniques into my life. I began to exercise more to provide my body an alternate avenue to the endorphins and adrenaline it so craved. I sought out friendships with folks who had a healthy sense of humor about themselves and the world, and who didn't resort to anger and conflict as a first response. I learned how to communicate my frustration, disappointment and concern without resorting to accusations and name-calling. I composed music and poetry that conveyed painful or intense emotions in constructive ways. I began to take more responsibility for my overall well-being and happiness, and gradually relinquished my codependent reliance on others to confirm I was lovable, valuable and whole. And as I began to see positive changes in my life, to experience healthy desires satisfied and unhealthy desires attenuated, my propensity toward aggressive responses began to fade. All the while, new information was being embedded into my "anger and conflict" semantic container – about when such reactions are effective and when they are not, and how best to navigate them.

What about all of that episodic material – the experiences that fed my previous conclusions about anger and conflict? It has been broken down into its component parts, analyzed for veracity and relevance to the present, and either redistributed into other structures in the mnemosphere, or reassembled according to a new thematic paradigm. It no longer exists as an amalgam of acceptable patterns of thought, emotion and behavior. The bully pulling a hurtful prank is no longer a reason to justify aggression, but a reason to exercise compassion and act in the best interests of everyone involved – including the perpetrator. Satisfying desires for excitement and challenge through anger and conflict becomes an example of uninformed and unskilled self-care, now replaced with more sophisticated nurturing mechanisms. Interpersonal injuries that evoked desires for revenge and retaliation now provide an opportunity for forgiveness, reconciliation and reasonable accommodation. As reflected by the stories in this chapter, the autobiographical material in this container has gradually shifted away from the self-aggrandizing and self-justifying to the humble, corrective and edifying.

This process is liberating, but it requires effort and, quite often, skilled external guidance. I could not have learned to unshackle myself from inappropriate anger responses without help; without the compassionate examples and techniques applied by the good folks at Fort River Elementary to start me down the path – and the many other helpful mentors, therapists and friends since then – I probably would have stumbled down a much darker road. Learning how to relate to people, how to mediate conflict, how to communicate without being defensive or accusatory, and how to diffuse my own anger response when it arises also contributed to my healing. I cannot claim that AMR has been the sole corrective influence in this regard, but it incorporates many of the lessons I learned along the way, and continues to facilitate healing and transformation in this arena.

My challenges with anger and conflict have made for a long journey, full of obstacles, twists and turns. Those who know me well can testify how, most of the time, lashing out combatively is no longer my strongest predilection.  I now prefer to humorize a frustrating situation, or cry my way through personal pain, or meditate my way out of anxiety, or take a time-out from stressful activities to find my center again, or appeal to the better nature of my fellows.  Do I still get angry at myself?  Of course.  Do I still confront people I feel have wronged me or someone I care about?  Yes, I do.  When I injure myself, do I curse loudly and vehemently?  Sometimes.  Do I still complain or accuse when I feel hurt or betrayed?  Sure, but my hissy fit will be expressed in the form of a lengthy email rather than a boisterous tantrum.  So I have now collected a series of observations and experiences to replace the vibrant patterns of anger and conflict in my early life.  I exercise, cry, meditate, sing and laugh.  And the more I replicate these calm an constructive replacement patterns, the calmer and more constructive my reflexes become.  I haven't struck someone in anger since I was a teenager.  Where I once might have escalated an emotionally bruising yelling match, I can now remain much calmer in the face of a storm.  And instead of beating myself up mentally for some mistake I have made, I more readily forgive myself and move on.  Simply put:  I am learning to let go.  All of this is possible because I have been able to create new patterns within my memory field, and therefore new patterns of being and becoming in my daily interactions.

# Chapter Six: Joy & Passion

There was certainly a lot of excitement in my early life – plenty of adrenaline-inducing activity to get my heart pounding and my mind racing toward screaming peaks of intensity. That in itself is a certain kind of joy. But the type of joy we'll be exploring in the following pages is of a deeper, quieter and more enduring variety. The profound contentment that arises from aligning our thoughts, actions and emotional life with elements of our being that are uniquely ours, elements which call to us from deep within, insisting that we express who we are in the most personal ways. Such experiences may be a complex intersection of dedicated study and effort over time – a fulfillment of hard work and long-held expectation – or an unexpected surprise that resonates with some as yet undiscovered aspect of self. These are the most satisfying moment for us, in part because they become tangible proof of our self-concept. They declare to the Universe our distinct meme of being, an affirmation of our personal "I am."

## Music

"Could you send Todd some sort of horn for Christmas? I don't know where he got the idea, but he keeps asking for one…" My mother wrote this to her parents when I was three, and similar comments are peppered throughout her later letters during our time in Eugene, Oregon. I loved to listen to any kind of music at that time, and once I acquired a record player at age five, I wore out every album that was given to me. I liked to sing along whenever anyone else was singing, and hummed to myself often. This was a little bewildering for both of my parents. They enjoyed music, and in fact were both gifted singers, but their appreciation was confined to quiet personal or social rituals and special occasions. My dad sang at Christmas and with groups of friends, my mom sang lullabies at bedtime and to herself when she washed dishes. Music had its place, and that place was relatively small. For me, however, music was an everywhere, all-the-time fascination. I proved this by incessantly playing the plastic horn my grandparents sent me, carrying it with me everywhere for weeks, until it finally died a predictable plastic death. My longing to interact with music issued from the very center of my being. Whenever I listened to music, my heart soared. Whenever I sang, I threw my whole self into each note. For me, music didn't just evoke or convey joy, it was joy itself. And it didn't seem to matter what type of music, either. The whining harmonies of bluegrass or the sorrowful grit of blues; the rich complexity of a classical symphony or the heady poetry of sixties' folk. I loved all of it and could spend hours-on-end lost in music's embrace.

Mystified as my mother was by the musical font within me, she tried to be supportive. When we lived in Manchester, Connecticut, mom bought me a paper drum set from Sears and enrolled me in a local church choir. We weren't churchgoers, and I didn't last very long in Sunday School – where I asked challenging questions kept sneaking upstairs to see what the adults were doing – but I did love to sing in the choir. The paper heads on the drum set only endured a few weeks, but I had a blast rocking the neighborhood. Also, in bopping around from one alternative educational program to the next, I was often exposed to new musical instruments. I first explored the piano in a daycare program when I was eight, and was instantly hooked.

Later on, living with my dad in Amherst, I would discover all sorts of new avenues to get my musical fix. My father wasn't very interested in fostering my musicality, and in fact issued a "no singing in the house" rule when I was eleven, but his girlfriend at the time, Kathy, was musical herself and seemed delighted to find a kindred spirit in me. Kathy had intended to sell her baby grand piano before I arrived, but after I demonstrated sincere interest and a good ear, she kept it in our spare room and encouraged me to play. She even paid a friend to begin teaching me rudimentary skills. That ended, however, when the teacher discovered that I had not been learning to sight-read as I had been telling him, but only mimicking him by ear whenever he played the pieces we were studying.  When my father and Kathy broke up, she even left the piano behind for a short time so that I could continue to play.  Once that piano was gone for good, however, I was devastated.  For a time after that, there was a desert in my soul.

The pull of music was strong enough that I could not go without an instrument for long, however.  First, I tried taking up the banjo.  In love with the folky sound, my father had picked one up for himself and tried to learn.  After he threw in the towel, I eagerly began plucking away, recalling my long hours of bliss listening to Pete Seeger on two of my precious albums.  I didn't get vary far on the banjo, but I did gain a new respect for those who could play the instrument well.  Then, at the urging of my school counselor, Ann, I tried cello.  This time I had a formal teacher who showed me how to bow and finger, but he was a sickly man who clearly didn't want to be there, and once again, this was much more difficult than I supposed, so I quickly lost interest.  After that, I returned to my search for keyboards.  I snuck into the school's theatre to play the sweet little baby grand there, but was soon found out and scolded for the trespass.  I found another piano at the Amherst public library, but this required special permission to use, and could only be played for a half-hour or so at a time.  I felt thwarted at every turn, and was one the verge of giving up, when I struck gold.

The object of my most ardent childhood affections

My dad taught psychology at the UMass Amherst campus, and one day during a long, hot summer when I was eleven or twelve, I tagged along with him as I had done many times before. Sometimes he would just work in his office, or in a research lab where they did tests on human perception, and often he would let me hang out or even help. Sometimes he would have one of his grad students entertain me with some trivial task, like feeding punch cards into the punch card reader for the IBM mainframe...but today there was nothing for me to do. "Why don't you go explore the campus?" My dad encouraged me.

"By myself?" I asked, incredulous.

"Sure, why not," he said. "Just be back in a couple of hours."

"Okay." And, with a surge of excitement, I left.

The UMass campus is fairly huge, at least from a young boy's perspective, and I wasn't sure where to go or what was safe to explore. So I just wandered around, climbing walls, jumping off of them, and generally remaining outside of the ominous looking buildings unless I had to pee. At some point I spied a huge structure that seemed different from the others. I stared at it for a while from a distance, then asked a passing student: "What's that?" "That's the new fine arts building," the student replied. Curious, I wandered closer. Most of the outside of the building was finished, and I was intrigued by the huge geometric shapes and smooth concrete leading up from the ground. Seeing an opportunity to refresh my climbing skills, I clambered up. The hot concrete made perfect traction for my sneakers, and I made quick time up to one of the lower roofs. Upon further exploration, I found an open metal hatch with a ladder that descended into darkness. It was too tempting to resist, so I started down.

I soon found myself in a concrete hallway, surrounded by all sorts of pipes and metal racks. The air smelled of wet metal, dust and freshly cured concrete. I moved forward cautiously, listening. Occasionally I heard a distant clanking, like someone pounding on a pipe with a wrench, but otherwise I seemed to be alone. I continued down the hall until I cam to a hefty cyclone fence gate. Beyond the gate was another hallway, with doors leading into spaces of varying size, some well-lit and others dim with shadow. What was in those rooms? They beckoned to me. I tried the latch on the gate, but it was locked. Then I looked up. At the top of the gate a space had been made for the large pipes that ran along the ceiling. There was easily enough room for me to squeeze through.

I clambered up the gate and slipped quickly through the opening, pausing only to listen for footsteps. I dropped into the hallway on the other side with a well-practiced roll to break my fall, then stood and brushed myself off. I grinned. This probably wasn't the sort of adventure my father had in mind for me, but it was sure a lot of fun! I wandered into the nearest open doorway and peered through the dimness. Across a huge expanse of floorless space, a wide wooden stage glowed warmly into the darkness. Centered on that stage, basking in a glorious halo of light, was the largest piano I had ever seen. Even from a distance, it was impossible long. Its glossy black surface gleamed majestically. Of course, I was immediately certain of what I would be doing for the rest of my outing.

Slowly I made my way across the intervening space. There was no floor, only a series of crisscrossing girders above a tangle of tools, dollies and construction materials. Eventually, there would be sloping rows of seats here, but now I had a relatively straight shot across the girders to the front of the stage. I clambered up onto the smooth flooring, still shiny and fresh, and walked to the massive instrument.

Standing before the piano, I looked around once to make sure I was still alone. Then I turned to gaze upon my prize. It was magnificent. Gleaming, glimmering bright, without a scratch or smudge or fingerprint on its inky surface. Carefully, holding my breath, I gently lifted the hinged keyboard cover and beheld the glistening keys. Bright gold letters on the cover read "Bösendorfer." I had never heard of that brand of piano before. I tried a simple chord – an octave-spanning A minor. A rich, even tone answered. But the piano's top was still down, muting the sound. Without hesitation, I lifted it, propping the heavy wood on its lowest support. Eager now, I returned to the keyboard, settling down on the black piano bench, and tried a few more chords while pumping the sustain pedal. What swelled forth were the most beautiful sounds I had ever heard.

For the next hour I played my heart out. Music filled the auditorium, a space that enlarged every harmony, held the softest note for just the right length of time, and fed my melodies back to me in ways I had never imagined. I was entirely smitten. I had no idea that any music – let alone music that I created – could sound like this...or feel like this. Eventually the elation in my breast overwhelmed me, springing from my eyes. I paused to wipe my face on my sleeve and take a long, calming breath.

The sound of a clearing throat. "Uh...sounds pretty good," a man's voice said. I looked around quickly, preparing to spring into a run. "Over here," said the voice. Then I saw him, standing down among the equipment and materials on the concrete in front of the stage. "I've gotta do some heavy work here, and it's gonna get loud. Do you...er...want me to come back later? I'm kinda on a schedule here...I—" He shrugged, clearly uncomfortable.

At first I was bewildered, then I understood. "Oh...yeah. Sure. I'm done anyway."

The man nodded. "Great. Okay, thanks." He stooped to retrieve a coil of extension cord, then headed further back into the gloom. I stood and watched him warily. Did he really think I belonged here? I probably needed to head back to my dad's office anyway. I sighed, closing the top and keyboard cover of the piano, then cast one last, longing glance upon my new best friend. No...there was something more than friendship here. Love? Lust? Longing? I turned and quietly left the stage, following the exit signs to an exterior door nearby. The bright sunlight bathed my face, but I barely felt it. The heat and radiance of the sun were no match for what I felt inside.

The rest of that summer was spent sneaking through the guts of that fine arts center. There were other pianos in other places, too. In fact, one section of the building had room after room of uprights – what I later learned were practice rooms for music students. But nothing compared to the majestic Bösendorfer, and whenever it was safe to do so, I would sneak back onto that sonorous stage. As it neared completion, however, the entire building became much less welcoming. Walls were installed, doors and hatches were locked, and, eventually, a lock was placed on the

Bösendorfer's keyboard cover. There were also more and more adults wandering the building, and more than once my presence there was questioned. Often, I was mistaken for a young female student. In fact, the professor who guarded the beautiful and massive pipe organ in the guts of the center actually took time to show me how to fire up the pumps and work the electronic registers…until he realized that I wasn't a flustered, flat-chested female student after all.

Once the summer came to an end and the school year began, my sojourn in the land of forbidden fruit was ended. But a pattern was set. No matter where I lived in the years after that, I could always find a keyboard to play – whether I was allowed to play it or not. There were pianos in libraries, public spaces, and other people's homes. There would be a harpsichord in Amherst High School, a Moog synthesizer in a Frankfurt community center, and a lovely selection of Steinways, Baldwins and other treasures in the University of Washington music school. Sometimes I had to sneak in after these places were closed. Sometimes I would risk a daytime exploit. Sometimes I would pay a dollar or two to rent some time. In High School, my humanities teacher, Jerry, introduced me to a friend of his who ran a jazz bar in Sachsenhausen, just across the Main river. Her name was Anita, and when she insisted I play for her patrons, I did so gladly. At first I was nervous – I had never played for such a large audience before. After a few rum-and-cokes, however, I really got into it. Today, I still search out keyboards to play, and have yet to set aside my passion for creating music.

§

I was also blessed with many wonderful opportunities to appreciate fine music as well. My father was an audiophile with diverse tastes, ranging from The Eagles and Fleetwood Mac to the McGarrigle sisters and Beethoven. He spent hours building components of his stereo system from scratch and encouraged me to do the same. He spent weeks working in the garage to replicate Fulton J speakers from clandestinely procured design diagrams – right down to the raw wool insulation. He likewise constructed a powerful tube amplifier from scratch, and built a custom tone arm for his Thorens 325 turntable.  Upon returning from a trip to New York City, he proudly presented me with the guts of a discarded Acoustic Research turntable, and we spent the next month building an oak case and balsa wood tone arm for it.  I then began collecting LPs, which I was allowed to play to my heart's content as long as I listened through headphones.

Dad also enjoyed live concerts, and he and his girlfriend, Kathy, would often take me with them.  I was exposed to many superb musicians making guest appearances or doing graduate performances at UMass concerts, and was delighted to find myself as an audience in the same performance halls I had been sneaking into for years.  Probably the most memorable of all these concerts was a PDQ Bach extravaganza.  The venerable Peter Schickele arrived late to the hall, bounding over our heads across the backs of the seats – in a tuxedo and high-top sneakers – to stumble onto the stage for a grand evening of musical hilarium.  I was often the only young person at many of these concerts, but to the surprise and relief of the nervous adults seated around me, I was always riveted from the moment the music began.  I remember on one occasion I made it all the way through Mahler's 3rd Symphony without a peep, falling asleep on the cold vinyl of the Dodge's back seat on the way home, only to have the dramatic symphonic phrases echo through my dreams.

My father also had many musical friends who encouraged me in various ways.  Two bona fide hippies who lived nearby, Eric and Judy, would have parties at their place that often involved music making.  We would all sit in a giant circle as various percussion instruments were passed around.  Then a couple of people with guitars, and maybe one with a fiddle or banjo, would start us off on a familiar folk tune.  On my first visit to this gathering, I stuck to my father's "no singing" rule until I was invited to join in.  Then I really cut loose, bellowing melodies and harmonies at the top of my lungs.  My father was appalled and told me to pipe down.  "Let him sing, Bill," Eric said, laughing.  "He's really putting his heart into it."  Though his expression remained sour, my father dismissively waved my permission to continue.  He actually had a great voice, so once he relaxed a bit he would often cut loose as well.  These sessions would continue well on into the evening, at which point someone would light up a hookah packed with home-grown cannabis.

This would make its way around the circle several times, and though I was never allowed to partake, I likely got my fill of secondary weed. By the end of the day, everyone was full to the brim with fellowship, music and heightened joviality. And then it was time to eat.

My mom also found ways to expose me to new musical experiences. During our years in Manchester, she would make the two-hour drive to up to Tanglewood in Lenox, Massachusetts each summer. There we would picnic in the lush green grass while the orchestra thrilled our ears, hearts and minds. I also remember those wonderful trees edging the main green, and how I would duck beneath their draping limbs to absorb each note, free of the distracting human conversations nearby. One year when we were seated particularly close to the concert hall, I caught a glimpse of the conductor being ushered from a limousine to the podium amid adoring cheers from the crowd. "Who's that?" I asked. "That's Leonard Bernstein!" the woman beside me declared. I had no idea who he was, but I thought he had an arrogant look about him.

By the time I was twelve, my father was fully alerted to both my appreciation of music and my ardent desire to create it. At the urging of his newest girlfriend, Jutta, he bought me a classical guitar and a few introductory books on chords and scales. I was not aloud to strum loudly and singing was still verboten – I was sternly reprimanded for this the few times I broke protocol – but I could play quietly in my basement room to my heart's content. And although the nylon string Yamaha wasn't a Bösendorfer, and didn't resonate quite the same way with my innermost muse as pianos in a concert hall, it was certainly something. By the end of my thirteenth year I was fully engrossed in my new instrument. To nearly everyone's surprise, including my own, I would be reading tablature, and then standard notation for the guitar, and learning surprisingly sophisticated pieces of music. I would continue to sing in school choirs and along with my guitar when I thought no one was around. I would start writing songs. I would eventually start jamming with friends after school. And as all of this built more momentum within my consciousness, music would be imbedded in my identity for the rest of my life.

A self-portrait with my first guitar when I was fifteen

## Words & Stories

My first visit to Amherst, Massachusetts, was in the Spring of 1971. I flew in on a plane by myself from Portland, Oregon, to join my dad, step-sister and step-mother in their home on Harkness Road, right on the border of Amherst and Pelham, Massachusetts. It was a beautiful spot of land on a sparsely housed stretch of wooded road, bordering a tangled swamp and hundreds of acres of mixed coniferous and deciduous forest. Although I was happy to lose myself among the swamp islands and endless dirt trails stretching out from our back yard, my new guardians would not leave me as unattended as I had been back in Florence. Instead, I was ushered into a daycare program with kids a little younger than I was. I remember being embarrassed and uncooperative at first, but I soon settled in to the new routine. In the morning, on her way to work, my step-mom, Mary, would drop me off. Then, usually around noon, Mary would return to pick me up and take me home.

Then, one day, Mary didn't show. The playroom slowly emptied out and the woman who watched over our kindergarten became more and more agitated. Finally she took me next door, to room a group of older kids underwent more orderly instruction. There an older woman in a light green dress began to argue with my kindergarten teacher, insisting she remain until my parents arrived.  Finally, after much kvetching and begging on the part of my teacher, the older woman acquiesced to watching me.  She was not happy about this, however.  When my kindergarten teacher left, the older woman marched over to me.  She had reading glasses that swept up at the corners like cat's eyes, and her blue-gray hair was pulled into a tight, uncomfortable-looking bun.  She looked me over sternly.

"You – what's your name?"

"Todd, I—"

"Yes, well you need to stay right over here.  Is that understood?"

I looked around.  There was a long table against one wall that was piled with books.  "Can I look at the books?"

The woman was flustered.  "Those are for older kids.  They don't have very many pictures.  You don't read, do you."  It was a statement, toneless and condemning.

"No."  I agreed.  I was disappointed that I couldn't look at the books, and it must have shown.

"Well…" the woman seemed to soften.  She marched over to the book table.  "Here, why don't you –" she shuffled through the piles, pulling books out here and there "—start with these."  She handed me a stack.  "Then come see me when you need some more.  Okay?"

"Okay."  The weight of the books in my arms was reassuring.

The woman began marching back to her class, her black high-healed shoes digging angrily into the carpet.  "Oh," she said, spinning back my way, "Don't make a peep over here.  This is quiet time."  She pointed at me with a scolding finger.

I nodded obediently.

For the next half hour, I sorted through the books she had given me. There were in fact very few pictures, so I made it through them fairly quickly. I could only guess what the stories were about. I stared at the swarms of letters on the pages, wishing I could understand them. I did know my alphabet from my mother's drills at the beach house in Florence, so I recognized individual letters, but I had no idea how they went together to form words. I stared some more. At some point I saw something familiar, a combination of letters I recognized. Perhaps it was "Stop," or "dog" or some other simple word, but as I stared at it, knowing exactly what it meant, something occurred to me. The letters that made the sounds for that particular word might make similar sounds for other words. In fact, all the letters of the alphabet that I already knew might create sounds the same way. If I could string those sounds together, I might be able to decipher words. Was it possible?

I picked another word at random on the page. "D…o…w…n." I let the sounds rumble around in my mouth. "D-o-n? D-o-w. Down?!" Yes, that was it! I giggled aloud, then quickly stifled my glee. I had to be quiet. I tried another. "F…i…s…h…." "F-i-s-ah? F-i-s-ha?" I shook my head; that one was hard. I tried another. "W…a…t…e…r…" I thought about it. *Wait here*? Was that it? Or was it *waiter*? Then I looked at the last word I had attempted, and something clicked. "Fish and water!" I declared. I knew I was onto something. I was ecstatic. I tried it again. And again. And again. At last, my first sentence emerged: "A fish swam down under the water!" Could it be this simple? Sounds strung together to make words, and words strung together to make sentences? And if I strung the sentences together…would that make a story?

I stared at the black letters on the white paper. Slowly, painstakingly, the words made themselves clear. It was like magic – marks becoming sounds that had meaning. I could barely contain my excitement, and pressed on further. There were a lot of repeated words, and that made things easier. After a short while, I was sure I had worked out nearly the entire page. It *was* a story, about a boy fishing in a stream. I laughed, jumped up, and danced in place with joy. I wanted to share my joy with someone, so I grabbed my book and wandered toward the voices in the adjoining room. I peeked through the doorway to find the woman with the blue-gray hair marching up and down rows of quietly seated kids. It all looked very serious, so I decided not to interrupt, and returned to my pile of books, settling down to read some more.

For a while I was lost in stories. There were talking animals, kids in city neighborhoods, adventures in strange places...anything and everything I could ever want. I had no idea how much time had passed, but I eventually made my way through all of the books the woman had selected for me. I looked up. There, just a few feet away, a whole new world offered itself to me. Images and characters and events I had never imagined were open to me now. I wandered over to the table and began sorting through the titles there. There were so many! The woman had said she would find more for me...but I could tell she was still busy. So, mainly by the pictures on the covers, I chose another few books at random and made my way back to my cozy reading spot on the floor.

Hours must have past. I was so lost in the elation of my new experience, I didn't notice the shiny black high-heeled shoes appearing on the floor just in front of me at first. When I did, I grinned. At last I could tell someone! "I got –"

"Yes, you did!" the woman interrupted, snatching the book from my hand. "I told you to ask me, not get them yourself young man."

"But – "

"Don't you 'but' me!" said the woman, wagging that finger again. "Now just be quiet and sit here. Your mother will be here soon."

Something inside me snapped. She wasn't going to listen to me. She wasn't going to let me read anymore. "She's not my mother!" I yelled, springing to my feet. The woman stepped back, then she squinted purposefully at me and grabbed my shirt. "Hey! Let me go! LET ME GO!" I struggled to free myself and she grabbed my arm as well.

"Now you listen here, *little boy!*" she hissed.

"WHAT ARE YOU DOING?!" I knew that voice, it was Mary, my step-mom, and I turned my head to find her standing in the door with an angry look on her face, which I also knew quite well. But this time, for once, it wasn't directed at me. "Let him go!"

"This boy – "

"I don't care what he did. You can't just grab him like that!"

The woman let me go. My mood changed instantly and I ran to Mary. "Guess what? Guess what?"

"Yes, well, if he's damaged any of these books you'll be hearing from me."

I looked at the pile on the floor where I had been sitting. "I was careful. I was *reading* them. *I can read!*"

The woman shook her head and frowned disapprovingly. I looked at Mary and she sighed. "C'mon, Todd." Mary said, turning to go.

"But I did!" I cried. "I DID read them!" I chased after her.

The blue-haired woman wasn't finished with us yet, and her loud black shoes stomped after us. "You can't just *leave* him here like that. We won't *babysit* him for you. That's not our *job.*"

"I'm not a baby! I'm *six!*" I yelled angrily.

"It won't happen again," Mary said flatly. "Let's go home, Todd."

Frustrated, I didn't want to get in the car. I wanted the wonderful truth – the ecstatic miracle that had happened to me that day – to come bursting forth. I wanted everyone to believe and understand. But Mary's expression held a dire warning. Her mouth was turned down, her eyes pinched. I held my tongue and got in the car. It was a long ride back to the house. Mary was upset and didn't want to talk. I asked her why she was late, and she wouldn't explain. I wanted to tell her about my day, but she said she was tired. She lit a cigarette and turned on the radio, so I looked out the side window. I loved to watch the trees fly by along the highway.  As I remembered the books and stories and magic, a kernel of joy burned small and steady in my chest, and I held it.

§

One of the greatest pleasures of my childhood was being read to.  This began with my mother and large picture books when I was two and three.  I even remember some of them.  My absolute favorite was a boldly illustrated story about two families – one family where everyone in was really fat, and one where everyone was really skinny.  I can still remember the people's expressions in the brightly colored drawings, and how I would laugh and grin as mom turned the pages.  Much later, when I was about eleven, my dad, his girlfriend Kathy and I would take turns reading from J.R.R. Tolkien's *The Hobbit* and *Lord of the Rings* trilogy.  We relished making up voices for each of the characters as we read.  I see these experiences as bookends for all of my family reading experiences.  To this day, I associate reading aloud with intimate togetherness.

Combined with my general excitement over the magic of words and stories, this is what drew me toward reading books.  And oh, how I loved to read.  After my eleventh birthday, I started to devour pages of everything I could get my hands on, and my world expanded exponentially every day.  I read late into the night, under my blanket with a flashlight.  I read during the day, before, during and after school, and whenever I thought I could get away with it, sometimes hiding my books inside of another book cover to avoid undue attention.  As you might recall from a previous chapter, one of my elementary teachers would confiscate any book she perceived inappropriate for young eyes.  My father, who always seemed suspicious of any daylight hours I spent alone in my room, would likewise discourage me from reading and invent some chore or other for me to do – usually outside – so that I could be more useful.  But he himself read copiously, and so I felt justified in persisting.  I also had support and encouragement from others in my life.  My dad's girlfriend, Kathy, was an avid reader and slipped me many of the books she had just finished.  Relatives and family friends who heard about my burgeoning interest also sent me books to read. Even my school counselor, Ann, gave me a book of poetry by Carl Sandburg for my eleventh birthday.

As we were encouraged to bring our favorite book to class with us for "reading time," I would usually schlep two or three different books along with me for that cherished ritual. From my earliest memories of reading, it was always my habit to have several books open at once. After all, sometimes I needed a break from the intensity of one story, and what better break than to immerse myself in another? I liked to have different flavors of reading running in parallel, too. Hemingway, Steinbeck and Hugo were serious, heavy hitters, and required the levity and playfulness of a Norton Juster, T.H. White or Mark Twain to counter them. Frank Herbert's *Dune* books had to be balanced with Mary Stewart's *Crystal Cave* series; Glendon Swarthout required the antidote of Arthur Conan Doyle, and so on. I read books like I ate my supper: a bite of meat, a nibble of corn, a mouthful of potatoes…and a swig of sweet, cold milk to wash it all down.

It wasn't until I attended summer camp at age twelve that I realized my passion for books was relatively rare among a broader set of peers. My school was full of smart, literate kids who loved to read, but they were exceptional in this respect. Summer camp, populated with a more mainstream population, had no such affection for words. In fact, the boys in my cabin – all of whom loudly expressed their hatred of reading – quickly realized that the best way to torment me was to hide the cherished copy of *Watership Down* I had brought to camp. I tried to combat this by hiding the book under the tent vent flap just above my bed, not realizing that I was exposing it to the elements by doing so. Within a week the book was warped and rippled, but even that did not deter me. I would read, come hell or high water, until the batteries of my flashlight were drained to nothing.

In different periods of her life, my mother wrote poetry and shared those poems with me. Both of my grandmothers also wrote me letters and post cards throughout my childhood, as well as the requisite greeting cards on special occasions. My aunt Wendy also contributed to this family tradition with post cards, notes and birthday missives, as well as encouraging me in my own writing efforts. And although those efforts were intermittent at best, I responded to this sharing and encouragement with my own letters and poems.   At first these were mainly out of a sense of obligation to return the affections of my family.   But then I began to write for myself alone.  I found a connection with my innermost self through the process of writing, and a strong inner voice that always had something to say.  Probably because my mother had always done so in her missives, I often mixed sketches in with my writing, and most of my early thoughts were written on large drawing pads amid doodles and hasty illustrations.

Here is one of my earliest poems, from about 1980:

### Why Have I Fallen?

Sometimes I am
a sack of nothing
blown tumbling, tearing,
through black desert.
Sometimes,
a tiny pine needle
nestled in the dirt
yellow like the inside of a beetle.
Sometimes,
a lump of sweet, soft butter
glistening on the patterned tile
sticking to the sole of things,
traveling in practiced patterns
over forbidden ground.

In time I would also begin writing love letters to the objects of my adolescent affections, and this added both an urgency and a more calculated aesthetic to my writing.  It was then that I began studying calligraphy and trying to master the art of dip pens, nib widths and India ink.  I think those romantic efforts were probably my most serious early attempts to capture my inner turmoil and longing – with precisely the right words, form and sentiment.  It was romance, in fact, that brought me my first bound journal as well.  One of the first young women to return my amorous affections did so in the form of a beautifully illustrated blank book with a cover she made by hand.  Insightful soul that she was, she encouraged me to put my endlessly rambling thoughts within those pages, which I began to do at age thirteen.  The craft that had evolved out of my letters, poetry and romantic communications would now be applied to other musings, as I tried ever more accurately to express what was within me.  I would spend hours working out my thoughts on paper, a solitary activity that was only rivaled by the hours I spent reading science fiction and fantasy.

The one constant throughout all of my reading and writing was a sense of connection.  Connection with my innermost thoughts and emotions, connection with the world around me, and connection with distant times, places and people.  The written word provided friendship in a way I had not experienced with flesh and blood.  When I wrote, my thoughts could be heard in a calm and receptive spaciousness.  When I read, I could explore the inner workings of others – be they fictional characters, friends or relatives – with the same contemplative openness.  When I read aloud or was read to, the shared transportation of the senses and imagination provided real-time connection with the people I most cared about as well.  This was in marked contrast to the awkward and often unsuccessful navigation of social situations during those early years.  In the hurried family and peer interactions of daily life, I cloaked myself in personas that protected, dazzled or deflected.  In the quiet moments of reading and writing, I could relax into a truer expression of who I was, and appreciate the unfiltered expression of others.  In this way, reading, writing and being read to unveiled a safe and limitless intimacy with myself, friends, family, romantic interests and the world around me.  As a result, all things literary were forever to be associated with an enduring sense of celebration, contentment and emotional release.

It seems appropriate at this point to share other examples of this early exposure to writing.  Here is an excerpt of a letter my maternal grandmother, Rita, wrote me when I was six:

> "There came next a strange box, done up in white and pink, that reminded me of the beautiful apple blossoms, on a hill back by my home, when I was a little girl; in the Spring, when the soft winds would blow,  and you could smell the sweet blossoms on the air.  These came from the box like a current of air, sound of the clear breath of Spring; the warm wind, and water running

down the brook, after the snow melts. But I listened now, and the north wind sounded cold as it blew the snow against the window, and I was glad to be warm."

There were other creative passions woven into my childhood, and many have remained with me over the years. I have continued to love words – the nuances, the etymology and usage changes over time, finding just the right word that means exactly what I am trying to describe, and so on. There was photography, a strong desire to capture a moment in time, a small part of a larger story, with an interesting composition, contrasting textures and intriguing angles of light. There was pencil drawing, calligraphy and oil painting. There was sculpting elaborate and fragile abstracts out of clay. There was videography and stop animation. There was acting and singing in elementary school productions. There were so many disciplines I enjoyed, and so many things I wanted to keep engaging in all the time, but it was really the act of conceiving, composing, aesthetically arranging and bringing into existence that fascinated and compelled me. Artistic expression connected me with a part of myself that I barely recognized or understood, but which I nevertheless intuited as vitally important.

## Practically Applied Improvements

From a very early age I enjoyed building and fixing things. For some reason, I was convinced that anything could be built from almost anything else, and that anything broken could be repaired. I don't know where this passion came from, but it has been with me as far back as I can remember. Lincoln Logs, Legos and Play Dough quickly graduated to hammers, nails, saws, chisels and any number of raw materials. Give me a garden spade, and I'd dig enough dirt to build a mud wall. Give me a sturdy cart, and I'd begin wheeling loads of wood and rocks hither and thither for various projects. I can't be certain, but I suspect my step-step-sister Shelly had something to do with this penchant for construction. She herself had a knack for making something out of nothing, and I was always impressed with her creations. Once, when we were six or seven, she made an elaborate dome in the back yard out of twigs and woven pine needles. It was large enough for us to both squeeze inside, and shone a brilliant orange in the midday sun. I have no idea how she managed this, and at the time I suspected it was some sort of magic. Shelly later studied fine art in college and continued to create interesting, beautiful work.

One summer in my seventh or eighth year, when I was spending the weekend with my paternal grandparents in West Hartford, Connecticut, I decided out of the blue that I wanted to build a model boat. I had no idea how to go about this, but was certain that I could, so I asked my grandfather, Ed, if he had any old scraps of wood I could use. Yes, he said, there were some pieces in a bucket down in his basement workroom. So down I went. Now an important point at this juncture is that Ed was a superb craftsman. His workroom walls were lined with all manner of fine woodworking tools, and he took great pride in his professional skills. As an understandable consequence of his expertise, he wasn't very keen on letting a young tyke use any of his tools. Which is why I didn't ask, but instead busily went about building my model ship with whatever I implements could pull down off of his carefully organized peg board.

After a few minutes of pounding randomly shaped pieces of wood together into the rough shape of a river barge, Ed came downstairs to see what all the racket was about. He walked into his workroom just as I was about to start carving a name into my "ship" with one of his prized woodworking chisels and a greasy, oversized hammer. With two very quick strides Ed was beside me, snatching the chisel from my hand and lifting me bodily off the ground by the back of my shirt. At sixty-five, he was still a healthy, strong man. I learned that day that he also still had the quick, violent temper of someone half his age. After I was finished trying to defend what I had done, and he was finished informing me of some workroom boundaries I was never to cross again, he took one look at my creation and decided it was time to begin my education in carpentry. This was the right saw to use, and this was how you drew it back-and-forth in long, even strokes. This was the right type of hammer, and this was how to hold it for maximum striking power. This was a finishing nail, and this was how you could countersink that nail. And so on. I ate it up. I wanted to know, and he was happy to teach me. I never did graduate to the privilege of using the finer tools in his shop, but he laid a solid foundation for my future endeavors.

There would be many other teachers over the next few years. When I was eight, one of my mom's boyfriends helped me build a scale model biplane, with a balsa wood frame and thin cloth skin coated with special, "aerodynamic" paint. It took us over a month to complete. I think it was one of my proudest accomplishments to date, and I used to lie in bed and stare at its gleaming, two-foot length, fantasizing about how it would fly. Unfortunately, the rubber band motor didn't quite provide the lift it required, and its virgin journey off of our second floor balcony ended in pieces on the parking lot below. Oddly, I really didn't care. It was an excuse to take it apart and built again, and I reveled in the exhilaration of watching it soar ever-so-briefly through the air.

My maternal grandfather, Louis, probably had something to do with my fascination with airplanes. He was a draftsman at Pratt & Whitney, and everyone on my mother's side of the family was very proud of what he did for a living. Exploring the letters my mother sent to her parents when I was four, I recently discovered a crude paper airplane I had made for Louis. When the carefully folded plane fell out of the envelope, I recognized it instantly. I remembered how many attempts I made to create the perfect gift for grandpa. How I tested each one to see how well it flew. How my mother had to scrounge through her art supplies to find more paper for me until, after four or five tries, I was satisfied with the result.

There is also a brief but happy memory of a warm summer afternoon spent with my father flying a simple, stick-and-wing glider on an empty lot. I must have been three or four, but I can still feel the sun stinging my eyes as I tracked the delicate wings against the bright blue sky, refusing to even blink for fear of missing a precious moment. And, later, there would be another memory of launching a red and white water-powered rocket from our back yard. The idea that you could make something fly on its own with a little preparation and careful transference of energy was very exciting to me. I think most of my enjoyment for sports like Frisbee and baseball arises from an appreciation of the same kind of physics.

At the more mechanical end of the spectrum, I loved to spend time with my dad whenever he worked on his car. I savored the smell of oil, gas, rubber and WD-40. I cherished the warm glint of his chrome wrenches.

I was in awe of the metallic massiveness of each successive vehicle – the Chevy, the Dodge, the Volvo. So I quickly learned the names and functions of as many tools as I could, and hovered nearby to pepper my dad with questions about what he was doing and why. This wasn't much of a bonding time for us, as my father often flew into fits of rage, cursing this or that godamnfuckingsonofabitchpieceofshit that had just gouged the skin off of all his knuckles. But it was a time to begin the slow journey to understanding how things were put together, and why they worked the way they did.

When I was seven, I was visiting my friend Evan, who lived at the opposite end of Harkness Road in Amherst, Massachusetts. It had been his birthday the day before, and his father had given him a brand new Radio Flyer wagon. It was a bright, glistening red on that summer day, and I marveled at it. "Can I borrow it?" I asked.

"What?!" Evan was incredulous. "I just got it yesterday!"

"I know. But I didn't give you anything for your birthday, and…I want to do something nice for you."

Evan considered. "I don't know…."

"I'll bring it back right away. Later today – I promise."

Evan seemed uncertain. "If my dad finds out I let you borrow it, he'll be pretty pissed."

"Please, Evan?" I really wanted some quality time with that wagon.

"What are you going to do?"

"It's a surprise!" I said. In reality I had no idea, but I really did want to do something nice for Evan's birthday. Especially if he was going to lend me his brand new Radio Flyer.

Evan sighed dramatically – something he picked up from his mother. "Okay. But you've got to bring it back before dinnertime!" He wagged his finger at me.

"I will! No ifs, ands or buts!" I declared, and immediately made off with his birthday present.

Walking the mile or so back to my house, I struggled to come up with an appropriate gift. But the harder I pondered, the fewer ideas seemed to present themselves. What could I do for Evan that could equal a Radio Flyer? As I approached my driveway, I began to get nervous and lose some of my effervescence. And then, as I stood before our garage door, it came to me in glowing ball of certainty. I would make the Flyer better! I would carefully take it apart, meticulously clean it, then paint every single piece of metal a lovely glossy black. I would put it all back together and deliver it to Evan's door – I could probably even finish by that afternoon. And Evan would love it!

We had the spray paint in the garage. We had sand paper. We had a few big pieces of cardboard I could use to protect the garage floor. It was perfect. It was almost as if destiny had arranged everything in my favor. At least, that's what I thought at first. The cleaning and disassembly went smoothly enough, and after a few false starts with half-empty paint cans, I found one full of glossy black paint. I was having the time of my life. I was *building* something, making it better for someone I cared about. The process was messier than I thought, and the paint didn't cover as evenly or as glossily as I'd hoped, but the result was okay. I stepped back and looked things over, wishing we had a few more cans of paint to fill all those red blotches poking through the black. But, oh well, it would have to do. I went inside to grab a sandwich and allow the paint to dry, filled to overflowing with constructive satisfaction.

When I returned to the garage, I ran into an unanticipated snag. I realized, somewhat regretfully, that I wasn't at all confident of how to put the Radio Flyer back together again. I did try, but somehow I had misplaced the cotter pins for the wheels. And one of the axles didn't want to slide back into place. And the wagon handle seemed to only attach upside down. It was frustrating. I chewed on the problem for over an hour, but I wasn't getting anywhere. In fact, all my fussing had also scraped up the new paint job. I bit my lip and cast about for a solution. The sun was going down fast, and I didn't have much time if I wanted to return the wagon before dinner. I stared at my hands, which were covered with black paint, and realized I was probably going to get in trouble for using up all the paint we had in the garage. Things were not looking good.

The return trip to Evan's house was difficult. First, there was keeping all those loose parts from sliding off the cardboard as I dragged it along the side of the road. Second, there was the fact that the cardboard itself was beginning to break down. And lastly, pulling the heavy load was becoming harder and harder as my arms and hands began to tire. At long last, just as the sun was slipping down behind the trees in Evan's driveway, I made a final heroic effort to get the jumble of wagon parts up to his back door. Evan must have seen (or heard) me coming, and ran out to greet me.

"Hey!" he said, beaming. "What's that?"

"It's your birthday present!" I said, still a little out-of-breath.

"But what is it?" He asked, still excited but perplexed. And then he took a closer look at the pile of irregularly painted parts, and his expression changed.

"It's your wagon!" I declared, still trying to sound upbeat.

Evan stared in disbelief. *"What did you do?!* What…" his voice broke, "My wagon! What?! *Why…?"* he held out his hands, emphatically beckoning me to explain.

"I thought it would look better in black, but it didn't turn out exactly like I hoped."

"It's all in *pieces!"* Evan cried. Then, glancing over his shoulder, his incredulity shifted to fear. "My dad is going to *kill me,"* he whispered.

"No, I'll explain to him," I said quickly. "It was…it was *supposed* to be a present. It was supposed to be…better." I glanced at the remains of the Radio Flyer and, when I searched my heart for the truth, could not deny its obvious lack of improvement. "I'll explain to him, Evan."

Evan was shaking his head, covering his eyes with his hands. "I can't believe you did this..." He squatted by the cardboard and fingered one of the wagon wheels. "You'd better go. Before my dad sees."

As it turned out, that was good advice. By the time I returned home, my father had already received a call from Evan's dad. No one, it seemed, could understand what the hell I was thinking, or why the hell I had done what I did, or how the hell I was going to make it right. After that, I was not allowed to borrow Evan's toys. A few weeks later, when I saw Evan's father again, I apologized, but he was still angry in that calm, passive way of his. "You have to learn respect for other people's things, Todd," he said in a soft, penetrating tone. And then he walked away, bowing his head in disappointment.

§

Those early years on Harkness Road in Amherst were a breeding ground for invention. In part I was driven by boredom. The summer was long, hot and humid, and I had not bonded with many neighborhood kids during my first attempt at Pelham Elementary's second grade. There was also an ongoing competition with my step-sister, who could create amazing and complex works of art out of just about anything; although she leaned more towards the aesthetic than the practical, Shelly was endlessly creative. And of course there was the pattern of observing what other children in the neighborhood were up to, and wanting to emulate that. Having little skill, little adult guidance or supervision, and an endless array of highfalutin dreams left me little choice but to experiment with the materials at hand.

When three brothers who lived nearby began racing a lawnmower engine go-cart up and down the street, I just had to have one. So I salvaged some wheels off of an old baby carriage, screwed them into the ends of two two-by-fours, and affixed the two-by-fours to a stub of ten-inch planking with carriage bolts. For a brake, I screwed a foot-long garden stake to the side of the plank, so that pulling it back would lever it against the ground. Using a rope nailed to the ends of the forward axle for steering, and plywood padded with a blanket for a seat, I eagerly set off to test my new vehicle. With much excitement and fanfare, I persuaded my step-sister to join me for the virgin launch. Once she saw my questionable contraption, she was skeptical, but she followed along anyway, probably to ensure I didn't hurt myself too badly.

We clambered up to the top of the nearest hilly section of road, and I invited her to climb aboard with me for the first run. Shelly adamantly shook her head.

"Suit yourself!" I said, a bit disgruntled, and set off down the hill.

To my surprise, my go-cart whizzed nicely down the grade. So close to the ground, it felt like I was really flying. I grinned and whooped and swung the cart from side to side, showing off. Then I pulled back on the brake, and slowly came to a stop. I jumped off and danced in place, waving ecstatically at my step-sister. She waved back, smiling. "It worked!" she cried, clearly surprised. I hurried back to the top of the hill.

"Want to try it?" I asked. Shelly looked nervously at the cart, but I could tell she wanted to have a go.

"Is it hard to steer?" she asked, wringing her hands.

"It's easy…see, like this." I showed her how, if she pulled on the right side of the rope, she could turn to the right. Then I had an idea. "I can push you to make it go faster!" Shelly shook her head. "It'll be fun, I can just –"

"No." Shelly said firmly. She had learned over time that not all of my ideas were good ones. "Just let me do it."

"Okay," I conceded. And off she went, veering wildly from side-to-side as she sped down the hill. At first I thought she was going to crash, and ran down after her, both frightened and giddy, but by the time I reached bottom of the incline, Shelly had safely steered the cart to the side of the road. "I thought you were going to crash!" I cried, grinning at her.

"Well, I didn't," she said reproachfully. Frowning down at the go-cart, she added matter-of-factly: "It's not very safe."

"Let me, then. C'mon. I want to try it with you pushing me."

"I don't know…."
"Just one more time! Then we can ride it together…"

Shelly looked back up the hill. "It was *kind* of fun…" she said. I was thrilled at the hint of enjoyment in her voice.

So we tried it again. And again. We quickly learned that the key to speed was to keep the cart moving as straight as possible – not always an easy thing when we riding it together, clinging to the steering rope with separate sets of hands, but a worthy challenge on a sunny summer afternoon.

After a particularly speedy descent, a loud, braying laugh intruded on our excitement. It was Robby, one of the neighbor boys about my age. He was standing in the grass on the side of the road with Greg, the youngest of the three brothers who owned a *real* go-cart with a motor and steering wheel. Robby kept pointing and laughing, and Greg started to smirk a bit as well. "What a piece of junk! *What a joke!*" Robby yelled through his laughter. "Would you look at that thing! Haaa haaa haaa!"

My step-sister faced them with a defiant squint, and I could feel my face turning red. She stuck out her tongue, and Robby laughed even louder.

"It's just to test," I declared defensively. "My dad promised…we're gonna make one with a motor." Of course, that wasn't true, but I was suddenly very embarrassed about my creation.

"C'mon, Todd," Shelly grabbed my hand, "let's go ride some more." And we started back up the hill.

The laughter persisted until we began our run. This time we really gained speed, flying by the two boys at a reasonable clip, screeching and hooting until we came to a rolling stop. As we started back up the hill again, Robby tried once more to disparage us. "That things gonna fall apart!" he said confidently, but much of the sarcasm had ebbed from his tone.  Greg was staring at the go-cart, considering.

"Can I try?" Greg asked.

"What?" Robby cried, "You're gonna *kill* yourself on that thing!"
But Greg shrugged and began following after us.  "Can I?"

I glanced at Shelly – she looked wary but deferred to me.  "Sure, I guess," I said, a little reluctant to share my new toy so soon.  Would he give it back?  Would he try to crash it or break it?  One of the other local kids had once insisted on riding my new bike into a ditch on the side of the road, breaking the frame in half.  My step-mother had purchased the bike only a few hours before it was ruined, and I was devastated.  But I wanted Greg to have a try; I was humbled that he would even want to.  I handed the steering rope to him and let him walk our go-cart up the hill.

§

There were many other projects over the years, and similar themes percolated through them all.  When I was in third grade in Manchester, Connecticut, I decided to make something special for our weekly show-and-tell.  I took the innards of a walky-talky out of their case, and carefully arranged them inside of a metal Sucrets box.  I carefully threaded some wire around the antenna connector and coiled it inside, then painstakingly cut a hole in the side to access the volume dial.  If I just wanted to startle people with a talking Sucrets box, I would leave it just like that and use its companion walky-talky to communicate from another room.  And, when I wedged some folded paper against the "Talk" switch to hold it down...voilà, I had a covert listening device.  For some reason, I was obsessed with becoming a detective that year.  I even made myself a fake detective ID and fake gun permit, complete with my photograph.  Perhaps this stemmed from my early experiences interacting with law enforcement, or my father's interest in mystery novels, or my mother's desire to be a police officer herself, or my boyhood fascination with guns – perhaps it was all of these things.  But when I brought my creation to school and demonstrated it, no one believed that I had come up with the idea myself. Everyone wanted to play with the device of course, and it started quite a ruckus among the other students as they competed for some walky-talky time. Then one of the boys in the class – a very popular and well-liked boy – declared I was a cheater and a liar, that this wasn't my original idea, and maybe I had just stolen it from somewhere. When I began to defend myself, some of the other kids joined in on my condemnation. The teacher, despite reprimanding my accusers for their rash judgments, nevertheless asked me not to misrepresent my own abilities again in the future. And this became a recurrent theme in my childhood: no matter what medium or method, over the following years my efforts to improve, fix or engineer things often met with similar resistance.

Even my German step-grandfather, who was usually supportive of my efforts in his quiet, non-interfering way, displayed some of the same skepticism one sunny Spring day in Frankfurt, Germany. He had been such a great companion on our walks, such a patient fount of German culture and vocabulary, I wanted to do something nice for him. He had been complaining for months about the cost of watering his garden and orchard, and kept speculating about different ways he could capture rainwater to supplement what the city was providing. There weren't too many things Joachim complained about, but this was one. At other times, he would just express a sad sort of resignation about something he would like to change, but didn't have time for – but he was truly irritated about the cost of Frankfurt water.

Our three-story stucco house on Hammerskjöldring, near carefully planned suburb of Frankfurt called Nordwestadt, was located on the site of an old foundry. Every time we dug in the garden we would discovery old fragments of iron, metal working tools or deposits of charcoal. There was also one prominent artifact still visible above the ground, and that was a huge cast iron cauldron half-buried amid the pear and plum trees. It was about five feet tall, with a diameter of perhaps four feet, and based on the thickness of its riveted sides it weighed in the neighborhood of six hundred pounds. It was an accepted fixture in the back yard, like a giant boulder, too bulky and weighty to do anything about but work around. One afternoon, as I stood near the back door looking out across the orchard, my eyes settled on the jutting curve of this rusting goliath, and the answer to my grandfather's dilemma became obvious.

It took several hours to dig the cauldron free of earth, and the more I dug, the more nervous I became about my endeavor. It was shaped like a giant cup, tapering at the sides to a curved bottom. Even if I got it out of the ground, how would I move it to its new location? I shrugged and kept digging. I hauled the longest, thickest pair of spare water pipes I could find from the basement, and pounded them underneath the prone side of the cauldron with a sledge hammer to create a set of parallel tracks. Then I took my grandfather's longest pry bar – a rusty steel rod as tall as I was – and began the slow process of levering the cauldron up the makeshift tracks. When it would only budge an inch or to with tremendous effort, I greased the tracks and quickly got it sliding more easily. Eventually, I pushed the behemoth all the way up onto level ground. Now, could I just roll it across the yard? I tried. Straining with all my might, I managed to roll the cauldron over to a walkway that bifurcated the orchard. But that was as far as I could go. No matter how hard I hove, the tiny concrete lip of the walkway was too great an obstacle to overcome. I stared at it in disbelief, bracing my bare back against the warm slope of iron, and tried pushing a little harder.

Just then, my grandfather Joachim appeared in the back doorway. "What are you doing?!" he said, laughing nervously.

"I'm trying to move this cauldron!" I said, breathing hard.

"That's too heavy for you to move, Todd," he said with certainty.

"Well…yes, it is. If you are just going to stand there and watch. Or you could help me before it rolls back on top of me!"

Joachim suddenly sprang into action – he was spry for a man his age – and with both of us straining to our limit we managed to overcome the half-inch lip of the walkway and roll the cauldron forward another couple of feet.

"Thank you…" I panted, resting hands-on-knees.

"What are you attempting to accomplish here?" Joachim asked, truly puzzled. "You could have just left this in the ground…"

"Well…wait and see," I said, and smiled at him.

Joachim didn't press me; as usual, he would leave me to my own devices. "Ah well. If you need help let me know," he said, and sauntered back into the house.

In another hour or so, I was ready to deliver the cauldron to its new home. I had dug a hole next to the corner of the garage, right where the downspout from the gutters emptied out onto the lawn. The trick was going to be getting the cauldron into that hole. Using levers and boards to lift and brace, I gradually stood it upright. Then I laid two hefty boards across the top of the hole I had dug, and shifted the cauldron slowly from side-to-side, walking it forward inch by precious inch. Eventually, just as the sky began to dim and my stomach reminded me it was close to dinnertime, I got the cauldron out onto the boards over the hole. Miraculously, the boards held just long enough for me to center the mass of iron before they splintered with a loud crack. The cauldron dropped into the hole with a loud thud, and after I worked the broken boards out from the sides, it settled perfectly upright. I was pleased.

"Joachim!" I called, running into the house. "Joachim, you should come and look!" I was excited.

Joachim rose from his desk and followed me out into the yard. He stared at the cauldron, confusion plain on his face. "How did you…?"

"Is that a good place? I wanted you to be able to collect all the water from the gutters, for the garden…"

My grandfather's new rainwater catch basin

"Yes, that's good. I can just run this downspout over to it. But…" He laughed nervously, irritation flitting across his features. "You could have hurt yourself," he said, frowning, "it wasn't necessary." Then he shook his head, barked another quiet, disbelieving laugh, and walked slowly back inside the house. Of course I knew what this meant. Joachim had reacted the same way when I bought him a hand-crank circular bread slicer for his birthday the previous year. Because of injuries and arthritis, he could no longer easily hold a knife in his hands, and regularly cut himself while carving off slices of rustic German bread. "Why waste good money on a fancy bread cutter?" he had declared, incredulous. "We don't need one of these!" But Joachim nonetheless took to using the circular slicer two or three times a day. Of course, we didn't need a rain barrel, either, but in the end the iron cauldron suited him just fine.

§

I had so much time to myself during my years in Frankfurt, this pattern would be repeated many times. A hundred-and-one ways to make apple pies. Have you ever tried an apple pie made with green peppers? Or designing the best water trap to allow gases to escape from fermenting apple juice – some tasty hard cider can be brewed on a windowsill, let me tell you. Or creating a battery-driven lighting system for my bicycle. Or perfecting an optimal pedaling method for maintaining high speeds on busy Frankfurt streets over long distances. But my favorite solution was something I designed for my Dutch step-grandmother, Maria.

Maria was generally a soft-spoken person, at least with me. After dinner, we would spend an hour or so watching news together on the TV. She would explain the political backdrop for each of the news stories, and clue me in on some of the European history that informed current events. It was a heady exercise. She seldom spoke about herself or her own history, however, no matter how often I pestered her. Where Joachim had let me interview him about his World War II experiences, Maria was reticent and deflecting, fluid and deft at shifting the conversation away from her past back to the present. One evening, as our little ritual of Q&A played itself out, I asked her why no one had realized what was happening in the German death camps during the war.

"Well now," she said, "there's knowing, and then there's *knowing*."

"What do you mean? How could people not know what was happening?"

Maria shifted in her leather chair and stared at the TV. "People didn't want to admit what might be happening, but they suspected. No one really *knew* for sure, though. Not until after the war."

"Did you know? You were a nurse, weren't you?"

Maria pursed her lips. Her gray eyes sparkled behind her glasses. "Yes, I was a nurse."

"So…did you know about the camps?"

"What was to know?" Maria's gaze remained centered on the television. "In America, did everyone know how slaves were being treated in the

South?  We had problems, and the problems were being solved, just like in America."

I wasn't following her.  Had I understood her correctly?  "You think the way Americans treated black slaves was…the same as how the Nazis treated the Jews?"

"Yes.  Why not?  You had your blacks, we had our Jews."

I was stunned.  I had never heard her reveal prejudice of any kind before.  She had always seemed reasonable and gracious.  "When you say problems…what do you mean?"

"Problems of life.  No work.  No morals.  Everything falling apart."  She gestured at the TV.  "It's getting that way all over again."

Then I realized that Maria had done it again.  She had managed to shift the focus off of herself.  I tried once more.  "So…when you worked at the hospital, did you – "

"We had so little," Maria broke in.  "No medicine.  Not enough equipment.  You know, we didn't even have a vacuum cleaner."

I was confused.  "Why would you need a vacuum cleaner – ?"

"I wish they would make a vacuum cleaner that was easier to use on stairs.  I think my back is going to go out if I keep carrying that thing up and down, up and down.  I even get tired from pulling it around the house, it's so heavy.  If old women are the ones using vacuums, why can't anyone make a vacuum cleaner for old women?"

It was pointless, so I gave up.  We sat in silence and finished watching the news.

The next day, I took a look at Maria's vacuum cleaner.  It was an ancient canister vac, with an extra-long hose so that she could, in fact, get half way up the stairs before having to carry the vacuum to the next landing.  I turned it on.  It was loud, and gave off the pungent wreak of old carpet, but it had great suction.  I turned it off and stared at it awhile.  Smiling to myself, I grabbed the vacuum and took it down to my grandfather's workroom.

The next day, my grandmother sought me out. "Have you seen the vacuum cleaner?"

"I'm making it better for you, Maria."

"Making it better?"

"Just another day or so and I'll be finished."

Maria looked concerned. "Please don't break it," she said.

It actually took two days, because I had to calculate the length of each of the blades on the centrifugal fan, and that required some help from a math teacher at school. I had done the rough math using simple arc geometry and some hand measurements, but I wanted to be sure. The math teacher got pretty excited showing me how to use imaginary numbers for a more precise calculation, and invited me to join one of his classes to learn more, but all I cared about were the results for this project. Once I had those, I could determine the volume of air produced by the fan at a certain rpm. As it turned out, this was a complete red herring, because all I really needed to do was construct a model and experiment. Still, taking the long way introduced me to a new and interesting mathematical lens for viewing the world.

The next day, I was ready to execute my plan. It took surprisingly little time, and within a few hours I had a prototype ready for my grandmother to try. I brought the reconfigured vacuum cleaner back upstairs and presented it to Maria. "There it is!" I said, grinning.

"What is this?" Maria asked, staring over her magazine at the mutated vacuum cleaner.

"It's your new vacuum. Come, let's try it out." I plugged the vacuum into the wall and handed the wand to Maria.

"What do I do?" she asked nervously.

"I'll turn it on, and then you can test it. See if it works on the stairs." I had a moment of self-doubt then...I hadn't thought about how steep the stairs were. "Ready?"

"Well...yes. I suppose we could..."

I turned it on. Just as it had in the workroom, the vacuum cleaner's exhaust port quickly filled the generous plenum. The improvised skirt billowed and the vacuum rose smoothly off the ground. The trickiest part, of course, was making sure the weight of the vacuum was perfectly distributed on its cushion of air so it wouldn't wander to and fro. I wondered if that would change as the dust bag began to fill up, but no matter...right now, it was hovering perfectly still above the hardwood floor.

"Oh, for the love of heaven!" Maria muttered. She was delighted. "And will it...?" She began to walk around the room, and the vacuum obediently followed her. Maria often laughed or smiled, but she never let her teeth show – they were gapped, a little crooked and badly stained with coffee; I think she was embarrassed by them. Today, however, she displayed them all in a wide and generous grin.

Over the next few weeks, the hovercraft-vacuum proved itself to be capable of many surprising things. It could, in fact, easily navigate the stairs, and Maria didn't have to pick it up anymore as she moved from floor to floor. It blew surprisingly little dust around in its wake, and made my grandmother's chores much easier. It was even quieter now, as the fan's noise was routed down into the muffling plenum. Unfortunately, my creation had two unfortunate side-effects. The first was that it terrorized our dog, Razi. Previously, he had always been irritated by the vacuum's noise, but now he became aggressive and utterly hysterical as he beheld the slow, predator-like drifting of the hovering canister across the room. The other minus was that whenever my grandmother rounded a corner a little too quickly, the vacuum became a kind of bola weapon, smashing into anything along in its wide, floating arc. After the hovervac nearly toppled an end table by careening into one of its beautifully carved legs, my grandfather politely requested I return to the appliance to its previous state.

So I did just that. For weeks afterward, I heard Maria casually dropping hints around her husband about how wonderful the hovervac had been, and what a shame it was that she didn't have something so convenient to use anymore – something made especially for an old woman.

## The Joy That Remains

What did I learn from all of these experiences? How did they inform my self-concept over time? How are these memories grouped to support my ongoing sense of self, especially concerning inviting joy into my life? First, let's take an inventory of the key impressions these memories have left me with:

- My own learning often requires an immediate, problem-solving situation to motivate me. I have a goal, an envisioned outcome, and I require information, skills and creative synthesis to achieve it. This, in turn, provides satisfaction upon completion of a given task – my new knowledge is useful, I know how to apply it, and that is in itself a chief component of my satisfaction. Knowledge for its own sake is interesting, but it doesn't seem beneficial to me without the context of a more immediate and compelling goal.

- Nearly everyone I have ever known has consistently doubted some aspect of my abilities, insights, knowledge, capacities or potential. In seemingly reflexive way, I have been offered skepticism and resistance to most of my ideas and efforts. Even smart, loving, accepting and supportive people – even those closest to me, who knew me the best – have had difficulty recognizing the value of my musings, the credibility of my claims or the helpfulness of my efforts. I'm sure that, at least in part, this is because I see the world differently than other people. In certain areas, I see possibilities instead of obstacles; solutions instead of failure; opportunity for improvement instead of futility. This has been a natural barrier that often coincides with many of the things that bring me joy.

- The felt experience of certain kinds of creative effort is the source of greatest satisfaction for me. It is how I feel when I play piano or guitar that matters, not how technically well I play. It is how a story affects my heart that draws me forward – how I feel about the characters, the wonder and mystery of the world in which they live, and so on – rather than the structure of the story or the beauty of the prose. It is the accuracy with which my words capture my own emotional intent that satisfies my itch to write. It is the emotional gratification of a well-composed photograph that inspires me, not its journalistic or historical value. The more technical and analytical aspects of these disciplines interest me greatly – immersing myself in them satisfies me on another important level – but it is not the spring from which my deepest joy flows.

- Helping others has always been a major contributor to my satisfaction as well. Whether I am successful or not, the initial spark for creating challenges for myself is the desire to somehow add value to someone else's existence. This, in turn, adds value to my own. And even when I am doubted, even when others deride my efforts, part of me is comforted by how often those efforts are ultimately embraced, expanded and relied upon by those who initially questioned them.

- It takes planning, study, consultation, cooperation, hard work and courage to accomplish almost anything worthwhile. At the same time, most of my effort has been solitary, because I could seldom find anyone who was willing to fully share my vision. Having passion isn't enough by itself, but it certainly helps...and the only person I could rely upon to be passionate was me.

What does all of this mean? There are many choices of meaning here. If all of my experiments had turned out the same way as Evan's wagon, I'm sure I would have concluded that I should avoid fixing things, stay away from tools, and desist trying to gift people with happiness through my handiwork. Thankfully, Evan's wagon was the exception rather than the rule. What if the foundry cauldron had fallen on me and broken some bones? What if my go-cart had crashed on its first run, or my step-sister Shelly had been badly hurt? What if my hovervac had burst into flames or somehow infuriated my grandmother?  In all of these attempts, the joy I received through my efforts was immediate.  Others benefited.  I benefited.  There was ample evidence that taking such risks in the future would serve others even as it entertained me.

Similarly, the consequences of reading and writing, playing music and composing songs were, for the most part, also positive.  However, there is a notable difference here.  In these areas, the element of service to others is a bit less tangible, and sometimes altogether absent.  Sure, when I have entertained folks at parties, or written a love song for a romantic interest, the music did benefit others.  When people have let me know that a book or essay has helped them in some way, that also reinforces the "value add" component of my creativity.   And of course there is nothing quite like the quality of intimacy that reading a favorite book aloud with loved ones can create.  Yet, in the main, these have been more personal, solitary and self-sustaining acts.  To make music alone in my room has nourished my heart and soul, but what if no one else hears it?  To write a poem that captures the reality of my inner landscape at that moment is cathartic and enriching for me, but what if no one else ever reads it?   Throughout my life, I have discovered that when the component of service is absent from my self-nourishing efforts, I tend to attenuate them.

What we begin to see among this grouping of memories are not only the sources of my joy, but also sources of impediments to joy, and this is very important.  Here again we encounter the dichotomy of patterns of memory as they are expressed in patterns of self.  Creative passion is vital, but so are social acceptance and, in a larger sense, confirmation that we can contribute something valuable to society.  Both bring me joy in different ways, but they have been very difficult to combine.  In my own life, the two have often been in direct competition with each other.  Only through persistent, disciplined focus in a limited number of areas have I been able to endure that long, hard journey that integrates my inner creative world with my social interactions.  On balance, I have sacrificed a great deal – family, financial security, intimate relationships, and bucket loads of social capital – in order to nurture my artistic muse.  At the same time, I have tried to compliment this with healing and compassionate effort towards others.  This remains an ongoing dialectic in my life.

That said, there are also memories where these seemingly competing avenues to joy coalesced into one magnificent and complimentary rhythm.  In my final years of High School in Frankfurt, Germany, I discovered a strong affinity for theatre.  I had dabbled earlier – as far back as fifth grade – but my High School experience was unique.  After a couple of productions at the school itself, and some acting competitions and workshops around Germany and England, I auditioned for an ISTA production of Arthur Miller's *The Crucible*.  It was a travelling troupe of actors gleaned from international schools all over Europe, and we would end up performing in several Northern European cities.  There is nothing quite like the bond between members of a travelling theatre troupe.  Nothing like the thrill of losing oneself in an emotionally intense role night after night.  And there is nothing quite like getting a standing ovation in Paris.  This seemed to be the perfect combination of artistic passion, social acceptance and service to others, and I was high on the whole experience.  I thought I had found a truly integrated bliss.

Alas, after my arrival in Seattle, Washington at age eighteen, I was confronted with the harsh realities about of what does and does not generate income.  The performing arts simply do not pay a living wage.  In my efforts to buy groceries, pay rent, and save up for my first car, my passions for theatre, music and writing were shelved in favor of jobs selling cameras, TVs, vacuum cleaners and, ultimately, computers.  In the process of assisting customers with their many questions,  I began to tutor people on their new electronic gadgets – help them print out their files, connect equipment, repair faulty floppy drives, etc.  And in so doing I returned to that other childhood passion:  fixing things.  Without my really planning to do so, this became a very lucrative career in information technology, and my main source of income for the next fifteen years.  And so simple survival dictated where I turned for joy to a large degree.

Ultimately, after allowing multiple dimensions of creativity to languish for close to a decade, I arrived at the conclusion that making lots of money and exercising one very narrow slice of my being – the satisfaction of technological problem-solving – was not equivalent to joy.  Sure, I could buy cameras and synthesizers and guitars and sophisticated word processing programs on really cool computers, but throughout my information technology career I simply didn't have the time, energy or emotional bandwidth for deep creative expression.  My life was consumed with highly structured *doing* within a very confined sense of self, and all the aspects of me that required spaciousness – my artistic muse, my spirituality, my aesthetic sensibilities, my desire to commune with nature – were not allowed to flourish.  Not surprisingly, I began having serious health problems.  And that, in turn, inspired a herculean effort to create a more balanced, multidimensional existence.

## Applying AMR

Has anything changed?  I still need to connect creative activities with service, but I have made much more room for them in my life.  I still have to make a living, but that is now balanced with making space and time in my life for my spirit, heart, soul and mind to breathe.  I still need to help people, but I allow myself more of those quiet, self-absorbed moments to write, read fiction, compose music and capture interesting perspectives with my camera.  In large part because of this, I have more joy in my life than ever before.  Life can still be stressful, but the stress in moderated by the contentment of both service to others and nurturing these important parts of self.

What I have really done is created space and time in my life for joy and passion, and vigorously defended those opportunities.  Whenever I write or musicize, I do so in a sacred physical space I have consecrated to that purpose.  I turn the phone off and won't answer my front door.  I no longer distract myself with the fantasy of making a living with my photography, nor am I compelled to perform theatre, music or spoken word, because performance is not the main substance of my self-nourishment.  I still seek to serve others with my work, and this book is certainly a testament to that, but I no longer struggle with the tension between making creativity a priority in my life and trying to garner acceptance and approval for this passion from others.  I have befriended writers, musicians, artists and patrons of the arts who understand, appreciate and support my desire to create.  My girlfriend, Mollie, is a visual artist who completely accepts my need for this self-absorbed time.  So for the most part these relationships allow me to pursue my dreams without insisting I conform to external pressures or expectations.  And since the default arrangement of episodic memory supports these conclusions quite well, I have not found the need to reorganize it.

This does not mean that the five core AMR practices haven't helped me with my creative or service-oriented efforts, or that I don't consider the five steps of the AMR process as I negotiate with my muse. In particular, it has been essential to generate goals, activities, environments and language that support my creativity. Yet so many of my accomplishments have been a product of sheer willpower – investing in a new idea with action, and then just holding on for the ride – that I sometimes prefer to flow with the momentum of my efforts rather than pause to evaluate my choices. I have written elsewhere that I believe artists are the priests and priestesses of the mystical continuum, and I still believe that to be true. In fact I would expand this to include any creative effort, for even technical problem-solving and scientific inquiry rely on intuition and mystical perception-cognition to synthesize truly ingenious outcomes. The impulse to create on almost any level is intimately bound with our spiritual ground. And of course the AMR practices and process are themselves a creative undertaking, relying on the same engines of volition, insight and intimacy with our innermost being to generate a revised map of self. Fore me, joy and passion have become inseparable from the ongoing journey of revising my identity, burrowing through autobiographical memory and exploring my metastructures of being – after all, these are where my most creative ideas originate.

Finally, we return to the application of compassionate affection to this particular family of episodic memories. There are probably two areas that are of most significance here. The first centers around my reaction to all the skepticism, incredulity and ostracizing of my early years. The more I encountered this, the more I tended either to become argumentative and strident, or to disengage altogether in a disappointed huff. I recognized that neither of these responses were particularly helpful, but I wasn't sure what else to do. As an adult, in the context of managing staff in the workplace and other relationships, I gradually learned that it was often important to allow others space and time for their own process, to empower them to make decisions or find solutions on their own. I could guide, encourage, suggest and collaborate…but it wasn't required that my advice be heeded or the validity of my insights be recognized. So, as I developed a keener compassion for my fellows, I began to let go of my need to be heard or appreciated.

This was further amplified as I began counseling couples and individuals, and teaching courses about mysticism and *Integral Lifework*. In such endeavors, everyone needs to find their own way via their own motivation, insights and strategies. I can offer assistance in the process, but that is all. Of course, in some of the other work I do, disciplines where I am viewed as an expert or go-to guy for solutions, I am expected to provide definitive answers, not manage a collaborative problem-solving process. So the opportunity for irritation and impatience is still there, lurking in plain sight. And as any of my friends could tell you, once I allow myself to be put in the position of being "the knowledgeable party" – or even when I feel particularly passionate about something – I tend to shift out of my co-creative mode onto a more pedantic soap box. So there is still room for improvement; I could still exercise more compassionate affection toward others during debates about politics, while defending Nature, or when offering opinions about movies, concerts, books or plays. There is always opportunity for growth.

The second area that demanded a steep learning curve was applying compassionate affection to my artistic impulses. Here I had to accept that I was allowed to care for myself, that I didn't need to feel guilty about nurturing my creative side. There are still moments when, as I sit down to read a science fiction or fantasy novel, or play my guitar, or write a poem, I find myself having to justify the indulgence. "It's okay," my inner voice will tell me, "You emptied the garbage, returned those phone calls, ran those errands, and scheduled your work for tomorrow. Now you can do this pleasurable thing. Really!" The compassionate affection here is directed at me, of course. Do I deserve to have joy? Do I deserve to relax? Does my muse deserve to be heard? If I truly care for myself, then joy, relaxation and self-expression will be a part of a balanced existence. And the more I engage this side of me, the more balanced, centered and happy I feel. I thereby create new patterns that demonstrate the importance of caring for myself, and the reflex to continue these joy-inducing modes encounters less resistance from the editor within.

## CHAPTER SEVEN: TRUST & INTIMACY

Some of the most formative patterns of memory involve how we experience trust. What have we learned is reliable and safe? What things did we discover can't be relied upon? Have we trained ourselves to deny or restrict some types of experience because we were betrayed or let down in certain situations? Do we now compensate for lack of trust in one arena, while trusting fully and unconditionally in others, because of events from long ago? In this way, trust comes to represent the level of intimacy, openness and vulnerability we allow to inhabit a given situation in the present. It also represents the nourishment potential of that situation. If I trust from experience that a carrot will nourish me and not make me sick, I am much more likely to be nourished by a carrot. If I know I can rely on a person to care for me when I am sick, I am more likely to allow them to care for me. If my past track record of following through on a commitment I have made to myself demonstrates I am trustworthy regarding my own well-being, my well-being will be facilitated by the trust I place in myself. And whenever I have been repeatedly disappointed or severely injured because I trusted something or someone, the nourishment I receive in those areas will become increasingly restricted the more that reliance is proven to be misplaced.

For the first year or so of our lives, trust is reflexive and nearly unlimited. Everything is assumed to edible – or at least chewable. Everywhere is safe to explore. Everyone is safe to be around, at least as long as one of our parents is with us. Every situation is given the benefit of the doubt of being safe, interesting, fun and nourishing until it is proven otherwise. The same is true of the information we absorb at that age. All language is normal and permissible. Everything we are told about the world is accepted as true. All explanations about the events we observe are believable.  Even our own imaginings – our own irrational fears, our own suppositions about cause and effect, our own conclusions about what is happening and why – are embraced as trustworthy and real.  And all of this openness, all of this eager inhaling of the world, allows us to be fed, to grow and be nurtured.  It allows us to have confidence in our own abilities, in the kindness and competence of others, and in the physical laws of the Universe.  It allows us to succeed as biological, socially cooperative organisms while at the same time celebrating the freedom of our will.

This all sounds exciting and natural.  And yet, what if that newfound confidence was never challenged?  What if we never failed?  What if our reliance on someone or something was never undermined?  What if, as a consequence, we never experienced boundaries to our freedom or our will?  On the one hand, perhaps that would provide us the momentum to achieve great things, unhindered by any checks or balances.  On the other, it appears that our current reality does contain inherent checks and balances, mainly so that no one individual or organism can dominate all others.  Perhaps if we were a primarily cooperative species rather than a competitive one, we wouldn't require such limitations.  But history informs us that without clear restrictions to our being, as enforced by consequences that are sometimes painful and even life-threatening, we would not succeed as individuals or a species.  We would be crippled by wild imaginings and incorrect assumptions that were never contradicted or adjusted.  Our ever-enlarging will would run amok, trampling everyone and everything around us.  We would consume things that are more harmful to us than nourishing, and our consumption impulses would quickly get out of control.

Thus a child of age two has already begun learning to test what should and shouldn't be trusted.  Is that stranger really safe?  Is this new food really edible?  Are the rules my parents have imposed on me really valid?  Is this or that behavior really inappropriate?  Perhaps this is a natural developmental stage that would occur regardless of the rearing environment.  But it also makes sense that, having already experienced the unreliability of certain things, children begin to decide for themselves rather than rely on blind and boundless trust.  There was the drink that was too hot and burned our tongue.  The box that was too flimsy to support our weight, resulting in a painful fall.  The words we spoke that made others laugh at us in an embarrassing way. A casual activity we chose to pursue that invited concern or anger from our parents. And so on.

So there is a dynamic equilibrium to trust. If we trust too little, we won't be nourished or supported. If there are no boundaries to our trust, we tend to become overconfident or take dangerous risks. Somewhere in between is a middle ground where we learn that confidence in certain circumstances must be moderated by caution, or renewed curiosity, or critical thinking, or careful forethought. Understanding how to navigate that middle ground is a major component of maturity as we grow up. Depending on how we were raised, our natural aptitudes and our early childhood experiences, most of us already have a rapidly expanding understanding of this middle ground – and its importance to our survival – by age five.

Of course, this is not always the case. Some children continue to rely on certain harmful assumptions or relationships even when their trust is gainsaid by negative consequences. For instance, children in abusive households might continue to believe their parents or siblings are being fair, kind, loving and just, even as the abuse escalates in frequency and severity. Children who have been conditioned to rely on the authority and guidance of other abusive individuals – relatives, babysitters, teachers, community leaders, etc. – may similarly continue to bear injury and exploitation without complaint. Why? Because in the only world these children know, their survival depends on perpetuation of these trust relationships, even though that survival may be fundamentally painful and miserable.

There are also instances where a child's innate wiring either pushes them to constantly rail against all boundaries imposed on their will, or, at the other extreme, acquiesce too readily to imposed constraints. In both cases, such children won't learn to recognize importance of a middle ground of thoughtful, negotiated trust, and have trouble navigating it later in life. In my worldview, almost all severe cases of such underdevelopment are the result of unsupportive childhood environments. Regardless of the cause, however, the impacts are devastating. Why? Because as we learn whom and what can be trusted, we also learn how to be trustworthy ourselves, and this progress defines many aspects of our character.  Our capacities for loyalty, honesty, integrity, kindness and devotion, for example, are defined by our exploration of trust.  So a young person who has not learned these things will struggle to be comfortable with themselves and others, and will likely find themselves disconnected from society as whole, or overly dependent others to define trust relationships for them, or be unable to relax into sustained intimacy.

We can apply this concept to later stages in life as well.  One way to look at adolescent rebellion is a renegotiation of trust relationships that were previously taken for granted.  We rebel because we need to redefine all mutual reliance according to our emerging definition of a more independent identity, a more clearly defined sense of self.  In this sense, parental or societal boundaries represent the trust agreements of our prevailing culture.  If we never rebel, if we never renegotiate trust, some part of us will always question our ability to create new trust agreements on our own.   Instead, we will be dependent on others to guide us through our most important decisions, because we never asked why things are the way they are – we never challenged the status quo.

As an adult, if I have not developed healthy and sustainable trust habits in relating to others and my own self-concept, I will not be free to live my life consciously or mindfully.  Instead, I will be trapped within a rigid and restrictive maze that leads nowhere but back on itself.  I might be paranoid and mistrustful in order to avoid risks.   I might be dependent or codependent to feel safe.  I might remain Pollyannaish and naïve so I don't have to think critically or examine my life too closely.  I might cleave to extreme or irrational beliefs for a sense of security.  And I will repeat this unskilled navigation of my relationships over and over again, even though the result is more often than not confusion, failure, isolation, disappointment, guilt, anger, hurt or grief.  In fact,  if I never address this pattern, my tolerance for cognitive dissonance will increase until I become numb to the stark contrast between my beliefs about the world and what is actually happening around me.  If this occurs, I am likely to cling desperately to my most incoherent and destructive illusions, because they are the only comfortable explanation for my own inadequacies and the apparent hostility of the Universe.   And, of necessity, I will defend these illusions vehemently, to my very last breath.

I believe this explains a lot of humanity's most intense struggles, both in the past and in the present. Trust, whether conscious or unconscious, is the chief operating component of all interdependencies in our lives. And our patterns of memory concerning trust determine the patterns of trust we experience in the present. What, then, are my own experiences in this regard? How did my childhood shape me? Did I learn to navigate the precious middle ground, or am I still lost in illusion? Let's take a peek at my past and see what we can see.

## Authority

When were are small, it can seem like nearly every one assumes they have authority over us. According to those who knew me as a child, I was apparently never comfortable with that assumption. In fact, I fiercely rejected anyone's attempts to corral or contain me. During my earliest years in Eugene, Oregon, there was plenty of loud rhetoric about sticking it to the man; resisting the establishment; not trusting anyone over thirty; tuning in, turning on, dropping out and so forth. Perhaps some of this worked its way into my developing psyche. But what reinforced this attitude more rapidly than the cultural memes of the time was the bizarre and often threatening behavior of the adults all around me.

Up until my reintroduction to elementary school in fifth grade in Amherst, most people in positions of authority and responsibility in my life seemed both untrusting and untrustworthy from my childhood perspective. My memories of them are replete with mistrust, betrayal and deception, which often seemed to result in emotional and physical harm to me. As much as I wanted to feel safe and cared for, I could not rely on others to provide such things. Certainly this was not always deliberate on their part – as with my parents, who were constitutionally incapable of creating a calm, stable and reliable environment for a child. With others, however, there was an added dimension of malicious intent. Many people seemed to resent aspects of my personality – I often engaged adults with a particularly grating mixture of precociousness, strident independence and vociferous or critical observations – and so I became the focus of pranks, bullying and anger from peers and adults alike throughout those early years. If only I could have kept my thoughts to myself, or presented myself as less observant and less articulate, or been less assertive and obnoxious, I'm sure my interactions with authority figures would have been a lot more pleasant. Then there were folks who were simply unsuited to be in positions of authority over anyone, who took out their frustrations on me because I was weaker, who were mean or abusive because, well, they could get away with it. And, of course, there were people I loved and respected who faltered in their kindness toward me, or injured me in ways they may not even have realized at the time, who nevertheless continued to represent an authoritative presence in my life.

During the last few years my mother and I lived in Eugene, I had a babysitter named Darlene. She was a lovely young woman with blonde hair and blue eyes who lived only a few blocks away from us, and she was one of very few people who could get me to do things I didn't want to do. I think I was probably smitten with her from the first day I saw her. She was certainly a godsend for my mother, who wrote frequently in her letters at that time how frustrating it was trying to find someone to babysit until Darlene came along. An earlier experiment had been the hippy commune next door to our house. The young students were generally high on something and inured to ideas of free love, so they let me wander around the neighborhood on my own reconnaissance. But once they discovered I was pilfering their penny jar for money to buy candy at the corner store, they scolded me for not appreciating communal values and sent me packing. We also tried a couple of stay-at-home moms who had kids of their own for me to play with, but that seldom worked out well. Not only was I difficult to manage, but I generally would lead other children into some sort of rebellious mischief.

Darlene was just twelve years old when she started babysitting me. In my memories of her she seems much older. She was already smoking cigarettes, wearing makeup and acting very adult for her age. But in reality she was just a teenager trying to find her way through the sixties. Sometimes we would stay at the house, and sometimes we would go hang with her friends, but I always felt safe around her. I trusted her. According to my mother, Darlene was one of very few people around whom I could just relax and be myself.

One warm summer day Darlene arrived late for babysitting. She was out-of-sorts, vexed about something, and as soon as my mother left the house, Darlene took my hand and swiftly led me back to my room.

"Hey!" I protested, startled by her sudden burst of energy.

Darlene let go of my hand and looked at me strangely. I had never seen that look before. She was smiling, but without any humor. Her eyes seemed larger, clearer and deeper than usual, like she was full of something that had to come out. "Want to see a match burn three times?" She asked. There was a forced lightness to her tone. I saw she was holding a cigarette and a box of matches in her other hand. I looked between the matches and her intense, searching eyes; between the cigarette and her unnerving smile. "No?" I said uncertainly.

"Sure you do!" she said enthusiastically. She knelt down beside me. "Here, hold your arm out."

I held out my arm. Darlene took a match out of the box and lit it.

"You know what a match is, right?"

I nodded.

"You know they burn?"

"Uh-huh."

Darlene grabbed my arm and ran the match beneath my hand. A flash of pain.

"Owe!" I tried to pull away, but Darlene held me firm.

"Wait! That was just the first time. Watch…it's like magic." But the smile was fading, replaced by something else. Something darker, fiercer and more menacing. She lit her cigarette, took a couple of puffs, and blew out the match. "See? The match isn't lit anymore." She pressed the smoldering tip into the soft flesh of my forearm.

"Darlene!" I screeched.

"Sshh. Be quiet now." She looked over her shoulder towards the front door, then turned back to me. "It hurts, doesn't it?"

"Stop it!" I said, getting angry now.

"Just one more…"

"No!" I tried again to pull free.

Darlene was concentrating, staring at my arm as if it were a foreign object. "This won't hurt much, and it's the last one. The last time," she said quietly. But she didn't seem to be speaking to me…she didn't seem to be in the room anymore. She was somewhere else, or perhaps someone else. Even so, I stopped struggling. She took the cigarette from her mouth and held its smoldering tip to my hand.

"Ooowwwwe!" I yelled, beginning to cry.

Darlene let go of my arm and stood.

"That *hurt!*" I accused, staring at the red spot on my skin and sniffing back tears.

She took a long drag on her cigarette and blew the smoke to one side. "It's a pretty neat trick, isn't it?"

I looked up at her. "You said it wouldn't!"

Darlene stared at me for a long moment, her expression first softening, then hardening again. "Todd. You're a big boy now, aren't you?"

I thought about it. "Yes!"

"Big boys don't cry every time they get hurt. Do they?"

I thought about that. "No. But – "

"But nothing," said Darlene, and she strode purposefully back to the living room.

§

One day, when I was about seven, my mother dropped me off with Jenny, a neighbor of my grandparents in Manchester, Connecticut. They had been neighbors for years, and Jenny and her husband, Byron, had provided a haven for my mother throughout her childhood, treating her like their own until they adopted a boy and girl when my mother was about twelve. Mom was so fond of them that her affections won me over as well, so that when we were introduced I quickly accepted Jenny as someone I could trust. It would only stay there for the afternoon, and Jenny seemed happy to have me. My mother had also confided that Jenny and Byron had special dust they could put in a fire to make the flames crackle and sparkle with rainbow colors. That sounded pretty cool.

I was there for perhaps an hour or so, following Jenny around the kitchen and the rest of the house, chatting away and very much looking forward to the fireworks that were promised. Suddenly Jenny's head snapped up from her work, and she scurried to the living room window. I heard a car pulling up outside, and wondered why Jenny was so distraught, pressing her hands to her breast and peering worriedly out at the street. "We have to go upstairs," she whispered. She hurried over to where I sat and tried to haul me up. "Get on up," she said "we need to go upstairs."

"Can I still see the fireworks?" I asked, not wanting to leave.

"Yes, yes! Now come with me."

We hurried up the stairs to one of the second floor bedrooms. Jenny fumbled with the latch of a floor-level cabinet and opened it. She was out of breath. "Todd, can you be a good boy and be very quiet?" She looked so worried. Her words were rushed.

I bit my lip and nodded.

"All right. Then climb in here. Right in here." She gestured through the open cabinet door, so I clambered in.

Jenny smiled hastily as I settled inside. "It doesn't look...there, see how much space – " We both heard the front door open and shut downstairs. Jenny's face betrayed her fear.

"I don't want to – " I began.

Jenny firmly covered my mouth with her hand. "Be quiet!" she hissed in a whisper. "Stay here and be quiet until I come back." I nodded as her hand pressed my face. I felt vaguely sick to my stomach, but I didn't know why. "He can't know that you're here! He – *please be quiet....*" She looked at me with worry, shook her head, then closed and latched the door. Her footsteps hurried off.

I looked around. A dribble of light leaked in around the edges of the cabinet door, enough to illuminate my surroundings once my eyes adjusted to the dimness. It was a spacious, dusty space, like a small attic. And it was stuffy warm. I pushed gently against the door, but it wouldn't budge. I considered pounding on it, or perhaps calling out, but Jenny's frightened manner and the urgency in her voice warned me against it. So I sat and waited.

A long time passed. I was sure she would be back soon, so I counted on my fingers. I caught myself humming and stopped. I tried to peer through the crack of the door, but there was only a sunlit bedroom with nothing moving in it. I listened, thought I heard voices, then all was silent. I waited. I waited some more. I felt around me and found a small sliver of wood sticking up from the planking. I picked at it. I started counting again, leaning back against a rough wood beam. I waited. The air was thick, hot and close. I fell asleep.

"Come on, dear..." Hands were pulling me, shifting me, and I flopped forward. I coughed. "That wasn't so bad, was it?" Nervous hands pushed matted hair on my forehead to one side. I felt a cool breeze and the hardness of the carpet. A trickle of sweat ran down my temple.

Something pressing against my lips. Something cool and round. I opened my eyes and drank greedily. The lemonade was liquid heaven. "That's good, isn't it."

I was outside the cabinet, in Jenny's lap. She looked different, but I couldn't tell why. Something had changed. She wasn't afraid anymore, but it was more than that. She smiled at me. I felt odd. Foggy. Sore. Exhausted.

I stopped gulping and clambered to a stand. "I have to pee," I said.

"Oh, well, yes," said Jenny.

§

When I was eight, I ran away from home. My mother had yelled at me because I'd forgotten to clean up my Legos. They were scattered all over the back patio in a chaos of red, white and blue, and she had stepped on them in her bare feet. She flew into one of her signature rages, promising there would be hell to pay if I didn't clean them up by the time she returned from food shopping. I was always trying to make her fall and break her neck, she claimed. When I began to protest that I wasn't finished building my Lego fort, she cuffed me angrily about the head and neck, screaming "Don't talk back to me! *Don't talk back to me!*" with each furious swat. Then she left for the grocery store, and I began plotting my escape.

Within an hour I was hiking over the Hockanum river on a railroad trestle. I'd grabbed some apples, some extra socks, and my dog, Soda Cracker, and stuffed them all into a vinyl duffle bag my father had given me. I liked the bag because it had a Dodger's logo on it, and because Soda Cracker could sit comfortably inside, her curious Beagle nose drifting from side to side as we walked. We made it as far as a small railroad yard before darkness settled over us, and to keep out of any rain that might fall in the night, we snuggled under one of the boxcars sitting empty on a side track.

We weren't entirely alone, as it turned out; there were others roaming the tracks. Men in big boots who talked quietly to one other as the rambled by with long, purposeful strides, heals and toes digging deep into the gravel. They didn't carry lights, so I figured that, like me, they weren't supposed to be there. The tracks weren't idle, either. Every now and then we heard a loud *thunk* of train cars mating in the night, followed by the slowly loudening squeal of escaping wheels. Soda Cracker kept completely quiet, and stayed in the duffle bag until she had to relieve herself, after which she returned to curl up next to me. Her silence warned me to keep quiet as well. We kept each other warm for several hours into the night. In the midst of our adventure there were comforting smells – sour grease, damp leaves, creosote and dirty gravel – and the familiar stillness of the New England woods. I thought that we were safe.

Then the car above us moved. Just a quick jolt and inching forward that signaled the car was now hooked to a train. I stared at an axle that was now moving closer to us, and realized with a shock that it was too low for either of us to squirm underneath. I had always assumed I would be able to duck a train axle if I ever fell on the tracks – now I realized I was wrong. Just as we scrambled out from beneath its bulk, the train car began to drift forward. We rushed across the yard to some surrounding trees and hunkered down to watch the darker shadows of the box cars slither forward through the night. I thought about how tired I was, and how thirsty. I hadn't brought anything to drink. At that moment Soda Cracker whined for the first time in our journey, and I glanced around hurriedly to see what might be approaching. There was nothing and no one in sight. "I guess you're right," I whispered to her. "It's time to go home."

We had been very secretive in our escape, but now I just wanted to take the fastest route back to the apartment complex. Navigating the railroad trestle and deep woods in the thick of night seemed foolish. So we struck out along the nearest road, walking as quickly as we could while the night grew colder and more still. I felt light-hearted and proud of what I had done, but at the same time a little guilty. I figured my mom was probably worried sick by now. I tried to speed up my pace, and thought about how I would maybe clean up those Legos on the patio before letting her know I had returned.

The policeman spotted us when we were about half-way home. I was already an expert at the "ducking headlights" game some of the kids in the neighborhood liked to play, and I quickly melted into the bramble beside the road before the cruiser was upon us. I waited, motionless, until I thought it was safe to reemerge, but this officer probably had some experience dealing with kids. When we returned to the road he was there waiting for us.

"Your name Todd?" The man's voice was close.

I was startled, glancing about for an escape, but there was no where to run. There was just a big policeman and his shiny cruiser, the eyes of each glinting softly in the night. "Yes," I admitted.

"You're mom's gonna be happy to see you," he said, stepping closer.

I couldn't believe my mom had called the cops. She hated cops. "I know," I said quickly, "We're on our way back."

The officer chuckled. "Oh yeah?"

"Yes!" I said confidently. "You can just let us walk back by ourselves."

"I don't think so," said the officer. And with that, he grabbed the collar of my jacket, swooped up my duffle bag complete with cowering dog, and tossed all of us into the back seat of his police car.

It was a short ride back to the apartments, but one of the longer ones in my young life. The officer told me how disrespectful I had been to my mother, running away like that. How evading a police officer was a crime. How, if he were my son, he'd give me a good whipping for it all, just so I wouldn't become a criminal. Did I know what a criminal was? And so on. When at last we stopped in front of my apartment, I positively ached to get out of that car. And there was my mother, silhouetted in the open front door, waiting. The officer let me out and I ran to her.

"I'm sorry mom!" I cried. Soda Cracker bound past me and disappeared inside.

"Oh, honey!  I'm just glad you're home."  She smothered me with a huge hug.  "Why did you disappear like that?"

"Ididn'twannacleanuptheLegosbutIwillnowI'msorryIwon'tdoitagain…"  It all spilled out in a rush, punctuated by loud snivels.

I heard the officer stroll up behind me.  "You ought to punish that boy," he said.  "You let him get away with that kind of crap and he'll just end up in jail someday."

"I was on my way back when he found me!"  I interjected.

"And I'm sure he'll lie his way right around that one, too."  The officer said, frowning.

"I'm not – !"

"Honey, go upstairs," said my mother.  "Go wait in your room."  She gave me a gentle push, and I went.

I listened to the officer droning on, with the occasional question or two from my mom.  After a while, I heard the door close, the cruiser pull away, and the footsteps of my mother slowly coming up the stairs.  She stood in the doorway of my room, wiping tears from her face.  She clutched a long belt in one hand.  "That cop…"  she began, her voice tight, "thinks I should beat you with this belt."  She looked down at the strap of black leather.  "He gave me his *own belt*, for Christsakes."

I stared at that belt, fixated, my chest growing numb.  "But mom – "

My mother shook her head.  "I don't know what I should do," she said.  And then, more quietly to herself, "I don't know what to do…."  Then, slowly, she turned and left.

I sat on the edge of my bed, holding my breath, waiting for her to return.  I was still thirsty, but I was too frightened to even think about getting a glass of water.  Soda Cracker, who had curled into a tight ball in the darkest corner of my bed, slowly unfurled and crawled quietly over to my side. I patted her head, scratched her ears, and whispered, "Good dog." She licked my hand. We sat there awhile. The clock by my bed said it was a little after midnight. Part of me was thrilled to have stayed up so late. I looked out the window of my bedroom at the streetlight in the parking lot. It glowed steadily, prodding the surrounding asphalt, trees and grass with a cold, blue-white light. That streetlamp had seen so much happen there in front of our home, but it just shone on indifferently into the night.

§

It was only a matter of time before my wild and willful nature collided with my mother's insecurities. At the end of my final year in Manchester, I received a dose of Ritalin from a psychiatrist who determined I was "hyperactive." I spent the rest of that day yelling random nonsense at the top of my lungs and running frantically around the house. This continued through the night, and although my antics were confined to by bedroom – using my bed as a trampoline – I managed to keep my mother and our neighbors awake most of the night. I finally collapsed, exhausted, just as the sun began to warm the sky. This was the final straw. My mother's friends told her I was possessed by an evil spirit. The psychiatrist suggested we adjust my dose of Ritalin. At wit's end, mom decided to have me committed to a children's ward at a hospital for psychological observation.

I have spent several months trying to discover where this hospital facility was located, but to date have been unsuccessful. My mother has, perhaps understandably, pushed memories of this time out of her mind. Perhaps someone who reads my description will be able to point me in the right direction. It was a lengthy drive from Manchester, perhaps thirty or forty minutes, and I remember a long, winding road through dense forest, and a tall, older style brick building painted white. There was a drab, brownish lobby and an elevator, and we made our way up to one of the upper floors. That was the children's ward, and I remember a long hall with a yellow vinyl tile floor, with a nurse's station on one side and rooms with two hospital beds each on the other. The windows of my room overlooked the trees and parking lot below, and there were many pale wood cabinets lining the floor and walls.

My mother cried as she said goodbye, promising to come visit me before the week was out. That was the first I learned I would be there for a week. I was distraught, but, as was often the case, I switched into my stolid caregiver mode so I could console and comfort my mother in her distress. "I'm sorry mom," I said. "I'm sorry." I must have done something really awful to end up here, I thought. That was enough to be sorry for. So I screwed up my courage and waved goodbye.

My first night was spent playing with a Matchbox car at the door of my room. It was late, and all the lights had been turned off except for those in the hall, so I squatted down on the linoleum and zoomed, vrrrooomed and puttered my car back and forth, back and forth across the tiles. A pair of thick calves sprouting from clunky white shoes appeared before me. I looked up.

"Lights out, young man. Time for bed!" She was an older, short woman with large breasts and squarish, thick-rimmed glasses. A nurse, I could tell by her uniform and cap.

"I'm just playing with my car," I said quietly. I was trying to be quiet because I knew the other kids were asleep. I thought it was strange that a nurse would talk at a normal volume with everyone sleeping.

"You can't be in the hall," she said, peering down at me. "You need to stay in your room."

I looked back over my shoulder. "I can't see. It's dark. That's why I came out here. I'll be finished soon." I returned to zooming my car back and forth.

"Oh, I see. You're one of the *those*," she said, and stomped off heavily down the hall.

Indignation welled up in me. "Yes," I said, a little louder than I meant to. The nurse slowed and turned to look at me. "I'm *one of those*," I said. And I went back to pushing my Matchbox car.

The next day a young man – a doctor, he said – came to ask me lots of questions.  He asked about school, about my mom, about what I was feeling.  He asked about the "incident" the previous evening when I talked back to the nurse.  He took a lot of notes.  I wondered if I was in trouble, but when I described the previous evening's exchange he seemed satisfied.  I asked him what there was to do at the hospital, and would I really be there a whole week, and when would my mom come to visit?  He said he would come back later that day to answer all my questions, but for now he had to go talk to other children.  So I was left with my cars, and the view out the window, and a bland meal on a plastic tray.

The doctor never returned.  I remember that first day fairly vividly.  There was a young boy a few rooms away who began to scream at about ten o'clock that morning.  There would be brief lulls when the screams receded to loud groans, but then they would start up again into full-throated hollering.  I poked my head out of the room a couple of times, but the nurses told me I had to stay inside.  "Why's that boy screaming?" I asked.  "He's having his dressings changed," said one of the nurses.  "He was in a fire, and has burns all over his body," she said.  I crawled into bed and tried to cover my ears with the pillow, but it was a thin, frail thing that wouldn't muzzle a mouse.  The screams continued well into the afternoon.

That evening they gave me some pills after dinner, and I fell asleep instantly.  When I woke the next morning, the young doctor was there again.  A nurse was with him, holding my arm and taking my blood pressure, listening to my heart, counting my heartbeats.  He smiled at me and I noticed he had yellow teeth.

"Good morning, Todd.  How are you feeling?"

I rubbed sleep from my eyes and sat up.  "You said you would come back," I said.

He seemed surprised.  "Did I?  Well, things became very busy yesterday."  He sounded a little stiff.

"You said you would come back," I repeated, still sluggish.

The doctor cleared his throat and nodded for the nurse to leave.  She frowned, gathered her papers and stethoscope, and quickly departed.

"I'm sorry I didn't come back," the doctor said, his tone mellowing.  "I'll try not to let that happen again."

I nodded, satisfied.

"Today we're going to do some tests.  How does that sound?"

"What kind of tests?" I asked, suspicious.  I wasn't very good at tests.  I got nervous and made mistakes, then got upset because I knew they were mistakes, and that made me more nervous.

"Just some standard physical and cognitive exams.  More questions like yesterday, and we'll check some other things to make sure you're healthy."

"Am I sick?  Is that why I'm here?"

The doctor hesitated.  "That's what we're going to find out.  It won't take very long, and then you can have the rest of the day to yourself."

I looked around the room.  "In *here?*"

The doctor chuckled.  "Maybe we can arrange some time outside.  Would you like that?"

I nodded solemnly.  "Yeah!"

"All right.  I have to leave again, but someone will come to get you soon so we can begin."  He began to leave, then remembered something.  "Do you need anything?  Anything…to be more comfortable?"

I thought about it.  "Can I open the windows?"

He shook his head.  "I'm afraid those have to stay locked.  I'm sorry about that."  He looked at me expectantly.

Then I remembered. "Oh! Slippers. Do you have any slippers? The floors are kind of cold."

"I'll see what I can do," he flashed a quick, yellowy smile, and was gone. I realized then that I had forgotten to ask him my questions again.

I remember only bits a pieces of that second day. Standing on a scale. A cold white room where they prodded my belly and poked my ears. I hated it when they poked my ears. A bright light and more questions about things I didn't always understand. The questions seemed like a big circle that never quite connected with itself. I was tense when all of this began, but slowly relaxed as the tests continued. And then it was lunchtime and I was back in my own room, sitting up in bed. Which is when the two men came.

They were big, dressed in white, and the were pushing a metal cart. They stopped outside of my room and I looked up expectantly. They looked in on me briefly and then stepped back out into the hall, muttering to each other in voices too soft to hear. I started to get out of bed, and I heard the young doctor. "You can go in," he said. And they did, wheeling the big metal cart between them.

"Hi Todd," said the doctor, entering behind them. "We need to do another test, and these men are here to help."

"Why?" I asked. I didn't like the men. They had a bland expression on their faces and wouldn't look me in the eye. One of them reached over and closed the door to my room.

"Well...we don't want you to hurt yourself, right? So they will help prevent any accidents." He waited.

"Okay." The doctor seemed nice enough. He hadn't hurt me yet. And he had apologized for lying to me. I supposed I could trust him.

The doctor nodded to the two men, saying to me, "All right, Todd. If you can just lie on your stomach for me."

I did.  The two men stepped to either side of the bed.  Their cool hands pressed lightly against my arms and legs.  I tensed.

"This won't hurt at all.  I want you to remain as still as possible."

I felt the cool hospital air on my back as my gown was drawn apart.  Then my legs were pulled open.  "Hey!" I cried out.

"It's all right, Todd.  Just try to remain still."

And then rubbery fingers spreading my butt cheeks, pulling me wider, probing.  "No!  Stop it!  *Stop it!*"  Hot panic coursed through me and I thrashed on the table.  The orderlies' fingers dug into my limbs as they gripped tighter.

"Just one more second," said the doctor, "and it will be over…"

"Noooo!" I was writhing frantically now, my whole body twisting and convulsing to escape those probing fingers.  I began to scream in earnest.  Just like the boy whose dressings had to be changed, only louder and, if anything, more desperate.  The probing continued.  I tried unsuccessfully to bite one of the hands that held me, tried kicking myself free, anything to escape what was happening.  The probing stopped, but still I struggled.  I was all panic and rage.  Metallic clinking sounds from the cart.  A sharp prick in my left buttock and a brief flash of stinging heat.

Then my mind clicked off.

The next thing I remember was waking in my bed, face up this time.  It was late in the day, and I looked groggily around the dim room.  There was a plastic bag full of liquid hanging beside my bed, and I followed its tubes downward toward my arm.  I could feel a thick layer of tape on my forearm, but when I tried to lift it I found my wrist strapped in place.  I woke up fully then, trying to shift on the bed.  My hands and feet were bound with leather straps lined with foam.  I pulled frantically against them.  Slowly, I worked one hand free of the strap by pulling out the foam.  Then I undid the buckles on all the others and launched from the bed.  My legs gave out and I tumbled to the floor, and the tape ripped off my arm with a flash of pain as I fell. I scrambled to the door and tried the handle. It was locked.

Peering out the window, I could see the nurses' station a few feet away. There was no one there, and no one in the hall. Maybe I could break the window? But it had wire mesh like the ones at school, and might be too narrow for me to squeeze through. What, then? I looked around the room, and my salvation became evident. Without a thought I ran to the second bed in the room and pulled. It was heavy, barely shifting on the linoleum, but using the handles of nearby cabinets for leverage, I managed to pull it in front of the door. Then I pushed my own bed against the other, creating what I thought was a formidable barricade. I'd show them! What now? I should hide. Hide so they thought I had escaped; so they wouldn't try any more tests. Standing on one of the beds, I clambered into a cabinet above the counter and closed the cabinet door. I smiled, pleased with myself, and nestled against the neatly stacked sheets.

Hours passed. Once I thought I heard someone working the door handle, but no one tried to enter the room. I was disappointed. Didn't they think I was gone? Didn't they want to look for me? I would hold my breath if they did, so they couldn't tell where I was hiding. But no one came. Occasionally I would open the cabinet door and peek out, just to make sure. Eventually, as real darkness began to creep into the room, I realized my error. They wouldn't believe I had escaped if the beds were up against the door! So I painstakingly returned the beds to their original places, then returned to my hiding place. More time passed. I had to pee, and I was getting hungry. Gingerly, I lowered myself down out of the cabinets. I risked a glance out the door's window into the hall, but all seemed quiet there. I tried the door latch. It was now unlocked.

I can't tell you how exciting that moment was for me. I could escape! I could get away from this crazy place with the screaming, burned boy and the rude nurse and the probing doctor with his burly helpers. With painstaking slowness, I cracked open the door. There was no one in sight. I crept barefoot out into the hall, my hospital gown flapping around me, and searched the area for a way out. Just a few feet away was a sign I recognized: Stairs. Checking one more time for witnesses, I bolted for the end of the hall and pushed open the heavy metal door. On the other side, brightly lit concrete steps descended. I took them two-at-a-time, jumping the last few at each landing until I reached the bottom.

As I pushed open the door to the lobby, I instantly realized my mistake. I couldn't casually stroll right out through the front door, not in bare feet and a hospital gown. But then again, why not? I started across the carpet. There were a couple of adults in the lobby. An older couple heading for the elevator, and a middle-aged woman in a light blue dress entering through one of the other lobby doors. I could see the parking lot beyond the glass doors of the entrance. I could feel the cool breeze waft against my face as the doors opened and a distinguished man in a pressed gray suit stepped through them. I made for the entrance.

"Ho ho!" said the man in the suit, blocking my way. "Where are you off to?" I tried to get around him, but he stepped back against the glass door, making it impossible for me to open it. I looked up at him. He reminded me a little of the East Indian doctor that used to visit my mom in Eugene. Dr. Singh. Dr. Singh would make Cream of Wheat with lots of butter and brown sugar for me, and I quickly became addicted. But this man was younger, wore that smooth, tight suit instead of Dr. Sing's loose and billowy garments, and he sported thick glasses that were much too large for his face. He peered down at me through those glasses with a quizzical expression.

"I'm just going for a walk," I said matter-of-factly.

The man smiled. "I see," he said.

Then the woman in the pale blue dress was there beside us. "I'm so sorry. It seems he snuck out of his room."

"They're hurting me, so I'm leaving," I explained.

"Hurting you?" The man gave the woman a questioning look.

"I'll look into it, sir. I'm so sorry. Okay now Todd, come with me..." the woman reached for my hand. I sprinted across the lobby.

Just then, the door to the stairs burst open and a young nurse rushed out, all out of breath. "There you are!" she said.

I looked from nurse to the woman in blue to the man in the suit. I was cornered, and everyone knew it. He smiled at me with real warmth. "Why don't we just take the elevator back upstairs together?" He offered. "And then maybe we can get you a bath?" He looked meaningfully at the nurse and she nodded.

§

For the next day or two there were no more tests. In fact I never saw the doctor with the yellowy teeth again after that. They even let me go outside for an hour or two with one of the young nurses. She was very pretty, and very nice. But she started to cry when I let go of her hand and ran across the parking lot, yelling that I wasn't coming back. When I saw that she was tearful and scared, I felt sorry for her and returned, promising not to run away. We walked a ways into the woods to the right of the building and discovered a huge concrete slab, cracked and crumbling, that tilted down a hill. I insisted on climbing the thing, and although she was reluctant and begged me not to hurt myself, she let me climb to my hearts content. I was very happy to be outside, and even happier to be climbing over jagged chunks of concrete. It must have been late fall, since the trees had no leaves but it wasn't very cold.

The next day I had a roommate in the hospital bed next to me. A boy my age with hardly any hair on his head, and skin so thin and pale you could see the blue and green veins through it. His name was Steven, and he was very sick, he told me. He said he wasn't going to live very much longer; even though he said his mom refused to confirm it when he asked her, but he had heard the doctors talking. I thought he was joking and told him as much, but he looked at me solemnly and said no, it was true. Later, when his mother came to visit she looked sadder than anyone I had ever seen, but I was nice to her because Steven encouraged me to do so. He also told me not to say anything to her about what he had told me. When she entered our room he did his best to look happy and smile. It seemed like he summoned all his strength to do it. She kept hugging him and touching his face, and completely ignored me at first. She also gave him a painted piece of cardboard with slots for different size coins, and some of the slots already had coins in them. It was so he could start a coin collection, she said. He thanked her and grinned, and after she left he stared at it for a long time, slowly sinking back into his pillow as exhaustion overtook his interest.

Then some orderlies came and wheeled his bed out of the room and down the hall. They were taking him for tests, they said, and Steven asked me to watch over his coin collection while he was gone. I didn't know when he would come back, so I made sure his coin collection was safe. Then the orderlies returned, and I thought they were coming for me, so I jumped out of bed and tried for the stairs again. They grabbed me and told me to calm down, but I just couldn't. So they strapped me to the bed again, this time using wash cloths instead of foam beneath the straps, so I couldn't wiggle my hands free. They didn't do any tests on me, but the new rigging worked, and I couldn't free myself. I tried for hours, rubbing my skin raw, until it started to get dark. I didn't like being strapped down at all. Eventually, the older nurse I had met on my first night there came and undid the straps, shaking her head and muttering under her breath. She had to change my sheets because I couldn't hold my pee that long. I had yelled at the top of my lungs that I needed to pee, but no one came. Of course, I had been yelling a lot, so they probably couldn't tell the difference.

Steven never returned to the room, but his mother came the next day. She looked even worse that she had before, and asked me where the coin collection was in a tired, raspy voice. I said I had promised to watch over it, but she said she needed it back. Reluctantly, I pulled it out from where I had hidden it under my pillow. As soon as I handed it to her, she burst into tears. "It's just bent a little," I said, not understanding. "Just on the corners." But she shook her head and thanked me for keeping it safe. I thought about asking her what she was going to do with the coin collection if Steven died, but I held my tongue. Maybe I would see Steven again, and I could ask him.

Later that same day a nurse I had not met before came for me. She was older than my mom, with thick mascara and makeup, and her brittle hair was a fake sort of blonde that showed other colors at its roots. I could tell from her voice that she smoked, and she seemed like an unhappy person. Or maybe she was sick. She led me down to the first floor, to a part of the hospital I had not yet seen. There was a long, dim hall with only a few doors on each side. We entered one on the left that opened into a brightly lit room with huge mirror on one wall. The walls were cinder blocks painted glossy white. There was a hospital cot opposite the mirror, and she asked me to climb into it. Behind the cot was a tall gray machine with lots of meters and wires popping out everywhere.

"What's that?" I asked, curious.

"It's a test machine."

When she said the word 'test,' I just about bolted from the room. Every muscle in my body tensed. "I don't want a test!" I declared.

The nurse smiled at me reassuringly, but it wasn't a genuine smile. "This is very safe. There is no way the machine can harm you."

I relaxed a little, still suspicious. "Does it take long?"

"It will be over in a blink," she said. She wouldn't look me in the eye when she said it, though.

I climbed into the bed and lay down. "What's the big mirror for?" There was something funny about the mirror. It was more bronze-colored than silver, and it was recessed into the wall instead of having a frame. It seemed more like a window.

"Oh, that's just so you can see yourself during the test," she said, but I could tell she was lying.

"No it's not," I said, challenging her. She started to speak, but just then the door to the room opened and an energetic young man walked in.

He was fit and tan, with black wavy hair and a huge white smile. He wore a white coat with a badge, like the other doctor I had met. "Hello, Todd!" he said, clapping his hands. He radiated warmth and confidence.   "You're absolutely right about the mirror!"   His grin widened.

"I am?"  I looked at the nurse, and she looked away.

"Yes.  That is actually what we call a two-way mirror, so we can see you, but you can't see us."  He offered this almost conspiratorially, as if it was a well-kept secret.

I was surprised, studying the glass.  I couldn't see anyone.  "Who's in there?"

The man chuckled.  "Oh, just a few doctors like me who are interested in helping you."  He waved his hand dismissively at the glass, then plopped down beside me on the bed.  "But, you know, they aren't very good looking, so we have to hide them behind a mirror."  His eyes were laughing, and even the unhappy nurse began to smile a little.  He was very charming, and I could feel my anxiety ebbing.  "Would you like to know what this machine does?" he asked, gesturing to the imposing mass of switches, meters and wires.  I nodded.  "Well…" he began, and proceeded to describe in great technical detail what the machine did.  I don't remember most of what he said, but I do remember that he spoke to me like an adult, as if he expected me to understand.  I was flattered. "So that is why we attach these tiny electrodes all over your scalp, so we can record how your brain is reacting to stimuli.  What do you think of that?"

I was impressed, but still a bit wary.  "Does it hurt?"  I asked.

The doctor considered, flashing a look at the nurse.  "Hmmm.  You know, some people don't like the way the electrodes feel against their scalp, and when we pull them off, sometimes it stings a little because of the glue."

"Glue?!" I sat up.

The doctor laughed.  He was joshing me.  "Just a little bit of sticky paste. Watch, I'll show you."  He grabbed one of the electrodes that was strung to the machine – I noticed then that they were all different colors, like

M&Ms or the stripes I had seen on the resisters of my walky-talky – and applied some "glue" to its surface. Then he playfully stuck the electrode to my arm. "It really doesn't hurt at all," he said. After a moment he peeled the electrode off. It didn't even sting. "You see? It doesn't stick to your skin very much. Which is why you must lay very still while we conduct the test…"

My stomach lurched. It must have shown in my face. He and the nurse exchanged glances.

"If you are uncomfortable, Todd, we can do this another time." He said it softly. I could tell he was being sincere.

"That's okay," I said. I took a breath, summoning courage. "I can handle it."

"Good. That's good," he said. He put a hand on my shoulder and smiled. "Let's get started then."

More people came into the room after that, stringing the wires all around me on the bed, parting my hair, gluing down electrodes all over my head. There were a lot of wires. While they worked, the doctor and nurse spoke quietly off to one side, occasionally glancing my way. Finally, everyone was finished and all but the nurse exited the room. As he shut the door, the friendly doctor poked his head back into the room and flashed a smile at me. "I'll be back right after we've completed our evaluation," he said.

I smiled back at him.

A moment later I heard the doctor's voice through a speaker set high up on the wall. "We're all set here, Miss Brown."

Miss Brown stood beside the bed, gently holding my left hand while she pushed some switches on the machine. An electrical hum filled the room, but I couldn't feel anything through the electrodes. I relaxed a bit. "It doesn't hurt at all!" I declared, glancing over at the mirror.

Miss Brown asked me to close my eyes, and I did. A man's voice I didn't recognize began giving me other instructions through the loudspeaker. "Who's that?" I asked, opening my eyes. The friendly doctor's voice cut in to reassure me: "This is Dr. Haines," he said, "He'll give you a few instructions to help us with the test. Okay?" I closed my eyes and let the man tell me what to do. Lie back, breathe this way, try to remember this or that…it went on that way for quite a while. I began to get restless. The friendly doctor's voice broke in, "Todd, is something the matter?"

"I need to move around," I said. I could feel my legs beginning to itch, the sort of itch that meant I needed to go play outside. The same itch that always afflicted me in school, when they asked me to sit still in class. The way they had itched on the plane, during the long flight out from Oregon to Massachusetts.

"Can you stay still just a little bit longer? We are almost finished."

"Okay," I said. I tried. It was hard.

Then the friendly doctor said, "Miss Brown, if you could please begin." At that moment, Miss Brown dug her fingers into my forearm. It didn't really hurt that much, but it was surprising. I opened my eyes.

"Hey…" I began. But Miss Brown wouldn't look at me.

"Increase the pressure, please," said the doctor.

The nurse's nails began to dig in harder. "Hey! That smarts!" I yelled, trying to pull my arm away. Miss Brown held if firmly. "Hey!"

"A bit more, please," said the doctor.

I stared in disbelief as Miss Brown's perfectly manicured nails burying themselves further into my flesh. I could feel the skin begin to tear. "Stop it! You're hurting me!" I tried again to wrench my hand away. "What are you doing?!"

Miss Brown wasn't looking at me, but when I glanced at the mirror, I saw black streaks of mascara running down her face. I kept yelling, she kept digging daggers into my forearm. I remember wanting to hit her, to make the pain end, and almost worked myself up into doing it, then I stopped myself. Then the voice, that evil, lying doctor's voice, calmly instructed from the speaker on the wall: "More, please."

I'd had enough. Summoning my strength, I drew my legs up against my chest and kicked out toward the nurse as hard as I could. The motion spun me on the bed, and bunches of electrodes ripped free of my scalp at once. The nurse gasped and flew sideways, stumbling toward the mirror, finally letting go of my arm to break her own fall. I was off the bed in seconds, tearing the remaining electrodes off my head and heading for the door. But the doctor was faster. He was there waiting for me, catching hold of my arms as I pulled the door open. I fought. I kicked his shins and clawed the hands that held me. I threw myself toward the hallway, desperate to be free, all the while screaming obscenities at the top of my lungs. I spit in his face. I bellowed. Then something the doctor said found its way through my rage.

"We'll have strap you down, Todd. Is that what you want? If you can't calm down, we'll have to strap you to your bed again…"

Abruptly, all the fight went out of me. "No…" I said. I was very still, waiting to see what he would do. He looked more surprised than angry. And maybe a little nervous.

"If I let you go, are you going to run?"

I shook my head, trying to seem compliant. His grip relaxed, and I tore free and ran. When I reached the end of the hall, I discovered to my horror that the door was locked. I glanced quickly back to see if the doctor was coming. He stood his ground, arms crossed, waiting. "Let me out of here!" I yelled, yanking on the door handle, then pounding on the door. *"Let me out!"* I looked at some of the other doors along the hall, calculating. I took a step toward the nearest possible exit.

Then the locked door behind me opened. Strong arms grabbed me. Struggling and flailing. Being held still. Then a paper cup of liquid.

"Drink this." I tried not to at first, but when they held my nose and head, I drank. It was sweet. And then I was being carried. Eventually, after a while, I found myself sitting in a cushy chair in a big office with high ceilings. The tanned, lying doctor sat in front of me at a giant desk. There was a name on the desk, and I remember asking what it meant, trying to sound it out and mispronouncing it, with the doctor correcting me. A foreign-sounding name. There were high windows and a lot of light from outside. And I noticed the doctor wasn't wearing his white jacket anymore. He was wearing a sport coat instead. He was looking at me, and waiting.

Gradually, each of my senses came back to me. I looked around. "This is a big room. Do you work here?" My voice was slurry. My head felt thick and slow.

"Yes. This is my office. I…run this hospital." He looked around. "This is one of the perks."

"A what?" I asked.

"A benefit of the position."

"Oh."

He steepled his hands before him on the desk. "How are you feeling, Todd?"

"I'm tired," I said sincerely.

"Do you remember what happened during the EEG?"

The test. I looked away. "Yeah." I remembered the streaks on the nurse's face. Her look of pain that mirrored my own.

"And how do you feel about that?"

I thought about it. "She shouldn't have hurt me!" I said with certainty.

"But it wasn't her fault," he said quickly, leaning forward. "She was following my instructions. Just doing her job."

I studied his face for a moment. He had been so nice, tricking me into cooperating. I wanted to hate him, but he had power over me. He ran the whole hospital. He could do anything he wanted. Had everything that had happened to me so far been his idea? Was everyone just doing their job? He looked so kind and calm, sitting there, waiting for me to respond. Was he lying now?

"What was I supposed to do?" I asked, letting him know I understood he was in charge. "She wouldn't stop!"

His eyebrows rose. "Well..." he began.

"What would *you* do?" I interrupted.

He took a slow breath through his nose and gazed at me over his desk. "I don't think I would have kicked Miss Brown," he said flatly. I looked at the ground, ashamed.

"Did it really hurt all that much?" He asked, his tone shifting toward sympathy.

"Yes!" I affirmed, and lifted my arm to show him the marks from the nurse's fingernails.

He grimaced. "I am very sorry about that, Todd." He seemed sincere; didn't he know it would hurt? And then, as my thoughts finally began to clear, I realized something. There was a reason I was sitting in his office, talking calmly with him, instead of being strapped to a bed. Maybe they had made a mistake during my test. Maybe *he* had made a mistake. And if there were mistakes, did that mean I wasn't all in the wrong?

"When is my mom coming?" I asked, testing the waters. "She said she would come visit."

"Mmm, yes. I advised against that," he said gravely, tilting his head to one side. "I thought you...could both benefit from a short vacation. So we could find out everything we needed to about you without any sort of...distraction or interference." He seemed so confident, so in control, but something was shifting between us. We looked at each other.

"So what's wrong with me?" I asked.

His hands and eyebrows rose abruptly. "Nothing. Nothing at all. You're a perfectly healthy young boy." He grabbed a file that was lying on his desk, and held it up for me to see. "All the tests are normal."

I was confused. Was he lying again? "But..."

"Did you think something was wrong?"

I shrugged. "I kicked the nurse," I said. Then I thought about it. "But...you made her hurt me." Something fell into place for me then. Something surprising and revolutionary. I slowly got out of the chair and stood. I walked over to the desk and reached for the name plate sitting on it. "It's heavy," I said, feeling its heft.

The doctor looked at me warily.

I set the nameplate down. "I want to go home," I said. It was more of a demand than a wish.

The doctor let out the breath he had been holding. "We're trying to make that happen right away. Tomorrow at the latest."

"Tomorrow?" I asked, thinking about the hospital room, the plastic trays of food, the screaming kids, the sad parents and strange smells. I could really use a nice hot plate of my mom's spaghetti.

"At the latest," he repeated.

I wandered toward the windows and tried to see the sky. "No more tests," I said with finality.

"No.  No more tests."

§

The predominant pattern in my interactions with authority figures as a child resulted in an observation that they did not have my welfare at heart.  They intruded on my freedoms, lied about their intentions, and tricked me into enduring situations that hurt me in some way.  They could not be trusted.  In my childhood perception, it seemed that even when I tried to do the right thing, the responsible and compassionate thing, I was punished for it.  And, of course, these figures demonstrated time and time again that they did not trust me, either.  They didn't trust what I told them was true.  They didn't trust me to make good decisions for my own well-being.  They didn't trust me to understand the complex reasons behind their actions.  When I think back on the consistent thread of betrayal and injury I experienced in the hands of those supposedly responsible for me, I am surprised I did not become a devout Libertarian, Randian Objectivist or radical anarchist.  I am also surprised I did not continue to create situations in my adult life where those patterns were repeated over and over again.  It would make logical sense for me settle into unreformed criminality, to rebel against rules of any kind and forcefully affirm that no one had authority over me.

But for many reasons – reasons hinted at when my life experiences are taken as a whole – this did not happen.  Instead, my mistrust of authority manifested in subtler ways as an adult.  In my resistance to what I though were unreasonable expectations in the workplace, for example, or my frequent head-butting with upper management.  In my disregard for class distinctions and indifference to certain longstanding social conventions and institutions.  In my propensity to seek out or create alternative methods of learning, healing modalities, employment and social activism.  In my reflex of suspicion whenever someone offered to help me.  In my deep skepticism of status quo assumptions about how people should live, what people should say to each other, and appropriate motivations for action.  I have by-and-large remained apart, isolated from the majority of my fellow human beings.  Although I have tried to join organizations, to jump on some social movement's bandwagon, to be a team player in the workplace, to adopt someone else's vision of how to live, it never quite works out in the end. I can't quite relax into structures that others have created. Instead I am compelled to reinvent the wheel on my own.

Sometimes this reinvention results in real innovation, and sometimes it doesn't. This has affected my personal relationships as well, even when there is no clear authority dynamic. Again and again over the course of my life, I have rejected the help and support of friends, family and lovers because I could not trust it to be beneficial. Either I didn't accept that others shared my values or had my interests at heart, or I didn't believe they were competent to be truly helpful. This deficit of trust has had a strengthening effect on my creative problem-solving skills and resilience to calamity, but a crushing effect on my ability to maintain close friendships over time. Of course, there are many other patterns of memory that contribute to how my friendships are shaped in the present, and that is what we'll cover next.

## Friendship

Perhaps the primary characteristic of all friendship is mutually offered trust. There are different affinities and attractions, different reasons to form the relationship, but being able to rely on each other for emotional support and shared experience is the foundation upon which all friendships are built. As with all relationship, this reliance is a two-way street. Perhaps we can't always provide the support our friends need, and perhaps they aren't always able to provide it for us, but there is an expectation that trust is equivalent and reciprocal between both parties. What were my experiences in this regard? Was I able to build trust relationships with others? Did I follow through on my end of the bargain, and did they? I will focus on my relationships with other children where the power relationship was equal. In any relationship where one person has more power – more authority, more positional influence or some other socially recognized advantage – the trust building process is riddled with other constraints, prejudices and expectations. Our genuine equals, our peers, offer us a blank slate upon which to create our own unique connections and interdependencies in a spontaneous and organic way.

I can't recall many memories of friendship before age twelve. I think this was because I moved between my mother and father's households so frequently, and because each family moved geographically fairly often as well. There are a smattering of interactions that are memorable, and I will relate some of them here, but nearly all of them convey a brief intensity that ended too quickly to blossom into lasting friendship. I think this had an enduring effect on friendships in later years. On the one hand, I acquired important skills to quickly create connections with people in new and unfamiliar environments. On the other, I often hold part of myself in reserve, not entrusting myself entirely to new relationships even when they offer unconditional trust to me. Along the same lines, the transience and disruption of my early relationships also helped me discern reliable candidates for friendship fairly quickly, while at the same time training me to avoid or resist relationships with people who didn't meet muster according to some fairly rigid metrics.

As a result, I have always had a small handful of close friends with whom I have invested my love and trust, and an only slightly larger group of acquaintances whom I hold firmly at arm's length. I am very tentative about extending offers of greater investment, and quickly withdraw if I detect hesitancy to reciprocate or chronic unreliability. In effect, I am not willing to take many risks with my friendships. I believe this is one of the best examples of cause and effect between early childhood experiences, memories of those experiences, and ongoing replication of those historical patterns.

When I was two years old, my mother used to visit once or twice a week with a friend in Eugene, Oregon. The woman had a daughter, a little younger, with whom I quickly bonded. The moms would build little forts of sheets draped over furniture, and the girl and I would scamper about on all fours, chasing each other to and fro beneath the bright white canopy. We were usually naked (or soon ended up that way as a result of our exertions), but at that age it was of course entirely innocent, and we would tire ourselves out with peek-a-boo and other high energy games. All the while our mothers would chat away, delighted to have their children entertain each other, and they would generally ignore us for hours until, exhausted, we were ready for a nice long nap. I remember all of this as vividly as if it were yesterday, I think because this was my first real connection with someone my own age.

At the end of a long, hot summer, there was a tearful conversation between my mother and her friend that would put an end to our weekly visits. The woman's husband had come home from the war, and she was very distraught about it. He had been wounded, and he was not the same. He was moody, and angry, and difficult to manage. And he drank too much. She didn't know what she was going to do, but we couldn't come over to the house any more. Her husband couldn't see people right now. They had to let him adjust. Maybe later. Maybe in a few months. Even then, though, we kids wouldn't be allowed to take off our clothes and play under sheets, she said. The husband wouldn't understand. She was unhappy about all of this, she didn't want these sudden changes, she felt guilty about her resentment and frustration. Over the course of the conversation, my mother became upset as well. All the while, their two children sat silently on the floor and absorbed what we could. There was sadness, and distress, and fear, and an a muddy sketch of the dark cloud that was descending over that household. One aspect of that afternoon would not become clear for many weeks, and that was how the four of us would never be in the same room again.

I think my memories of this experience are instructive for any adults who interact with children. Kids get it. They may not understand all the subtle nuances of adult communication, but they grasp the broad strokes, and learn from them. What did I take away from this? That friends could be taken away quite suddenly. That blossoming friendship, innocent nudity and playful joy were conditional and possibly even shameful. That something called Vietnam did bad things to good people. That things I liked and wanted didn't last. For weeks afterward, I would ask my mom when we would visit our friends again. Was the man there better? Could they maybe visit us instead? And mom would quietly say that no, we wouldn't be seeing them anytime soon. Maybe someday. Maybe someday. Eventually, I stopped asking.

§

For the remainder of our stay in Oregon, there isn't any sustained connection with a peer that would qualify as friendship. There were the failed attempts at fitting in at school. There were the hours exploring the beach in Florence with Puma. There were occasional visits with other families that only proved how different I was from other children. There was the intermittent and often combative connection with my step-sister, Shelly, whose companionship I enjoyed, but with whom I constantly vied for attention. There were days and weeks of time apart from other children. There was one girl on a farm that I met during my fifth year, the daughter of one of my father's friends, with whom I recall an intense period of sharing, but it was one afternoon to contrast an endless series of afternoons alone. By my sixth birthday, I had never experienced any kind of enduring connection with any of my peers, and felt closer to our dogs than to most other kids.

That all changed when I arrived in New England. Although it was still a rural lifestyle, my father's house on Harkness Road in Amherst, Massachusetts was surrounded by all manner of kids my age. There were Robby and his sister, who lived directly across the street. There was Greg and his older brothers, just a few houses down. There was Ben and his gaggle of siblings, who lived on their farm a mile up the road. And there were an endless assortment of interesting new acquaintances at Pelham Elementary School – Mary, Evan, Elizabeth, Nick…so many. My life was suddenly awash with new relationships, though I of course had no idea how to navigate them. There were established groups, clubs and cliques I couldn't begin to comprehend. There were old and new alliances, unspoken boundaries and rules, and a whole language of colloquialisms – all equally beyond my ken.

During my sixth and seventh years I tried, and tried mightily, to trust and be trusted, to find my own level amid a sea of excited childhood energies. But it was difficult. Those who were present when I arrived at second grade recall that I made a big splash. One childhood acquaintance remembers: "When the teacher asked us what exciting things had happened to us over the summer, you stood up and declared that a Bluebird had flown in your bedroom window and stolen your watch from beside your bed. We all laughed, and the teacher tried to correct you, but you stubbornly stuck to your story…." As I said, I tried.

At this point my mother moved back to Manchester, Connecticut, and once again took custody of me. Even know she recalls the reason she returned. Ever since my departure, she had been having distressing dreams about me; about how I was suffering and afraid, and how she needed to rescue me from some vast, dark and horrible conspiracy that was scheming to crush my spirit. And who knows, perhaps Pelham Elementary would have been my undoing. There was, after all, a fifth-grader whom I found shooting up on the playground one day. He was sitting in the lawn, calmly injecting himself, while other kids looked on in horror. When I asked him what he was doing, he said, "Hey, man, it's just grass….you want some?" Or perhaps it was the antagonism between my step-mother and me that my mother sensed. Mary was, after all, despairing over how to manage a very strong-willed child, a boy who seemed hell-bent on thwarting all her motherly plans and who lead her daughter into all sorts of trouble. Or perhaps memories of my father's stern parenting or my paternal grandmother's controlling behaviors were what spooked her so thoroughly. Or maybe it was just irrational paranoia.

Whatever the reason, I left my new found world of peers in rural Massachusetts for a very different landscape in Manchester. Here I encountered all the tensions of inner city life. For the first time in my experience, people were treated with radical difference based on how they spoke, where they lived, how they dressed, and the color of their skin. I was introduced to all of this in the first home we rented in Manchester, a second floor one-bedroom in the Parkade Apartments. It was a confusing and frightening time, with a lot of rapid adjustment to a whole new set of cultural standards. And it all began in second grade, at Wadell Elementary.

I quickly befriended a boy named Todd in my first week of school. Not only was it thrilling to meet someone else with my name – that had never happed before – but he had already established an outcast status similar to mine. Todd had some sort of disorder that gave his body odor a bitter, almost skunk-like quality. The other kids shunned him instantly, either taunting him or bullying him. Whenever he passed gas in class, only one or two of the teachers had the authoritative presence to restrain the students from bursting into screeches, groans and giggles. Todd would then be asked to step out into the hall for a moment, and return when he was ready to do so. His humiliation could be seen plainly on his face, and I think that is what prompted empathy in me. I thought I understood quite well how he felt and what he was going through. In reality, I didn't know the half of it.

At some point in those first couple of weeks I began defending Todd. He never asked me to…in fact, he seemed additionally mortified when I began telling the other kids to shut up and stop teasing him. But it created a bond of sorts between us. Eventually, one or two of the teachers began to recognize my seeming need to help Todd, and his need for relief from ostracized isolation, so they encouraged us to get acquainted. Whenever Todd was sent out into the hall, I was asked to join him there. At first, Todd resented my presence and wouldn't even speak to me. Then, after several gruff and cajoling attempts to get him to smile, he finally began to soften. Then, one day, when he was experiencing a particularly bad and recurring bout of gas, the teacher asked me to escort him to the nurse's office.

"I don't want to go!" Todd announced. This shocked everyone – the teacher, the other kids, even me. Normally, Todd never talked back to the teacher or anyone else. Instead, he bore his humiliation in angry silence, directing all his frustration inward. But not this time. "I'm not going!" He said, finding a louder voice.

"We've discussed this, Todd," the teacher said sternly, "and this is what you are supposed to do." She looked at him frankly.

Todd stared down at his desk, trying to bore a hole through it with his eyes. His hands gripped the metal sides, the muscles in his neck visibly straining through the skin.

"I'll go," I said softly. "I'll go with you."

Todd looked away, but his muscles began to relax. He got up and made his way hastily to the door. I looked up at the teacher, and she nodded permission, then quickly glanced out the window in discomfort. I rose and followed Todd out into the hall. We began making our way toward the nurse's office in silence.

"It doesn't matter what they think," I began.  It was a tack I often took with him.  "They're just jealous because we get to leave class."  I grinned his way.

Todd stopped and spun to face me.  "*You* don't have to go to the nurse's office.  *You* don't *have* to!"  He was angry.  Really angry.  I had never seen him so worked up.

"Okay!"  Why was he yelling at *me*?  "Sorry...I – Why don't you want to go to the nurse's office, anyway?"

He flailed his arms.  "Why should I?  Nothing anybody does works!  They don't know what's wrong.  They don't know how to make me better..."  And as abruptly as his anger had flared, it evaporated.  His hands fell to his sides and his pale blue eyes just looked at me, waiting.

"Well...maybe it will go away by itself," I suggested.

Todd frowned, then sighed.  "I doubt it."  Then he started off down the hall again, and I followed.

This was the foundation of my first tenuous friendship in Manchester, and our interactions continued for the next week in this vein.  We would hang out on the playground and talk about getting together after school, but Todd was so busy with doctor's visits and other activities that he rarely had time just to play.  He was also very nervous about my coming over to his house, and said his parents wouldn't let him come over to mine.  "Why not?" I asked.  But he would never explain.  "They just wouldn't," he said.  He avoided telling me where he lived as well.  So we shared what time we had together and talked about what seven-year-old boys talk about:  our latest toys, the sports we liked, the newest kids to arrive in our class, and so on.

Then, one day I proposed we meet on a weekend.  We could rendezvous somewhere away from where either of us lived.  "I don't like being around where I live, anyway," I said.

Todd was curious.  "Why not?"

I smirked. "Everybody's always *fighting* over there. The grownups are yelling at each other and cursing all the time. Kids are fighting with each other. There are gangs –"

"Gangs?" Todd smiled a big, white-toothed smile at me, not believing.

"I dunno…clubs, gangs…you know, you've got to pick sides."

Todd nodded. "Yeah. So…where do you live, anyways?"

I was surprised I hadn't told him. "The Parkade Apartments."

"The Parkade?" Todd laughed. It was the first time I had ever heard him laugh out loud. "That's where I live, too! Which side are you on?"

"Over by the brook! And the tunnels…"

"Tunnels?"

"Storm drain tunnels. Haven't you seen those?"

Todd shook his head.

"Oh, you gotta see those. I'll show you. They start at the brook, and go on forever underground. It's really cool…can you play on Sunday?"

And so we made our first play date for that coming weekend. Why had we never seen each other before around the apartments? It didn't matter. We were now unspoken allies, carving out our own recreation amid the ongoing family, clan and tribal wars of our neighborhood.

That Sunday I woke early, eager to get through breakfast and out the door. I told mom about my new friend, how is name was Todd and that we were in the same class. She was happy for me and sent me on my way, equipped with an offer to invite Todd over for lunch. I strode through the apartment complex with a new sense of place, a new kind of belonging. I didn't run into any of the other kids – it was early yet – but I wasn't so afraid of them now. I had a friend. I was beaming with newfound confidence as I approached our appointed meeting place – the

Big Lawn, one of the large green courtyards in the middle of the
complex. Then again, what if he wasn't there? What if his parents
wouldn't let him play today? I quickened my pace, and soon I was
running.

As I rounded the end of the building I searched the Lawn. At first, I
didn't see him. Would I have to wait? What if he didn't come? And
then I spotted him sitting by the street on the curb, and I ran over to
where he sat.

"Hey Todd!" I said.

He looked up. He didn't look happy.

"Can't you play?" I asked.

He shook his head and looked away.

"How come?"

He seemed to be struggling for words. He looked past me down the
street. I followed his gaze and saw someone sitting in a car parked on
the opposite side of the road, watching us. A silhouette in the
windshield, backlit by the morning sun. Was that his dad? His brother?

"What's going on?" I asked.

Todd stood up. "You gotta leave me alone," he said, but there was no
force behind it.

"Huh?"

"I said," Todd glanced again at the parked car, "You gotta *leave me
alone.*" This time he said it loud, with force. "*Just bud out!*" His fists
were clenched now, and he took a menacing step toward me.

"Are you crazy? What are you talking about?" I was stupefied. I stared
at him, barely noticing the small crowd of boys gathering on the far end
of the Lawn.

"Go on! *Get outta here!*"  He raised his fists, as if to fight.  And then he cracked.  A single tear worked its way down his cheek.  Then another.  With a choking sound, Todd dropped back on the curb and buried his face in his hands.  I heard a car start and looked down the street toward it.  Whoever had been sitting and watching was now pulling out and heading our way.  Further up the Lawn, the crowd of boys had grown to ten or twelve, and they were slowly making their way along the green toward us as well.  Every one of my instincts told me this was a bad situation about to get worse.

"Todd!" I yelled, pointing up the lawn.

Todd looked up at me, then at the car, then back over his shoulder.  "See what you did?  Do you *see*?"

"No!  What?  I didn't – "

"You're *white*.  White folks always say they done nothing wrong.  They never see.  *Ever*."  This wasn't the calm, contained, even-keeled Todd that I knew from school.  This wasn't the same person I hung out with on the playground.  This was somebody else.  What was he jabbering on about, anyway?

The car had almost reached us and was slowing to a stop.  I ignored it.  I was calculating how fast I would have to run to escape the gaggle of tough-looking kids that were almost upon us.  For some reason, though, the gang had stalled in the middle of the lawn.  They were staring at the car behind me, then at Todd, then at me.  Their young faces were full of fear...and hate.  Todd looked up, saw the car and scrambled to his feet, quickly wiping the wetness from his face.  He took a couple of deep breaths, steadying himself, and then he looked me in the eye with renewed conviction.  "I can't be your friend...anymore," he said, and then he turned and ran.  Todd wasn't running very fast as he made for the corner of the nearest apartment building, and a couple of boys on the green took a half-dozen steps toward him, mocking him as he went.  Then they gave up the chase.  I heard the car behind me pull away, but I never did get a good look at the driver.  I was preoccupied with the steely glares of the kids about to surround me.  I had waited too long.

"You're new here, aren't ya?" said a wiry, black-haired boy of about nine. He wasn't the oldest or the biggest in the group, but he had the confident air of a man in charge. I looked at the others. Now that the car had taken off, they're faces held nothing but contempt.

"So what?" I asked, distracted. I was still reeling from what had occurred between Todd and me.

"So I always get to fight the new kids," said the boy, "that's what." The others chuckled. *"Put 'em up!"* One of them yelled.

I was nonplused. The leader eyed me, then barked a laugh. "He doesn't know what that means!" The others laughed with him. "Like this," he raised his fists in front of his face, knuckles high – just like Todd had done but with much more panache. He looked like a fighter on an old boxing poster. Having missed my opportunity to run, I decided to make the best of it. I tried to copy his stance. To a boy, everyone burst out laughing.

"No no! Not like *that*," said the leader. He was genuinely amused with me. "Here," he took a step closer. I stepped back into the street. "Don't worry, I'm not gonna hit ya. Here, like this…" He folded his fingers down first, then his thumb over the front of his fingers. "See the difference?"

I looked at my own hands. My thumbs were buried against my palms, my fingers curving over them. I quickly copied his version of a fist instead.

"That's right. See, you hit somebody the way you had it, and you'd break your thumbs."

"I bet he still sucks 'em!" said one of the boys.

"I know how to fight…" I mumbled, trying to salvage my pride.

The gang leader smirked. "Yeah, sure." He seemed very relaxed. "So what are you, anyways?"

"Yeah," another boy chimed in, "how come you're hanging around with niggers?"

"I'm not!" I said. I had no idea what a 'nigger' was, but I was pretty sure I'd never spent time with one.

"We just *saw* you!" another voice chimed in.

I was confused, and it must have shown on my face. The leader waved the others quiet. "We're Italian," he said matter-of-factly. "The Big Lawn is *our* turf, kapish?"

I didn't kapish, but I nodded anyway.

"So what are you? A mick?"

"Maybe he's a *kike!*" yelled one of the boys.

"Is that it? You a kike?"

The hostility in their expressions had faded, replaced by curiosity. It seemed like the storm had passed. "I don't know," I said honestly. I had no idea what any of those words meant.

"Well, he ain't Eye-talian!" someone said, and that brought another round of guffaws.

"Listen," the leader said, "maybe you can practice some, and *then* you can fight me."

"I'll practice on him," said one of the boys. Nervous laughter all around.

"Naw. He's just a kid. He's got guts, though, standing up to me like he did," said the leader. "Gotta give it to him." He cocked his head to one side and eyed me, smirking.

"Or he's stupid."

"Not stupid," the leader said, cutting off my defensive retort with a meaningful look.

An awkward silence. Not knowing what to do with my fists, I shoved them in my pockets and stared at my feet.

The leader took a breath. "Let's go," he said. "See ya around, short stuff. Just remember who's boss."

"Okay," I said sullenly. Then, after a moment: "I'll practice!"

The leader grinned back at me, then led his crew off across the Big Lawn. I started in the opposite direction toward home. I walked slowly, in a strangely disconnected state. I didn't know what to make of anything that had happened that morning. I only knew I had somehow lost a friend, and probably gained a few new enemies. I would ask mom about it. She usually understood things people did and could relieve those vast mysteries to my mind and heart. The morning air was crisp and the sun had already burned the dew off the grass. The Parkade Apartments were waking up. I could hear pots clanging through kitchen windows, children yelling at each other, and parents yelling at their children. I could smell bacon frying and toast being browned. Maybe mom would let me watch Sesame Street later on, but first I would have to do my chores. For a while I had tried to get the kitchen garbage into the dumpster, but it was too high for me to lift the paper bags, and more than once I dumped scraps and leavings all over myself. So I kept finding new places around the complex to stash the smelly sacks instead. Now I had to watch over my shoulder even more warily than before. I sighed and wondered about what the boys had asked me. Was I a kike? A mick? What was I? Todd called me white, and maybe that's what I was, but even though I had never really thought about it before, I was pretty sure you couldn't sum up a whole person with just one word.

§

And so it went in Manchester, with countless false starts in friendship for the remainder of my stay there. There were two brothers, Nicky and

Johnny, who were neighbors of my maternal grandparents on Horton Road. They were friendly enough to begin with, and we had a number of interesting adventures, but at some point they had a falling out with each other and started using me as a tool for retaliation. Things got surprisingly nasty surprisingly fast. Then there were the slightly older kids who invited my trust with the sole purpose of making me the butt of some joke or prank. And of course there were the nice, genuinely friendly kids whose parents did not approve of my wild ways. Always, it seemed, I was the unwelcome newcomer, the outsider looking in, the kid who didn't fit.

There was one other avenue to finding friends, and that was the time I spent at my paternal grandmother's in West Hartford. During the summer months, I might stay for a week or more at their old red Colonial on Wood Pond Road. The lake there offered plentiful opportunities to recreate and connect with other kids. This was, however, a very different environment from the gritty streets of Manchester. The beaches were thronged with carefully groomed, well-spoken children in immaculate, pale outfits. They played tennis and sailed. They swam in straight lines and knew the difference between side stroke, back stroke and crawl. They were reserved, rigid, and harshly judgmental with each other. They seemed to be competing for something nearly all the time, but I could never figure out what it was.

Needless to say, my uncouth manners, lack of refined clothes and ignorance over the subtleties of various sports instantly set me apart. I wasn't worth the effort, not even to ridicule. I simply wasn't part of their game. My grandmother tried to insert me into her church activities, using her clout on the church board to enroll me into an already overfull summer activities group. I quickly demonstrated my skepticism about all things religious, and was constantly sneaking out to the courtyard on the church grounds to get away from the stifling Sunday school structure. Why should I go to school in the summer? So that arrangement didn't work out so well, either.

All of these experiences contributed to a recurring pattern in memory: I could not easily develop trusting relationships with my peers. From my end, people seemed unpredictable, social etiquette inexplicable, and friendship generally unreliable. From my read of others, I could be trusted in private with awkward secrets, but seldom did that translate into publically acknowledged trust; for the most part, I was treated with hesitant or intermittent affection. But I did crave acceptance, I wanted to belong, so I found myself in an endless cycle of trying, failing, and trying again, strung taut between ignorance and stubbornness. Of course, part of me also longed for the salty breezes of Florence, the sting of sand on my cheeks, and the expansive freedoms of those adventures, solitary but for the loyal courage of my dog Puma. But that life was gone, and with it the only steady and grounded sense of self I had ever known. Who was I here in Manchester? I was many things, but none of them me. I was a series of hastily assembled personas that interfaced with alien surroundings in order to survive. I was everyone that I had to be in the moment, and no one that I wanted to be. So, in the end, I also did not trust myself to be myself.

§

Finally, my first year after returning to Amherst when I was ten, things began to change. Upon my arrival, I was too wild for the other professor's kids and too articulate and pensive for the local farmers' children; I wasn't a scholastic achiever and I didn't play hockey. I was the frequent target of jokes, pranks and ridicule, although my reputation for wildness made even the boldest bullies avoid direct confrontation. Then, in my second year at Fort River Elementary, I met Dean. We liked each other instantly, and began working on Audio Visual projects together. Soon he invited me to his house, and I met his two fine brothers David and Scott, his warm and compassionate mother Bonnie and her friendly boyfriend Gaton. For some reason – I think because we all appreciated a similar wry and sometimes edgy sense of humor – we got along exceedingly well, and I ended up spending a lot of time at their house. Dean and I cooked meals together, explored the surrounding woods together, introduced each other to the music we liked, debated every subject under the sun, wrestled occasionally and laughed a lot. I felt closer to Dean than I had to any other boy up until that time, and I enjoyed his family better than I did my own. After a year or so, I began to believe that friendship could be something reliable, something worth nurturing and protecting, something that brought joy instead of disappointment. Just maybe something I could trust. It would to erode some of my uncertainties about relationships.

After all, this friendship was just one flickering candle in a vast, dark plane. In the following years there would be additional successful relationships, adding warmth and light to my experience, but even these could not effectively change my governing beliefs about the fragility and impermanence of connections with other people, or a narrative self that cast my relationships in terms of incompatibility or absence. One new pattern did begin to percolate through my unconscious substrata, however, and that was a tenuous insight that true friendship, affinity and camaraderie was possible for me, just exceedingly rare and precious. So although I had trained my heart to resist opening itself to others, it now knew that real intimacy was possible, that with the right person and in the most fortuitous circumstances, I could actually relax my defensive personas and just be me.

## Sexuality

To understand the psychosexual dynamics of my family, we have to begin with my father's mother. Rachel was an ingeniously controlling matriarch who thoroughly enjoyed manipulating every member of her clan. Though she often strove to achieve what she thought was best for everyone within the radius of her extensive and often intrusive ministrations, she also had a devious and mean-spirited sense of humor. I recall how, one Easter when I was twelve, she invited my father's former wives and girlfriends to stop by for a visit. Of course none of them knew that the others were coming, but when they arrived they were delighted to gossip about my Dad amongst themselves. Grandma Rachel absolutely glowed with pleasure as each surprised face appeared in her kitchen, adding furious momentum to the event. I stood among them, nervous but excited, listening in on the giggles and stories. When my own mother arrived, she took one look at the group of women and burst out laughing. "I can't wait to see Bill's face!" she said, beaming.

Eventually my father returned from his trip to the store, stumbling into the packed kitchen with an armload of groceries. "What the...?"

"Look Dad!  My whole life is in this room!"  I declared.

"Yes Bill, isn't it wonderful?!"  Rachel said, eyes bright with laughter.

My Dad looked around in shock, mouth gaping.  "Shit…."  And then he was out the door, bags of food still in hand, shaking his head in disbelief and cursing to himself as he jogged down the driveway.  The jubilant teasing of a lifetime of lovers followed him all the way to his car, and in a squeal of tires he was gone.  He didn't return for several hours.

This was Rachel's enduring quality:  the ability to get people's goats, and get them good.  When it was someone else, it could be quite entertaining, but woe betide those who thought they could escape her vindictive opportunism.  Yet she held so much power over our family that we would all gather at her home for holidays whether we wanted to or not; it was  our familial obligation, our tribal tradition.  And there was an almost comfortable routine to how things played out.  If any gifts were involved, Rachel presided masterfully over their opening, instructing each of us in turn which gifts to open when, then teasing and cajoling both the giver and receiver while laughing uproariously at our gift choices and reactions.  I can recall her berating cackle echoing through the house as if it were yesterday.  On other occasions there would be the requisite battle of wills between Rachel and her husband Ed, who seemed to be continuing their sniping match from the previous Christmas.  This would escalate into increasingly hostile quips, until at last Rachel would sneak a Louis Armstrong album onto the old record player in the living room.  This made Ed so nostalgic he would give up the battle, retreating upstairs for the remainder of the day to hide a solemn face and dampening eyes.  And finally there would be Rachel's favorite pastime:  pitting one family member against another with a question here, a word of gossip there, all salted heavily with her amazingly canny insinuations.  All of this made the holidays quite memorable, but also quite stressful.

My father and I pose for a Christmas picture at grandma Rachel's insistence

My father passionately hated to attend these functions but felt unable to decline, so he medicated himself with alcohol, sometimes calling upon the liquid courage to spar with his mother, and sometimes just passing out on the couch. The women at these gatherings, especially the new girlfriends or wives, were completely baffled by our family dynamics, mainly because Rachel made it her mission to win the confidence and even admiration of the fairer sex, while at the same time demeaning and alienating my father, uncle and grandfather. At first, when I was very young, I was insulated from all of this. I had so much other drama and conflict in my life that Rachel's home seemed like a luxurious haven on a beautiful lake. She seemed warm and nice to me, even protective. In the week or more I spent there each summer, I would sail in the Sunfish, swim across the warm waters of the lake, watch TV and make fat sandwiches for myself from Rachel's well-stocked kitchen. As I got older, however, I eventually became the object of her sharp-edged humor. By the time I was ten, I was so stressed about any visit to Rachel's that I would vomit repeatedly on our long drive from Amherst to her West Hartford home.

Rachel utilized a powerful combination of genuine affection, conspiratorial confiding, and blatant sexuality to slowly bring me under her control. As far back as I can remember, she made me believe that I was special, that I was her confidante, her favorite and singular grandchild. I was the only one she allowed to watch her dress and put on makeup. I was the only one she beckoned to speak with her through the half-closed bathroom door. I was the only one she visited late at night, in a robe that fell open when she sat on my bed, for whispered conversations. I believe now that many of her riskiest behaviors were fueled by a deep unhappiness and too much alcohol, but that does not dilute the confusion she introduced into my childhood. There was the curious shock of her nakedness as she dressed in front of me. There was the thrill of being the exclusive recipient of her most secret thoughts and aspirations. And there was the guilt-inducing arousal as Rachel moaned and gasped through that open bathroom door, clearly wanting me to know that she was pleasuring herself just an arm's reach away.

Over time, the expectations she placed on my young shoulders became more and more adult. Too adult for a preteen boy. And that of course is the error residing at the heart of all child abuse: to burden children with emotions, knowledge, sensations, situations, responsibilities or relationships that are simply beyond their years to comprehend, integrate or manage. And so we arrive at why I have led with Rachel in our discussion of sex. Although my time with her was not my first introduction to sensuality, it was nonetheless more formative than many earlier events. Rachel enticed me not with lewd invitations, but with an offer of protective trust, of emotional intimacy, of ongoing friendship, support and affection. Amid her combative and controlling matriarchy and a wealthy array of superficial socializing, Rachel remained lonely, fearful and desperately in need of love. She really did care about me, I'm sure, but for whatever reason – probably because she herself was sexually abused as a young girl – she sought to heal her pain and isolation through inappropriate intimacy with her grandchild.

§

There were other sexual experiences when I was very young, some of them easy to recall, involving children and adults both within and outside of my family. The details of these encounters are less interesting than the episodic memory patterns they created. By age eleven I was well-versed in the associations between secrecy, pleasure, fear, lust and shame. These would in fact become more rigidly chained associations as time went on. I was certainly more informed about human reproduction than any of my peers, who seemed utterly clueless about both sex and their own confused longings. What got me into trouble was that as a result of my experiences, I had already begun sexualizing many of my interactions with other children and adults, openly discussing sex with anyone who was interested. This was, I would later learn, a sign of my exposure to adult sexuality and the premature encouragement of my own sexual feelings in those contexts.

What I also learned early on was that many of my friends and acquaintances throughout childhood had sexual secrets of their own. There were two friends, brothers age ten and eleven, who fondled each others' nipples until they both achieved erections. There was a sixteen-year-old babysitter who hid me in the bushes of a public park while she and her boyfriend had sex. There was a nine-year-old pal of my step-sister's who asked me to watch her jump up and down naked on my step-sister's bed while she touched herself. There was the thirteen-year-old boy from across the street who, it turned out, relished doing exactly the same thing. There was a college-aged woman living in the apartment downstairs who woke the whole household with boisterous orgasms. There was a fifth grader who tried to grab other boys' penises in the restroom while yelling "Pork 'em! Pork 'em!" There was the giant cucumber hidden in an adult friend's dresser drawer, proudly displayed and explained to me. There was the shifty old man who visited the playground to grope under the skirts of the toddlers playing there. There were games of "doctor" and "show and tell" with willing neighborhood girls. There were seemingly innocent baths and showers with other kids and adults in my family. There was the close family friend who confessed to having sex with dogs when he was a teenager. And so on, to the point where all the varied truths of human sexuality became much stranger than fiction.

All of this observation and interaction occurred before my own puberty, so when my hormones kicked into full gear, I had a pretty good idea of what to do. A very adult idea. By then, however, I was no longer living in the ghettos of Manchester, where sexual interest and exploration seemed to blossom early for many kids. I was now among the well-educated, upper middle class children of Amherst, Massachusetts. These were nerdy professors' kids who had the same sexual feelings as all children, but substantially less of an idea of what to do about them, and a considerably larger accumulation of conflicted emotions. There were of course a few hearty farm girls who were quite knowledgeable about the birds and the bees, but although I was fond of farms, barns, hay lofts, horses and even some of these young women, I wasn't drawn to these easy flirtations. Following in my father's footsteps, I wanted more challenging and intellectually stimulating dalliances. So, after a few failed attempts to initiate sex with girls my own age, I sought out older girls and women. When I was twelve, I had my first steady girlfriend, a nineteen-year-old artist who was happy to kiss and fondle and explore.

Within that same year, I tried to woo someone even older. I had just turned thirteen, and was living with my foster parents, Rick and Marge. Denise, a lovely single Italian woman in her early twenties, was renting an apartment in our house. We quickly became friends, and after a few months I began making advances. Denise firmly resisted, and while being careful not to bruise my young ego, spoke frankly of her preference for older men. Then, one night when Marge and Rick were out for the evening, my foster brother, sixteen-year-old Randy, decided to get me drunk. We traded shots of Jack Daniels and blackberry brandy until neither of us could see straight. Then we went for a joy ride in the family Ford Grenada, fishtailing it into a tree. Then we jumped off the second floor balcony onto the asphalt driveway several times. Then we mooned passing cars for a half-hour or so. After that, there is a long black, silent space, and I have no idea what happened.

I awoke in the living room, shirtless and still completely drunk. Denise sat across the room, watching me with a worried look. I didn't know how she had gotten there, or how I had gotten there for that matter, but I was really glad to see her. *"Denise!"* I slurred.

"Hi Todd," she said, her worried look intensifying.

"Hey!" I said, trying to get out of the chair. I couldn't quite manage so I sank back into the soft leather cushions. "Huh...."

"How do you feel?" she asked. She was wearing a loose white blouse that clung in just the right places. I stared brazenly at her concealed breasts.

"I feel...great!" I said, meaning it. "Hey..." I tried to hold her eyes in a meaningful look. Denise's eyebrows rose. "Would you like to make love?" I asked.

Denise smiled, unsurprised. "Todd, we've already talked about this..."

"Yeah...but look at this!" I fumbled awkwardly with the fly of jeans, and after a few tries was able to pull my flaccid, thirteen-year-old manhood into view. It looked pale, small and ill-mannered...not at all how I felt. I tried to will my organ into readiness, but it remained limp, then rapidly retracted itself back into my pants like a hairless, frightened mouse. I looked up at Denise, who was trying unsuccessfully to hide body-jolting laughter behind her raised hands. "Not much to look at," I said, "but it will doooo...the job!"

Denise shook her head. "Todd, I...think you're too drunk to do anything right now." She tried to look serious.

"No I'm no-ot!" I protested. But even as I began to formulate my next argument, a wave of nausea coursed through me. "Uh..." I reached for Denise beseechingly with both hands, my face contorting with panic, and she herded me into the bathroom just in time.

I spent the rest of the night vomiting all over the place. Into every corner of the bathroom. On the hallway carpet. All over myself. Denise had to wash my bed sheets three times, staying up with me all night long. I don't know what happened to Randy. I think he tired of my dilapidated condition and found some other drunken fun. By morning light I was thoroughly exhausted. Rick and Marge, who returned early the following morning, had no idea what had happened, and let me stay home from school because of my flu-like symptoms. Looking back, I'm sure I had sufficient alcohol in my young body to poison myself or worse. But I survived. And because of Denise's kindness and discretion, my dignity survived as well. She continued to resist my adolescent amorousness, and in fact my experience with her helped me understand that caring and sex did not always go hand-in-hand; that unconsummated feelings of attraction could be channeled into kindness. I also learned that whiskey and blackberry brandy do not mix particularly well. To this day, I can't stand the smell or taste of either.

How was this experience typical? Mainly because it reflects my confusion of companionship, friendship, love and sex that would persist well into later years. I would continue to look for both love and intimacy in inappropriate places, discovering even when I did connect sexually with someone that what I longed for was not there. I wanted to trust and be trusted, but sex did not reliably afford those consequences. In the moment, it did feel like the greatest vulnerability that could be offered or accepted, but it could also become a barrier to real intimacy – a substitute for authentic and open sharing.

## To Trust or Not to Trust?

These patterns of memory guided my relationships for decades. I reflexively mistrusted authority figures and social institutions of any kind, always seeking the agenda behind what I knew must be deception and manipulation. I would reinvent the wheel whenever possible, confident that the institutionalization of anything is a sure sign of its corruption or inadequacy. Too often, I also sabotaged, disengaged or undervalued my friendships, sure that I would be abandoned, misunderstood or hurt in some way. For example, instead of returning to New England after my five-year stint in Frankfurt, Germany, I impulsively headed to the West Coast to the disappointment and consternation of my extended family and childhood friends in New England. More through negligence than deliberate effort, I then severed contact with my High School friends, and, a few years later, did the same thing again with friends I made in my first few years in Seattle. My romantic relationships fared no better, with my repeating the same dysfunctional dynamics again and again. I proved to myself and everyone around me that I could neither fully trust nor be fully trusted.

Sex became one of my closest allies in these trust-disrupting efforts. With it I could ruin a close and satisfying friendship by sleeping with that friend's sister. By instigating romance with a coworker, I could make my work environment uncomfortable enough to necessitate leaving my job. I could destroy the safety and effectiveness of a writer's group by having sex with one of its members. I could sabotage my spiritual community and relationships by chasing after the scent of a woman's hair. I could risk my access to various support systems through risky sexual behaviors. I could torture myself with sexual premeditations, disrupting my equilibrium and undermining supportive platonic relationships. And so on well into my early thirties, when I finally began to learn some hard lessons about what sex was really all about…and what it wasn't. You could even say that my sexual habits up until that time were a structural barrier to my overall well-being and success in life.

What changed? Over time, I began to establish more trust in platonic but profoundly intimate relationships, and gradually relied less and less on sex as a means of substituting for that trust. The pull to introduce a sexual element into that intimacy still lingered, but since I was now receiving the quality interpersonal connection I had always sought, I could more easily manage those impulses. This is actually a principle of *Integral Lifework*, where once we learn how to effectively nourish ourselves in all twelve dimensions of self, our self-sabotaging behaviors and habitual substitutions naturally attenuate. Still, the memory patterns surrounding trust and intimacy persisted just below the surface in my unconscious substrata, threatening to undermine everything I was learning.

Ultimately, the first real progress regarding trust was a result of the five core AMR practices. When I first began applying them, I didn't realize they were acting in concert to help me relax fearful, controlling and sabotaging behaviors. Eventually, it became obvious that the more I conditioned my mind, heart, spirit and body to let go of previous patterns and associations, the more I could achieve a sort of neutral equilibrium. In that processing space, those strong, self-protective impulses softened into choices; I could relax my previous reflexes and generate more constructive responses. In other words, I could begin challenging the set organization of my episodic memory and the way it supported various metastructures of being. I could begin rearranging my sense of self, and begin to trust more easily.

## Applying AMR

All such patterns of experience, memory and emotion are inherently neutral until we start contextualizing them – that is, until we start formulating values around them and energizing them with our conclusions. Most of the time, we do this unconsciously, as a matter of habit, from internalized cultural attitudes, self-protective reflexes, and the valuations we learned from our family of origin. But when we begin to create new contexts consciously, when we begin to consider "what does this really mean to me right now?" for each past and present situation, then those unconscious determinations begin to lose their sway.

The events of my childhood led me to believe that most people could not be trusted, especially folks in positions of authority, and even those in my own family on whom I was most dependent. They also encouraged me to assume that all friendships would end painfully, and that intimacy always led to betrayal. Further, I could conclude with reasonable certainty that in almost every situation, people wanted something from me and would do or say almost anything to get it. So these were the default semantic themes and metathemes with which I tried to navigate my adult life. They informed the narrative self I projected into the future, my emotional disposition in every relationship, and even the spiritual ground with which I tried to connect. My initial conceptualization of "God" was of a stern authority figure who ruthlessly manipulated human beings to His own ends – just like everyone else who wanted to get close to me.

To challenge these beliefs, I had to shift each processing space within me into new orientations. With neutral awareness practice, I began to create some distance between my emotional center and mental processes and the intensity and immediacy of past betrayals in my memory field. With gratitude and compassionate affection practices, I learned a new road to intimacy and vulnerability that did not rely on the actions or affections of others, and so dissipated some of the energy I had invested in past failures. Through therapeutic breathing, I found ways to work through the panic and fear of past trauma, so that my body could be more relaxed when confronting stressful situations in the present. And through cognitive restructuring, I began to choose new context and meaning for a wealth of formerly antagonistic episodic material.

Using these tools, my grandmother's manipulative antics and simmering hostility become something else entirely: evidence of her own intense suffering and a paucity of effective healing and coping mechanisms, which of course had nothing to do with who I was at that time, or who I am now. The mishandling of my care at the children's hospital likewise becomes an instructive lesson about the inadequacies of psychiatric diagnosis and treatment at that time, and perhaps the surprising ignorance of many of the people involved, but it no longer equates all authority with the automatic assumption that such authority will be abused. All those memories of awkward interactions with other children from my childhood no longer mean that people can't be trusted or that I will always be on the outside looking in, they mean that I have unique experiences and sometimes a lack of socialization or specific training that makes my interactions and friendships more challenging, but also often more authentic.

What goals, activities, environments and language helped me integrate this shift in my conclusions? Surrounding myself with people who share many of my most important values, for one. Among other things, my current community of support greatly esteems art, creativity, spirituality, nature, intellectual inquiry, and deeply open conversation. Through self-employment and avoidance of authoritative or controlling organizations, I tend to remain removed from hierarchical or oppressive environments.     Instead,   I   try   to   create   mutually   respectful interdependencies with others through my personal and professional associations.  My personal goals include helping others find effective ways to cope with antagonistic patterns from their past, heal their hurts and transform their lives.  Although I can still be critical, I also routinely express my trust in the abilities of others, and my own confidence in fulfilling whatever trust they place in me.  And a favorite activity of mine is also to openly confront the inadequacies or ignorance of any authoritative institution – not to rebel against its authority, but to help that authority become more effective in its goals.  For instance, the way I vote, the way I engage traditional medicine, the way I earn and spend money, and the way I utilize and respect the rule of law are all intended to refine the positive impact of those institutions rather than undermine them.  Instead of giving myself over to the care of those who have power over me, I chart my own course as much as possible and engage everyone I can as equals.

When grandma Rachel was in hospice, I flew out from the West Coast to visit her in Connecticut.  She was very weak and hadn't been eating for a few days, and she drifted in and out of lucidity.  We had not spoken very often in those last years, and she knew that one of the reasons I had moved to the West Coast was to distance myself from her influence.  But there we were, sitting together in her room, gazing up at the many family photos my uncle had nailed to the wall across from her hospice bed.   Even in her frailty, she wanted to look her best.   She kept complaining about not having her makeup or nice cloths to put on for us, and I was transported back to the days she would invite me in to watch her "put on her face."  This was the same woman who had manipulated and controlled so many members of our family, still embarrassed about her freckles.  I took her hand in mine and smiled at her.  She smiled back and gripped my fingers with all her strength, holding onto me as if her life depended on it.  In those few intimate moments an understanding blossomed in my heart that I had only intellectually embraced up until then:  that a fullness of compassion could overcome pain, resentment and mistrust; that love could rebuild all bridges and heal all wounds.

Do I still struggle with trust sometimes?  Yes, but as I slowly gather evidence of success in my relationships using these new orientations, I begin to trust myself and others more and more.  And that is really the essence of the transformation: as I become more intimate with and compassionate toward my innermost self, I am more comfortable being intimate with others; as I learn to trust who and how I am from moment to moment, I can more readily expand that trust into wider and wider circles of affection. I am not perfect, the world is not perfect, and my friendships are not perfect. But as I continue to engage the five core practices of active memory organization, that imperfection becomes more acceptable to me. Indeed, I am even beginning to appreciate the possibility that my vision of an ideal self in this arena could actually harmonize with my real self.

And thus we come to the end of the part of the book that exemplifies different semantic containers I have constructed over time to navigate my existence. There are of course many more containers, some of just them as important and as powerful as the ones enumerated here, which contribute to my metastructures of being. The ones I chose to include here have been helpful in defining and resolving common barriers to well-being, and specifically those that disrupt self-care in the twelve dimensions of nourishment. Of course, these containers will not remain static, but will constantly recombine, reprioritize themselves, and reintegrate with my ever-evolving sense of self. As I revisit them in the coming years, I'm certain I will find new meanings and associations for the episodic material that is still a potent part of my memory field.

# FIVE CORE PRACTICES: RESOURCES

With a theoretical framework established, and a few chapters of autobiographical material for examples, our focus now will be finding practical resources that facilitate the application of AMR principles. There is easily enough material on this topic for an additional book. However, a lot of that material is already covered elsewhere – in my own writings and the excellent work of others within their specialties – so instead we can simply take a gander in various directions to see what is available. We will review a smattering of personal disciplines and resources that develop and expand the five core disciplines of active memory reorganization that we've outlined thus far.

## Neutral Awareness

Neutral awareness practices are any disciplines that help us distance ourselves from reflexive reactions to interior or exterior phenomena and processes, and to diffuse the energy of all associations. These include a number of widely utilized approaches, each of which often has a unique appeal to one person or another. As with all of AMR practices, what resonates with us at a particular time in our lives, or in a particular stage of our healing and growth, will inevitably change over time. We need only begin experimenting to know what works best for us. Of course this entails a certain amount of stick-to-itiveness, as neutral awareness is not, for most people, a natural inclination of consciousness. The following are some examples of methods that, with repetition, will help develop neutral awareness:

- Jnana Yoga techniques such as neti-neti.

- Buddhist vipassana meditation.

- Sufi muraqaba meditation.

In my book *Essential Mysticism*, I offer a number of exercises – such as "returning to emptiness" and "presence and absence"– that are intended to help stimulate neutral awareness. Here is one such exercise from that book called *"Who am I right now?" Self Inquiry*:

1. Objective: Between 15 and 75 minutes of continuous meditation each day. If you can, insulate this with a buffer of five minutes before and after so it never feels rushed, and so you have time to reflect on your experiences.

2. Find a quiet place to sit and relax, and begin your meditation with an inner commitment to a broader goal beyond healing or personal edification, but which is also inclusive of those outcomes; i.e. "May this be for the good of All."

3. Relax every part of your body. Start with your hands and feet – perhaps moving them or shaking them a little to release tension – then your arms and legs, then your torso, head and neck.

4. Breathe deeply and evenly deep into your stomach, preferably in through the nose and out through the mouth, so that your shoulders remain still but your stomach "inflates." Practice this until you are comfortable with it.

5. With your mind's eye centered in the middle of your chest, just above and behind your sternum, silently ask yourself "Who *am* I right now?" As words, images, feelings or experiences arise within you, create space for them in your mind and heart without judgment or analysis, and just rest in them for a moment. What arises may reflect the past, the present, or a desired future. If nothing happens at first, simply keep breathing and ask again, perhaps changing the emphasis on each word, as in: *"Who* am *I* right now?"

6. After you have rested in each event a while, let it go. That is, release any attachment or certainty you might have about these private thoughts, and gently set them aside. Avoid forcibly rejecting or denying what you find, but allow it to be deliberately tenuous,

questionable, optional. You might resist wanting to let go of what you find. Nevertheless, it is important to release all that you encounter – try breathing it out with your exhale. Comfortable in your uncertainty, expand the question by emphasizing other words, such as: "Who am I *right now*?"

7. Repeat the cycle of questioning, acknowledging without judgment, and letting go. If anything resurfaces repeatedly, try confronting it by asking "Why?" Rest in the response you receive to this question just as you rested in your previous inquiry, and then let that go as well. Continue questioning with new emphasis: *"Who am I* right now?"

8. If you become disquieted, uncomfortable, jittery, or severely disoriented, try to relax through it. If uncomfortable sensations persist or become extreme, cease all meditation for the day.

9. Give yourself space after your meditation to process what you have experienced. Just *be* with what has happened without judgment or a sense of conclusion.

As with all of the core AMR practices, there is a continuum of qualities of experience rather than arrival at some definitive experiential destination. Our objective is to increase our ability to gradually detach our awareness from the material we are observing, so that it has less and less emotional content, distinct meaning, or implications for our self-concept. It just is. Where these practices eventually lead us will vary greatly depending on our receptivity and stage of development. As one flavor of mystic activation, we may come to glimpse our own spiritual ground through such practice. But along the way it will also help us reform unhelpful beliefs about ourselves and others, and perhaps open a window into our innermost unconscious substrata.

### *Gratitude & Compassionate Affection*

At first it might seem as though gratitude and compassionate affection practices are aimed only at transforming our reflexive emotional disposition, conditioning it into a more positive or productive spectrum of responses. And although this is an important aspect, these practices can also have a penetrating impact on other metastructures as well. As I practice compassion for aspects of my being, my past and my present, I begin to mold my narrative self in positive ways. I might reform some of my governing beliefs in the process, or at a minimum help them become more malleable and less rigid. And such efforts also help me release and process somatic memories as well. It all depends on the focus and intensity of my felt sense of gratitude. Here are some resources for learning various forms of gratitude and/or compassionate affection practice:

- Gratitude exercises and training – abundantly discussed and promoted on the web in recent years – and in particular those that invoke positive feelings of gratitude rather than gratitude as an intellectual exercise only.

- "Giving thanks" as part of daily spiritual rituals that are deeply felt as opposed to rote. These could be of any tradition, though the most readily accessible in the West are often Judeo-Christian.

- Bhakti Yoga.

- Sufi cultivation of *ishq*, the passionate love of Allah.

- Buddhist metta bhavana meditation.

One exercise that has had a potent effect in my teaching and coaching, and which can be found in my other books as well, is the following gratitude mediation:

1. Objective: Between 15 and 75 minutes of continuous meditation each day. If you can, insulate this with a buffer of five minutes before and after so it never feels rushed, and so you have time to reflect on your experiences.

2. Find a quiet place to sit and relax, and begin your meditation with an inner commitment to a broader goal beyond healing or personal edification, but which is also inclusive of those outcomes; i.e. "May this be for the good of All."

3. Relax every part of your body. Start with your hands and feet – perhaps moving them or shaking them a little to release tension – then your arms and legs, then your torso, head and neck.

4.  Breathe deeply and evenly deep into your stomach, preferably in through the nose and out through the mouth, so that your shoulders remain still but your stomach "inflates." Practice this until you are comfortable with it.

5.  In the middle of your chest, just above and behind your sternum, gradually fill your heart with gratitude. It need not be directed at anything or anyone, but you could shape this as an offering to the Source of Life, or Nature, or Deity, or simply to the present moment.

6.  Begin with a small point of feeling, and allow it to slowly spread with each breath until it fills your whole being. For some, it may be helpful to visualize this spreading gratitude as light emanating from a point in the center of the chest. Maintain this state for as long as you can.

7.  As other images, sensations, feelings, or thoughts arise, let them go and return to your focus of gratitude.

8.  If you become disquieted, uncomfortable, jittery, or severely disoriented, try to relax through it. If the sensations persist or become extreme, cease all meditation for the day.

9.  Give yourself space after your meditation to process what you have experienced. Just *be* with what has happened without judgment or a sense of conclusion.


In step five of this meditation we can introduce different things to be grateful for over time. To begin we may want to focus on positive generalities, such as a pleasurable experience, our health, our loved ones, a beautiful day, etc. As we strengthen our thankfulness muscles, we can become both more specific and perhaps a bit less trite. We can offer gratitude for challenging situations that have helped us learn and grow, for the reminders of our frailty or mortality, for humbling events and so on. Ultimately, we can focus our thankfulness on the core material of our memories that shaped us – even if that material is difficult or painful. And as we surround everything with gratitude – all the ups and downs of life both past and present – we instigate transformative processes within every region of our mnemosphere. As we begin to change the context and valuation of how we came to be, we strengthen our confidence and appreciation about who we are.

Why are gratitude and compassionate affection tethered to each other? Because one inevitably leads to the other, regardless of which door we enter first. The key is to begin somewhere, and allow our hearts to practice the felt sense of these conditions on a regular basis so that one or both of them can consistently and easily arise. Eventually we can reap the benefits of compassionate affection for every facet of our past, and every facet of self. To forgive, let go of pain, resolve our grief and shame and begin to heal is all dependent on our capacity for gratitude and compassionate affection. The goal here is to develop those responses first independently of challenging mnemonic material, and then to slowly turn the spotlight of our heart's greatest power on the burdens of our past. At first, we may only be reducing the acuteness of our emotional pain, but ultimately we can fall in love with everything and everyone that once caused us distress.

## Therapeutic Breathing

The positive benefits of therapeutic breathing have increasingly been recognized by the mainstream medical community. From dissipating anxiety or stress to lowering blood pressure, controlling our breath can have immediate positive results. The enhancement of spiritual practices through controlled breathing has also been utilized in many traditions. The primary element of most techniques is a slowing of inhalation and exhalation. Often other components are added, such as visualization, silent mantra meditation, or rhythmic breathing. You may have noticed that the previous exercises contain a controlled breathing element. This is because therapeutic breathing greatly enhances the other core AMR practices. Here are a few resources offering different breathing techniques:

- Hindu pranayama.

- Qigong breathing exercises.

- Zen breath-counting meditation.

- Abdominal or "diagphragmatic" breathing.

- Holotropic Breathwork and Rebirthing Breathwork.

I am a fan of *four-fold breath*.  The practice is simple:  just breathe in slowly, hold your breath for the length of a breath, breathe out slowly, then rest for the length of a breath.  Continue this for several minutes until you are comfortable, breathing as evenly, deeply and slowly as possible.  This not only slows down breathing, but initially requires a steady focus on the breathing itself.  When we then add an additional locus of attention while continuing the four-fold breath – a space in our body, a specific memory, an imagined outcome, our spiritual ground – we can unify the breathing with that locus...essentially breathing our conscious attention through whatever we are holding in our mental concentration.  When the locus is some part of our body where we have tension, illness, injury or scarring from previous injuries, this technique can help access and process somatic memories.  When the locus is our spiritual ground, not only can we deepen our conscious connection with spirit, but also begin to unveil the karmic barriers that we must inevitably work through.


## Cognitive Restructuring

Because of its effectiveness, different variations of cognitive behavioral therapy have been utilized to treat everything from PTSD to depression to longstanding personality disorders.  The basic tools are the same for all of these approaches, with variations tailored to address each condition.  In AMR, the same CBT tools can prove useful in assessing how our episodic memory is organized, then to move specific material from one semantic container into our integrative buffer, and ultimately into a different or newly created semantic container.  For example, we might use the *downward arrow technique* to discover linkages between certain memory patterns and the semantic themes and metathemes that led us to conclusions about ourselves or the world around us, then decide whether those linkages are really rational or valid in the present.  We might journal our moods and *automatic thoughts* to discover patterns in our internal processes and evaluate their effectiveness.  We can challenge the core beliefs that have energized autobiographical memory in unhealthy or self-limiting ways by evaluating the evidence that supports or refutes those associations.  And we can reinforce new memory organization through deliberate exposure to new experiences that reflect and support that organization, then track and assess those experiences over time.

AMR's cognitive restructuring also adds elements of another cognitive approach called Motivational Interviewing. Here our focus is aligning the AMR process itself with the personal values and goals that are most important to us. Does the identity we have formed from our past arrangement of episodic patterns support the values and goals we hold dear? If not, how can we resolve discrepancies between what we feel is most important and how we inadvertently create barriers to those priorities through the organization of our memory field? Because memory is self, the more we can align the various operations of our mnemosphere with our values, the more successful we will be in realizing our goals and living our ethos from day to day. In addition, Motivational Interviewing provides other tools to help overcome ambivalence to these self-creating efforts and begin actualizing a change plan. Although many of these MI tools are defined in the context of interaction with a professional coach or counselor, they can easily be learned through self-study as well.

Resources for better understanding all of these elements can be found among the many superb texts on CBT and Motivational Interviewing. Here are a few I recommend:

- *Building Motivational Interviewing Skills*, by David B. Rosengren

- *Motivational Interviewing: Preparing People for Change,* by William R. Miller & Stephen Rollnick

- *Mind Over Mood,* by Dennis Greenberger & Christine A. Padesky

- *Making Cognitive Behavioral Therapy Work: Clinical Process for New Practitioners,* by Deborah Roth Ledley, Brian P. Marx and Richard G. Heimburg

- *Cognitive Therapy of Personality Disorders,* by Aaron T. Beck, Arthur Freeman & Associates

An additional component of AMR's cognitive restructuring is the use of *Integral Lifework's* primary drives and fulfillment impulses to evaluate and organize autobiographical material. Our most formative experiences will naturally arrange themselves around one or more of our fulfillment impulses (see chart in Overview), because we are hardwired to learn effective ways to satisfy them. By evaluating which *active expression* a particular memory appears to support, or the *felt sense* it seems to evoke, we can quickly identify the fulfillment impulses most relevant for that episodic material. After all, these impulses greatly influenced how we integrated and prioritized our experiences to begin with, whether we were conscious of the process or not. As we reconsider that valuation, revising context and exploring dichotomies in order to reorganize our memories, it is important that whatever conclusions we come to, and whatever homes we create for each family of experiences, align with these native support structures.

For example, my own "freedom and adventure" semantic container includes memories that support the fulfillment impulses of Discovery, Autonomy, Affirmation, Mastery and Effectiveness, among others, but it is Discovery and Autonomy that I have chosen to emphasize in my active memory reorganizing. Likewise my "shades of pain" container references Avoidance, Belonging, Exchange, Perpetuation, Effectiveness, Mastery and Understanding, but I have chosen to prioritize Understanding and Mastery, with a little Avoidance thrown in for good measure. And in my "joy and passion" family of experiences, I have decided to emphasize Fulfillment, Sustenance, Affirmation and Union above any other impulses those experiences might inform. By clarifying the felt sense and active expressions I would like to associate with each memory, I feed into my desired organization of that material.

One outgrowth of this fulfillment analysis is the clarification of a natural dichotomy in attitudes, conclusions and behaviors that the same episodic material creates. Once the contrast is clear, we can differentiate, honor and integrate both ends of a dichotomy's spectrum without repressing or denying any of it. How we energize and prioritize each semantic container in our memory field is therefore the result of a deliberately chosen emphasis – a mental and emotional tilting of the scales – that frees us from unconscious defaults. By thinking about the interconnectivity or our thoughts, emotions, reactions and memories in this way, we begin to shift all of our interior processing away from reflexive, avoidant, passive and closed cycles. Instead, as it becomes more active, questioning, mindful and open, we continually strengthen the mechanisms that provide us with powerful insights and the creativity of transformative consciousness.

Finally, as I consider the twelve dimensions of nourishment and how to best care for myself in each area, I will also include this context as I organize my autobiographical memory, as well as using the conclusions I reap from those memories to guide my self-care routines. For instance, my "faith and mystery" container is full of interesting tidbits that contribute to my Authentic Spirit dimension. My "safety and fear" container has helped immensely in how I enrich my Supportive Community and Playful Heart nourishment centers. And of course all of this interior work with my past has supported positive results in the Restorative History and Empowered Self-Concept dimensions as well. Really, there are infinite interdependencies here, but if I focus on just a few if these relationships, I can much more easily and fluidly maintain harmony and integrity in my mnemosphere and my life.

## Reinforcement & Accountability

This facilitates the integration of all four previous core practices. In order for any new patterns of self to reliably take root in our thoughts, behaviors, emotions, physiology or spirit, they must be reinforced through the goals, actions, environments and language we choose for ourselves. First we set our intention, then we maintain our attention, then we follow through – over and over again until the new modes of being become our effortless habits. The central factors in all reinforcement and accountability are our relationships: our community of support, our work environment, our romantic partners, and our daily interactions with others. These interactions define the quality of everything else.

This principle is already expressed in CBT and Motivational Interviewing, and discussion of goals, change plans, and exposure to situations that challenge or revise reflexive responses are the subject of much discussion in these disciplines. Spiritual practices inspired by gratitude and compassionate affection likewise tend to encourage expression of those sentiments in interpersonal language and the cultivation of loving relationships and supportive environments. Various neutral awareness practices are designed to continue that awareness as we transition from internal observation to external actions. To be mindful or watchful of our speech, thoughts, attitudes and efforts from moment to moment, and to observe them without judgment, helps us maintain integrity with who we authentically are. In other words, practicing neutral awareness allows us to shed our personas and insecurities and become more present to everyone and everything around us. And therapeutic breathing allows us to enhance these other practices while responding to stressful situations with more equanimity, confidence and clarity of focus. In concert, all of these core practices lead to transformative actions and interactions.

Once again, however, the greatest contributing factor to the success of reinforcement and accountability will be the quality of our relationships. In *Integral Lifework*, several critical nourishment centers are grounded in how we connect with other people. Playful Heart, Supportive Community, Authentic Spirit, Restorative History, and Pleasurable Legacy all have explicit interpersonal components as an integral part of the nourishment process. Really though, all dimensions spring from relating, connecting, exchanging and embracing; the intended harmony of all nourishment centers is purely a function of loving relationship. So if we want our ongoing efforts in active memory reorganization to be fully supported, we will need the accountability of our friends, loved ones and chosen community. Isolation and introspection will bring us clarity, insight and conviction, but interaction with others is what amplifies and solidifies those *ahas* into a sustainable trajectory.

What happens when our relationships do not support our consciously chosen identity? Our natural propensity is to create survival personas that help us provide for our own needs, and this is especially true if we perceive ourselves to be in unpredictable or adversarial environments. I am the Fighter who must always be on alert, because no situation or relationship is safe. I am the Hermit who removes himself from society to avoid the complications of interpersonal demands or societal expectations. I am the Perpetual Failure, helpless amid the storms of life, certain that my hopes cannot be realized. I am the Dare Devil, always looking for new heights of feeling and new extremes of experience to medicate my anxiety and boredom.   I am the Social Elitist, insulating myself from the struggle to survive with material wealth and social privilege.  The critical feature here is that we will adapt to whatever relationships dominate our lives by donning a false front, a conforming personality that we believe empowers us in our most familiar contexts. In order to relax our survival personas and express an identity that resonates with our most healthy, sincere and complete sense of self, we need to change that context, relinquishing antagonistic relationships and building supportive ones.   This means creating new friendships and revamping existing ones, and sometimes even exiting relationships that resist reformation.   As fundamentally interdependent, highly social creatures, we will never free ourselves of a self-limiting past if we subject ourselves to the same patterns of interaction over and over again.

In terms of resources to support reinforcement and accountability strategies, we can refer back to the resources for each of the previous core practices, and to the sections of my book *True Love* that address relationships.  It would also be helpful to explore the idea of survival personas included in *True Love*.  What ultimately holds us accountable is of course our own conscience and the commitment we have to our own well-being.  Our primary metric for this accountability is the ongoing exploration and evaluation of our narrative self, our governing beliefs, our somatic memory, our spiritual ground, our emotional disposition, our integrative buffer and our unconscious substrata.  Thus we come full circle to the beginning of the AMR process, and the unique progression can begin again.   As we understand who we are   through the associations of autobiographical memory, we can test that understanding against any new associations we have created with active memory organization; we can compare our chosen identity with the goals, actions, environments and language with which we populate our conscious world.  We can compare our real self with our ideal self.

In my own life, reinforcement and accountability have manifested in many forms.  As bosses, coworkers and employees.  As psychotherapists and spiritual counselors.  As close friends and lovers.  As teachers and students.  In certain situations, divination has proven to be a powerful reminder of the inner and outer paths I have chosen.  Ultimately, it is my conscience and self-discipline that holds me to account.  By revisiting the

AMR practices and process without shrinking from what they reveal, each one supports all of the others, taking up slack where the others leave off. And should I fail to attend the quiet reminders of my conscience, my loved ones will step in to shed a little light on my responsibilities. If my friends turn a blind eye to some darkness I have yet to face, my students and clients will challenge me to face those shadows. Without fail, even when I give up a struggle to rectify an unhealthy pattern or initiate a more positive and constructive direction for my life – even when I despair or turn away – I am held to account by a conspiracy of circumstances, an abundance of synchronicity that demands reengagement. It seems as though the very fabric of the Universe is designed to help us move forward. So despite how difficult this may sometimes be for us, on the other side of resistance and confusion and willfulness is an abiding gratitude that the road goes ever on and on.

## Other Options

AMR is intended to be an open framework, driven by principles rather than precepts. When we encounter more effective techniques or approaches better suited to our particular strengths or families of experience, this framework allows plentiful room for incorporation of new ideas and methods. The efficacy of any system should be measured and revised according to the quality of its outcomes, rather than reliance on past successes or rigid tradition. That said, to remain AMR, an underlying cadre of cohesive intentions should persist. Are all metastructural regions being addressed? Are all dimensions of nourishment being attended? Are new associations for past and present episodic material being established and sustained? Are the related barriers to well-being and wholeness being removed? If all of this is true, then there seems unlimited freedom for adjusting methods and applying new modalities.

Remember also that another benefit of the core practices outlined in AMR is their value in assessing progress over time. Each is grounded in introspective, internally empowering disciplines that clarify conditions of mind, heart, body and spirit. Instead of relying on external dependencies for exploration, diagnosis and treatment, these practices encourage us to rely on ourselves. We are not submitting to someone else's ministrations, or relying solely on technology or pharmaceuticals to regulate our interiority, or in any way relinquishing responsibility for our healing and transformation. So a goal of accountable self-reliance in the therapeutic process is another characteristic that any AMR technique should retain.

In some situations, complimentary modalities may be required to relieve acute distress in one or more systems of being, but those interventions should be temporary until we are able to execute every aspect of AMR with a modicum of self-sufficiency. For example, if I am in intense physical or emotional pain, I may need a superficial, externally dependent remedy that provides enough relief for me to sustain interior focus. If I am too angry, tired, confused, impulsive, addicted or depressed to move forward with even the simplest steps of an AMR regimen, some externally dependent mitigation may be required. Professional guidance or training in the AMR process can be helpful at any time, and especially at the beginning. Still, once active memory reorganization takes root, it should self-perpetuate without any requirement for long-term external support other than the systems of accountability we choose to keep in place for ourselves, and which we regulate with our own conscience and discernment.

## Afterthoughts

Not all memories endure or have an impact on our development. But when certain conditions are met, our memories play a primary role in constructing and maintaining our self-concept and self-worth. What are these conditions? It varies dynamically from one person to the next, and one set of circumstances to the next, but there are commonalities. Sometimes a single, particularly informative experience can change how we view ourselves and the world around us. Sometimes, when certain experiences are repeated often enough, they begin to form familiar patterns that influence our development. Sometimes strong emotional content is all that is required to encode a potent and enduring memory.

The impact of any memory on our being also depends on our own receptivity to that impact. The intensity of any experience is subjective, based in part on how open, sensitive or interested we are in whatever is happening to us. And our receptivity is likewise wildly variable, depending on our current state of mind, our native curiosity and perceptive abilities, our willingness or capacity to be vulnerable, our attitudes and beliefs about the source of any influence, our emotional disposition, and so on. And of course the repetition of similar flavors of experience can also be relatively arbitrary. All of this, in turn, is filtered through the beliefs we already hold about ourselves, and is further contextualized by the cultural backdrop – the memeplex of societal values, morals, expectations, prejudices, etc. – within which we are operating at any given time.

With so many complex and seemingly random interdependencies in play, it is difficult to fully anticipate what impact a future event will have on our development, or even what formative residue our current experiences are leaving behind. It is much easier to interpret these influences in retrospect.  But there is a challenge in attempting a retrospective interpretation as well, because all of the same variables that influenced us in the past can influence us in the present.  That is, we will tend to unconsciously reinterpret all of our previously constructed associations according to our current level of receptivity, the perceived frequency of certain memories, our emotional state, and their subjective intensity or relevance.  Through these conditions we will prioritize our memories to support our current understanding.  So unless we are particularly conscious and careful about how we evaluate and re-assemble our memories, we can fall prey to any inaccurate, self-limiting and even destructive patterns that formulated out of families of experience from our past.

This patterning is cognitive and behavioral, but it is not limited to these arenas.  It is also deeply systemic and somatic – patterning that influences our very physiology and how each molecule of our body navigates and reacts to its environment.  It is spiritual patterning as well, training the metaphysical components of our being how to interact with the physical world – and how our mind, heart and body should interact with spirit.  So the associations we generate over time not only shape our values, assumptions and beliefs, they also shape how our physiology functions, heals and grows, our access to emotional vocabularies, and the course of our spiritual journey.  How we integrate our experiences and reinforce them through memory creates a path for our continued adaptation and growth.  To whatever degree we can consciously perceive and manage this process, we will influence the quality and effectiveness of our efforts in every dimension of self.

As with nearly everything other facet of being when we are young, our memory encoding and management style are both fairly flexible and fluid.  Then, slowly at first but with every-increasing speed, things begin to rigidify.  Associations become more firmly entrenched.  Attitudes and assumptions about our experiences become more reflexive, and the wheels of accepting and fully integrating new experiences and information turn much more slowly.  Our sense of self becomes more solid and generally less permeable, and our reactions more predictable.  There may be aspects of our being that remain flexible, but for the most part we increasingly seize up.  This is not an inherently unhealthy thing; it helps us navigate the world more efficiently.  Imagine if we had to carefully assess whether each breath was really necessary before taking it, or research which types of foods were the most nourishing every time we sat down to eat, or painstakingly analyze which types of people we enjoyed more than others every time we sought out social interaction. This constant reprocessing would certainly interfere with our effective survival, so naturally we learn to repeat successful choices and patterns. In terms of the basic perpetuation of our species, that which becomes reflexive can help us become more effective, and thus secure a place for the next generation.

But, as we've explored, there are costs to this efficiency. What if our reflexes are fundamentally unhelpful, and we just don't realize it? What if rigidified patterns of being are degrading our life, interrupting our healing or disrupting our evolution? Perhaps poor sleeping habits are making us overtired. Or negative thought cycles are preventing us from mending our relationships. Or self-destructive behaviors are sabotaging our goals. Or karmic baggage is undermining our contentment. In order to break free of the patterns that lead us toward these unfortunate places, we can become more flexible and fluid in both our modes of being and our self-concept. We can revisit the conclusions that corralled us into counterproductive conditions, the important life experiences that led us to those conclusions, and the way we have organized memories of those experiences to support our beliefs.

Just as with any organic system, there is a dynamic equilibrium between extremes that helps us create positive an supportive patterns of memory, and, in turn, positive and supportive patterns of self. We shouldn't compulsively annihilate all reflexive responses, but neither do we need to cling to them. In a happy medium of conscious reflection, insight and active memory reorganization, we can find our way to a self-nourishing oasis between extremes, and thereby engage the adventure of this existence with more vigor, competence and joy.

### Permeability & Balanced Self-Nourishment

It is relatively simple to chart the correlation between active memory reorganization, removing barriers to self-care, and fully nurturing ourselves in all twelve dimensions of *Integral Lifework*. Simply taking an inventory of how effectively we are nourishing ourselves in each dimension will begin to shed light on how our consciousness interacts with each region of our mnemosphere;  and as we explore different semantic containers, our style and prioritization of overall self-care will likewise become clear.  We could even define many of the barriers to nourishment as interrupted communication between different metastructures or supportive structures.

One goal of AMR is therefore to increase the internal permeability of the mnemosphere; that is, to encourage fluid and open exchanges between all of its metastructures, supportive structures and shared components. Regions should freely interact and contribute to consciousness through shared processing space.  Semantic containers should not contradict or compete with each other.   The agents for all structures and metastructures should have unrestricted access across every region, so that every aspect of self can be harmoniously coordinated, with appropriately supportive data available to each.  In Jungian terms, the process of individuation – of self-integration into a well-functioning whole – could be described as the harmonious interaction and amalgamation of our metastructural regions, supportive structures and agents.   When such boundaries remain impermeable, we can inadvertently energize patterns of memory and self that interrupt, combat or otherwise antagonize each other, disrupting that integration.

That said, some amount of segmentation and compartmentalization represents normal, healthy functions of mind.  We will "chunk" incoming information into smaller bits to encode it more easily.  We will differentiate, contrast and compare data to make decisions or enhance self-nourishment with dialectic tension.   We will create semantic containers to organize our exposure to new situations, environments and information.  But the danger of strict compartmentalizing is that we in effect cripple our own self-nurturing capacity and the integrity of our self-concept;  we may assign equal attention priority to fundamentally incompatible aspects of self, or excessively energize dissociated material. In its most extreme manifestations, this lack of permeability and balance often results in psychological disorders, spiritual crises and chronic physical illnesses.  Even in its less virulent manifestation, the resulting cognitive dissonance, emotional paralysis, black-and-white reasoning, intolerance of change, nourishment deprivation, physiological depression and lack of purpose will nearly always limit our ability to grow and thrive.

By regularly engaging in the five core practices and five step process of AMR, we therefore unleash the magic of our conscious attention on this inner landscape, energizing our most potent autobiographical material, then building positive associative connections around it. At the same time, we de-energize harmful material and associations to the point where they no longer hold significant influence in our memory field; where in fact they are relegated to our integrative buffer for thoughtful reprocessing. Wherever there is disconnection, competition and dissonance, we excite a healthy interdependency of all metastructures within our memory field, fully connecting, integrating and harmonizing them all.

In order to achieve reliable, balanced holistic nourishment, AMR offers an indispensible set of tools that reinforce another common thread as well: a building up of our reliance on interior qualities and capacities that coincides with letting go of our dependence on externals. As one example, if we have internalized cultural memeplexes that disallow full-spectrum nourishment, AMR deconstructs and neutralizes those memeplexes. As another example, the fifth core practice and the fifth step in the AMR process focus on consciously aligning externals with the healing and constructive choices we have created within. Over time, we learn to quickly recognize what is authentic nourishment through its resonance with each dimension of self that we have brought into balance. We no longer navigate the world through the pronouncements and inducements of others, but through the confidence and vision of a internally strengthened self-concept.

Much of my other writing has promoted mystic activation as a critical component of self-care; that is, the evoking of spiritual perception-cognition as a crucial factor in nurturing the self. In the framework of active memory reorganization, mystic activation has additional relevance because it has the potential of delinking the mnemosphere from our cognitive axis, and liberating our attention from the contextual backdrop of memory. Mystic activation strengthens our capacity to shift episodic material from one container to another, not only by encouraging the expansion and utilization of our integrative buffer, but also by putting us more intimately in touch with the content of other regions. In their most disciplined forms, the first four of the five core practices of AMR are in fact powerful mystic activators in themselves. This is something to consider for more advanced applications of both active memory reorganization and the holistic nourishment of all twelve dimensions of being.

## Lingering Questions

The application of AMR to my own autobiographical material has led me to certain conclusions about my own nature and the nature of being human. It has helped me better understand my strengths and aided my charting a focused and purposeful course through this life. It has also allowed me to integrate many otherwise difficult and inexplicable experiences without much cognitive dissonance, aided in the healing of many old wounds from childhood, sharpened my mind and expanded options for how I process new experiences. Not only do I feel more complete and harmonious within myself, but I have a much clearer idea of how and why I feel this way. However, even with all of these benefits, there remain many questions I have not yet answered about my past, my purpose and my identity. Most of these questions seesaw between what is inherent to my nature, and what has been nurtured into prominence through my experience.

Some of the questions may never be definitively resolved to my satisfaction, but I believe it is important to ask them. Much of my past writing has been the consequence of concerted efforts to find answers, and I suspect future works will be inspired in a similar fashion. I leave a few of these questions with you now not only to demonstrate the importance of this additional semantic container in my life, but also because I believe not having come to certain conclusions is just as important as arriving at a few useful assumptions. It is helpful to avoid becoming overly comfortable with our beliefs. After reading the stories in this book, it may even seem as though some of these questions challenge or contradict certain generalizations I have made. And that's just fine, because the essence of AMR is a continual re-visioning of self. In some way or other, we are always reorganizing our memory to adjust to the present; that is an incontrovertible consequence of being alive.

So here are a few queries I hold in my mind and heart to keep the eternal fires of transformation burning bright, and to remind myself of the limits of my own assertions:

- How can I be certain I have really befriended all of my demons and weakened the manacles of structural limitations resulting from past experience, as opposed to rationalizing my way around them, living in an unaware denial, or compensating for them with distracting substitutions?

- What have I forgotten that might assist me in my efforts to heal, grow and transform? What memories still require reorganization to better support a more effective or informed self-concept? What is working well, but requires more accountability and reinforcement?

- What if, after I have reorganized my memories to support a more positively envisioned self – and become comfortable with the new arrangement – I begin to forget supportive episodic material? Is it crucial I somehow refresh my memory in a conscious way, or can I rely on my unconscious substrata to support my chosen priority and organization of semantic containers?

- Is it necessary that I consciously understand the nature of all of my experiences and beliefs? If I live in harmony with myself and others, should I still exhaustively examine my interiority? Is there a danger of undermining both well-being and effectiveness if I linger too long – or with too much intensity – in the depths of self?

And so we arrive at the culmination of this particular effort. As with all of my work to date, depending on the day of the week, phase of the moon or my state of mind and heart at any given time, my own judgments about the work I have done will vary widely; I am alternately an enthusiastic fan and my own harshest critic. However, I hope you will find something here to take with you in your journey, and that your inner flame rises steadily to the challenges ahead. For now, you have a snapshot of my inner space that seems stationary and immutable. Moving forward, these conclusions will of necessity adjust and evolve to integrate new insights and discoveries.  As I call upon my memories to support and expand my sense of self, I will continually reinvent T.Collins Logan to conform to the expectations I generate.  This is the nature of self, the nature of memory and the nature of human understanding.   Like observing a speeding train, our interpretation of who we are and the meaning of our experiences depends entirely on our frame of reference.

Taken by my biking buddy Eric on our train ride from Lyon back to Frankfurt

www.ingramcontent.com/pod-product-compliance
Lightning Source LLC
Chambersburg PA
CBHW021614270326
41931CB00008B/697